Strength Basing, Empowering and Regenerating Indigenous Knowledge Education

Riteway Flows

I0025369

John Davis

Routledge
Taylor & Francis Group

LONDON AND NEW YORK

Designed cover image: © Getty Images

First published 2024
by Routledge
4 Park Square, Milton Park, Abingdon, Oxon OX14 4RN

and by Routledge
605 Third Avenue, New York, NY 10158

Routledge is an imprint of the Taylor & Francis Group, an informa business

British Library Cataloguing-in-Publication Data
A catalogue record for this book is available from the British Library

Library of Congress Cataloging-in-Publication Data
Names: Davis, John, 1977- author.
Title: Strength basing, empowering and regenerating indigenous knowledge education : Riteway flows / John Davis.
Description: Abingdon, Oxon ; New York, NY : Routledge, 2024. | Includes bibliographical references.
Identifiers: LCCN 2023041523 (print) | LCCN 2023041524 (ebook) | ISBN 9781032288352 (hardback) | ISBN 9781032288369 (paperback) | ISBN 9781003298717 (ebook)
Subjects: LCSH: Aboriginal Australians—Education. | Torres Strait Islanders—Education. | Ethnoscience—Study and teaching—Australia. | Culturally sustaining pedagogy—Australia. | Culturally relevant pedagogy—Australia.
Classification: LCC LC3501.A3 D38 2024 (print) | LCC LC3501.A3 (ebook) | DDC 371.829/9915—dc23/eng/20231127
LC record available at https://lccn.loc.gov/2023041523
LC ebook record available at https://lccn.loc.gov/2023041524

ISBN: 978-1-032-28835-2 (hbk)
ISBN: 978-1-032-28836-9 (pbk)
ISBN: 978-1-003-29871-7 (ebk)

DOI: 10.4324/9781003298717

Typeset in Optima
by Apex CoVantage, LLC

Strength Basing, Empowering and Regenerating Indigenous Knowledge Education

Strength Basing, Empowering and Regenerating Indigenous Knowledge Education demonstrates how to bring Indigenous Knowledges to the forefront of education practice and provides educators with the tools to enact culturally responsive curricula and pedagogies, ensuring positive educational outcomes for Aboriginal and Torres Strait Islander children and students.

In this book, John Davis presents Indigenous Knowledges – ways of doing, creating, and learning – combined with contemporary education practice, to develop a culturally responsive pedagogy that builds on the strengths that Indigenous Australian students bring to the classroom. Setting Cultural Proficiency as the benchmark, the book offers educators a lens through which to review their education practice. It moves beyond the deficit model of Indigenous education by challenging non-Indigenous educators to reflect on personal biases and to raise their expectations of Indigenous students. Not 'tacked on' to an existing curriculum, or specific to a single school term or unit of learning, Riteway places Indigenous Knowledges at the centre of education. The approach is holistic and adaptable to any educational context, from the early years right through to tertiary education.

Providing a roadmap toward transformational education for Aboriginal and Torres Strait Islander children and students, this book will be essential reading for pre- and in-service educators alike.

John Davis is an expert, experienced educator, teacher, manager, and school principal. John is a senior research fellow at the Indigenous Knowledge Systems Lab (Deakin University), a regular media commentator, and the former CEO of the Stronger Smarter Institute.

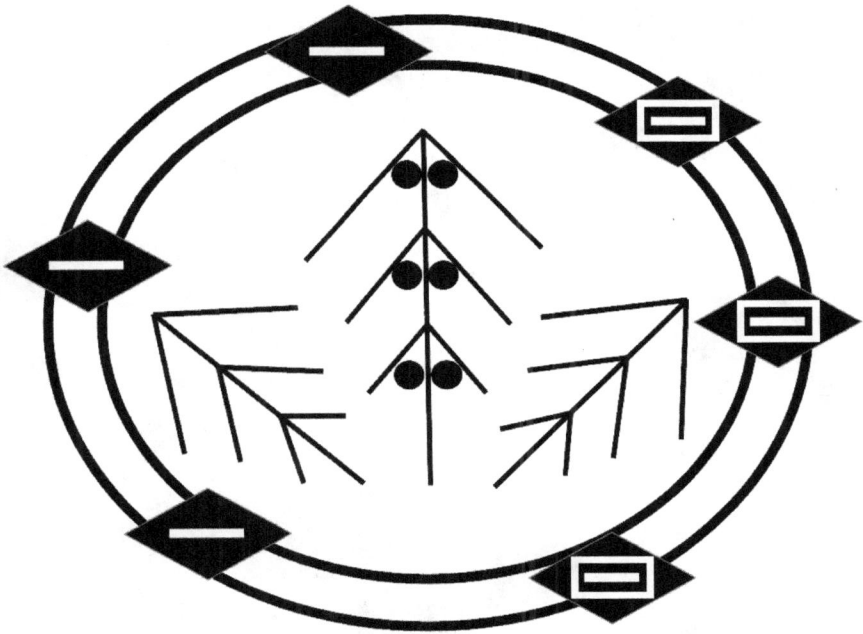

'Strength Basing, Empowering and Regenerating Indigenous Knowledge Education . . .'

Contents

Contents

Figures

Concept/Context . . . Dgagunbara – Research Fullas

Figure 0.1 Concept/Context . . . Dgagunbara – Research Fullas.

Knowledge Maps

JD's 'Place Bases'

Figure 0.2 JD's 'place bases'.

JD's Eagle Flights – Stronger Smarter

2006

- National program training – SSLP at Cherbourg teaching coordination/ leading 'Next Steps'

2007

- Regionalisation of SSLP models, Weipa 'Teacher Training' meets, and middle-level professional development, LAS support
- Newcastle Regional SSLP at Williamstown
- Orange 'follow-ups' – Indigenous Student Leadership sessions
- Broome Regional SSLPs – last foundational steps for Institute
- Alice Springs 'Tri-State Forums'
- Menindee 'Tri-State' Stronger Smarter consultancies and 'follow-ups'; re-engaged from

2016

- Stronger Smarter specialists
- Nesting and creation of Trans-tasman Indigenous Principal voices – NATSIPA and Te Akatea international conferences
- Creation and lead of Stronger Smarter masterclasses launched at UQ

2018

- Keynote address at Waitangi, as well as Australian Indigenous principal exchange in Waitangi Hut
- Cairns Indigenous Empowerment Conference address
- Tasmanian Catholic schools follow-ups
- Taribelang Bunda Aboriginal Corporation programs, Bundberg QLD
- Warril Yari Go Stronger Smarter programs, Logan City, QLD

Place Bases: Logan, Yugambeh Ngima Yuggera Country

YACCA (Youth and Community Against Crime). NGO auspices and young people–led. Learnt community advocacy, strength-based approach training: collectively created largest youth disco – safe space gathering based in Logan City, Beenleigh. YACCA group members formed 'Club Vision'. Across the Beenleigh/Eagleby area (reporting highest crime waves at that time), led by visionary local Ms Sandra Fields, collective yarns with hundreds of young people nominated then chose 'representatives' for our local YACCA youth-led community voces. Our group and dance that we created

Figure 0.3 Place bases: Logan, Yugambeh Ngima Yuggera country.

to combat 'boredom', a regular theme shared by young people as to reasons for extra-criminal/curricula activities, was called 'Club Vision'.

A specific training ground and safe space for middle-tier and younger people leadership that embraced our voice and showed us who were more supportive elements and organisations across our broader community mesh-work. Anecdotally, members of our community action group have become law enforcements, radio hoists, NGO service providers, and CEOs/principals of local schools/community orgs, **1993–1997.**

Murri Group Program. First formed by Uncle Duncan Williams – Yugambeh. Gathered and learnt from master didj man Johnny Briggs – Yorta Yorta. Uncle Duncan and YACCA gifted and gave me my first ever didj (which I still have), **1993–1997.** Murri Group morphed into 'Murriland', led by my brother Will, which became the template for his school programs, 1998–2023. The 'safe space' created still exists in local Beenleigh Highschool, and Will has taken the model to build a broader community-controlled language nest and education program. It operates now, once a week, for all local gundoos (jarjums).

Knowledge House at Loganlea SHS, 1999–2023. Knowledge House conceptually was seeded in 1999 through the creation of 'Nyumba Bugir Anga' – teaching clearly model. Gaining a permanent teaching position 'across the river' in Logan central hubs, I nested with families and local community for nearly a decade. The initial 'Nyumba Bugir Anga' programming led to the creation of Knowledge House. In my second stint, returning from country service to my home community, I respectfully asked Elders and local Indigenous community orgs in relation to what they saw as needs for our local school-aged jarjums and families. If they thought a regular schooling circle design would assist and empower. Through Indigenous community consultation, the 'action' output of this research became the Knowledge House model. With community consultation and agreement making reached, the programming that we led collectively as Knowledge House staff created a more culturally responsive and culturally safe education pathway. 'Unlocking the door' was a key component, and this was family-based learning and sharing opportunities – the Coochie Mudlo nest – once a year.

Consulting and co/designing with students, who held regular Knowledge House circle meets, meant Indigenous voices were heard. An output of these meets was enactment. One thing being heard, another process having projects lifted and enacted. Meaning-making, we led more safe space creation through teacher resource library, student resource library, Barinj 'Big Boomerang' Bush tucker gardens, and our ever-successful Kap Mauri – whole-school cook-ups. Working individually and insularly is so important, then opening up, breaking bread with our wider school community. To be able to fly from the nest, the nest must be right. A code/switch mantra which worked well with jarjums was, 'Don't shit on your nest. . . . Birds don't shit in their nest.'

For multiple Loganlea school events, Indigenous gatherings were held and Indigenous community would host our whole school for Kap Mauris. The blend of the macro and micro programmatic planning and outputs so essential to maintain and lift in a third space – the cultural interface. Outside the school gates, we couldn't control the alt-right formation of 'Aussie Pride' gangs and parties, the Pacific Islander presence, which would lead to massive riots across town on Logan City. What we could control was our inner Loganlea circle. And the ripple that creates and brings as positive energy and positive flow is the central spring from which that energy comes.

Honour and respect flows to Traditional Owner Aunty Eileen Williams, Aunty Pat O'Connor, Torres Strait Islander (Bowie families), Wakka Wakka and Mona Mona IK experts in dance and culture, Uncle Country Matheson (RIP) and Wakka Wakka dancers led by Livo Riley, then the transition to Nunukal Yuggera dancers, Uncle Eddie Ruska dancers, Timothy White as a lead dancer and Durithunga student leader, Community Durithunga leaderships across the rivers, Uncle Fred Masters, my mate and mentor who drove me to work when I didn't have a car – great family role model and phenomenal spirit whom I'm blessed to still have weave in my life. Community Elders and supporting Indigenous community orgs; Yugmabeh Community Centre (now taken over by multicultural services) in Kingston; Uncle Martin Watego (RIP), who wove with Logan Elders originals, like Jutja Pa Paddy Jerome. Knowledge House staffer originals, Larry Johnson, Gooreng Gooreng; Kelly and Lisa Masters, Kooma; Aunty B Wilson, Bandjalung; and Petah girl Hegarty, Wakka Wakka ngin Cobble Cobble, as well as Aunty Rachel Tisdale. Am blessed that into the future, this model, full circle, definitely flows. One of my boys, Rueben Mani, is taking on teaching as a first career choice. He is based alongside his yadgie Meli, in part-time work at Loganlea and can see, taste, and feel the space his Yaboo helped co/create with community. And more importantly, he is part of the next generations to take footprints of 'next most powerful steps' for safe space creation and articulation.

Community Durithunga Logan City–wide. Indigenous-only educators' leadership circles. Spanning over decades from the ASSPA era (1990s) to the launch of ACARA (2010s). Durithunga grew in a region for education that had one of the highest Indigenous populations but little to no Indigenous education services – structurally, from within the education organisational organism. The model which was developed in the state systems mid-1990s was not centred on need or highest populations but built on a historical and truncated HR model which 'assigned' individuals to large 'grouped' school cohorts. This would mean Indigenous school officers, often not education-trained, would service multiple school sites across education districts. This 'multiple service' model is applied across other social service sector areas, like policing and health. 'Liaison officer' roles are probably the most 'sort-after' yet least-renumerated positions in the country. And as 'sort-after', most oversubscribed. The 'stress' and fracture pattern of the 'work' is not on Indigenous commitment; it is on the systemic racism – lack of full-service resourcing. The community workers employed are often placed between a 'rock and hard place'. If we stay, we 'tick the box' of servicing our communities, albeit massively under-resourced; if we leave, another gap is created in HR. Much love, strength, and positive energy for our mobs who put their hand up time and time again. Fuck the system that perpetuates the stagnations.

Federally Indigenous-funded, ASSPA, as a 'community-controlled' or individuated response, was place-based and individuated-based on the local school's context. Seeing this strength, a number of Logan-based Indigenous educationalists sort to build a more sustainable model of support and guidance for each other as educators in the system and our learning communities nested within districts. Brokering language use and site use of the Yugmabeh people, we sat circle over many years, forming and actioning Indigenous

Figure 0.4 Community Durithunga Logan City–wide. Indigenous-only educators' leadership circles.

education programmatic responses based on not what was directed, not given by the district or educational jurisdictions. We sat circle and grew, Durithunga, our way of Indigenous education leadership because we drew on the strength of our identity as Aboriginal and Torres Strait Islander people.

A 'strength-based map' of Durithunga educational impacts is shared via a co/researcher (kolab) reflections – Professor Annette Woods working side by side with myself as a chief investigator for a successful longitudinal study of and on social justice education through multimodal literacies, called URLearning (Davis & Woods, 2019). Through the advocacy of independent community, Indigenous educator voices, we were able to advocate for better Indigenous education representation in the region and supports. Over the years, this has built to service a successful Indigenous education regional office, with multiple-level Indigenous officers, 2020, and a doctor in Indigenous education as the director. A far cry from the Durithunga 'change' context that created the need for Durithunga business in late 1990s, and still no community-controlled voice in education in the region (2023), though a continued educational challenge in the south-east and in Queensland. The state never likes to cede full power.

The power within Durithunga circle and legacy of works by its leaders is shown through the recent Springer article reflections and is blueprinted through the deeper Indigenous Language program weave works that have occurred and durithunaged well after Durithunga leaders planned and developed them. Real-time cases now, models of local impact collaborations, now decades strong, themselves include the Knowledge House model, Bulkari Jarums, Faithy Green. Koa ngin Kabi, Bariebunn Boul Gary Crosby – Larrikia and Yugmabeh as a LOTE at Waterford West primary, as well as Murriland at Jinndi Mibunn. PhD-level research on Community Durithunga is the foundation for the Stronger Smarter Institute's 'masterclass' design and activity. Community Durithunga Research, specifically the IRMs, are a core focus at IKSL. Despite migloo gaze, our models of strength continue to grow and flow. Because they are grounded and kinnected to the original thinkers, makers, creators, and designers of such a large and beautiful social meshwork – the mist nets of our Indigenous communities.

Further sites of wanjau include*:

Mackay North High – Aboriginal and Torres Strait Islander Studies First Year Centre and Senior School.

UNESCO, Paris, France, International Forum on Indigenous Education, Special Rapporteur.

SIKAT, Indigenous Australian Cross-Cultural Exchange with the Philippines: WIPC.

Waterford West SS, **Bariebunn Boul** and LOTE and QUT Longitudinal Study, PhD outputs.

Hymba Yumba Community Hub, Sustainability through Centring Indigenous Knowledges, Alternative Education Program, Independent Schools Queensland.

State-Based **EATSIPs,** ACARA influencer, ten-officer-led foot-printing statewide. Foundational steps through to enactments. Core target was Indigenous staffing model: Indigenous teacher–led strengths and capacity-building.

State-Based Indigenous Languages – **ACARA influencer.**

Warril Yari-Go Karulbo – Logan City Indigenous Community–Controlled Leadership Circles (now named Gnirigomindala Karulbo).

Indigenous Knowledge Systems Lab – IKSL nested within NIKERI at Deakin Uni – JD is a foundational research fellow alongside Dr Chels Marshall and former NIKERI Professor Gabby Fletcher. The Lab is and has been created by the energies and flows of the founder, Dr Tyson Yunkaporta.

*NB not all sites of 'praction' are included in the preceding knowledge maps. EATSIPs, for example, our ten officers covered hundreds of schools in the 'state-wide' model. The focus of and for sharing here is with 'places' where there has been a deeper, longer connection and kinnection – more demonstrable of Riteway flows.

About the Author

John Davis is an expert, experienced educator, teacher, manager, and school consultant. John is the former CEO of the Stronger Smarter Institute, an organisation that works with educators to improve the educational outcomes for Aboriginal and Torres Strait Islander children. He is a regular media commentator, including regular appearances as a panellist on ABC's *The Drum*. John is currently a senior research fellow at the Indigenous Knowledge Systems Lab (Deakin University), an activist, public-facing think-tank rooted in research that leads with the insight that Indigenous Knowledge carries the patterns, systems, methods, and protocols to make regenerative models of production, trade, economics, governance, and technology function sustainably at scale. John is passionate about our people, our languages and culture, and working and moving our ways forward as best practice in education and community development.

1 Language Weaves

◉ Language Weaves

The *Language Weaves* to follow provide a translation of text for readers of this research, a translation of how we '*roll our tongue*' in academic writing (Davis, 2018). In respects to that 'roll' or language code switch between Standard Australian English and Indigenous languages, through the book is reference to the broader 'Indigenous' classification for us as a people – First Nations and Traditional Owners. In a broader regional grouping or collective, I often use First Nations – First Nations 'Voice' for Australian Parliament (as an example). And for specific place and relational reference, more localised, I refer to Traditional Owners of the land.

Ideally, a 'language list' or explanation of Indigenous Knowledge (IK) terminology is available up front in my (and our IK) writings to lessen the distance between the non-Indigenous reading audience. Sometimes the version of language in part of my articulation of 'our way' our languages is a script different from the general typed font. I've chosen in this text not to italicise the difference. The process of and focus on *Riteways flows* is the only combination of words which will be italicised through the text. Most terminologies are explained within text, and further reference can be made to PhD work (Davis, 2018) on context/meanings. For ease and weaves of the languages in this text, they are recorded and referenced in what follows, **alphabetically**.

Bala:	A Torres Strait and Pacific – namely, Melanesian – relational term meaning 'brother'.
Bandjalung:	Refers to the First Nations group of northern New South Wales. This is the language or regional

DOI: 10.4324/9781003298717-1

boundary for Murri and Kooris. Regionally, the New South Wales boundary relates to Kooris, and north of their rivers like the Tweed, we are referred to as Murries. Our people also have a 'shared space' relational term – the space in between; a lot of the old people from, in, and around Logan City (Davis, 2018) would refer to each other as 'Goori'.

Barinj: Yugambeh language referring to 'large boomerangs'. There's a 'place' at Knowledge House, Loganlea State High, that Indigenous family groups planted local trees and plants in the form of 'barinj'.

Barkandji: Western or red sands people of far western New South Wales.

Barrunga: The species classification/name of the native rat kangaroo. Barrunga's big mimburi was the western plains of the bunyas. Was as the plainlands look and feel different now post-colonisation. However, our re-firing country should in time bring back right conditions for this important species to flow more strongly again.

Batchalla: Saltwater Pacific Ocean people of Murri country. Batchalla are the Traditional Owners of Hervey Bay and regional townships.

Bauluan: Barrungam First Nations language translation for grassland balds, or 'open country'/space.

Boobargun ngummunge: Barrungam translation/meaning for the Bunya Mountains. Refers and references the great trees and fruiting nuts as 'the place of mother's milk'.

Boul: Refers to a circle in design and thinking. Draws on Yugambeh and Barrungam languages.

Budin Guju: Barrungam translation for 'big carpet snake'. This is in direct correlation to the importance of this animal as a Barrungam Cultural Indicator Species. The 'big snake' relates to the broader story and pattern of relationships and formation of country to the Dreaming.

Budin Yadga: Barrungam relational term for 'big brother'.

Budin Yadgie: Barrungam relational term for 'big sister'.

Bunya Bunyas: Translates/relation term referred to as a place name for and of Boobargun nguumonge.

Carbal: Barrungam (and multiple Murri) language translation for 'carpet snake'.

Coochie Mudlo: A Nunukal and Yuggera First Nations reference for the ceremonial island on the saltwater country of the south-east. Specifically, a place called Redlands in Queensland.

Cultural Burning: The act of practicing or praction of fire stix knowledge on country. It is cultural and delineates to First Nations 'fire ways' when it involves First Nations leaders up front and is practiced or burnt through an Indigenous cultural lens. The actions of applying and doing. Steffenson refers to this process as 'practions' (Steffenson, 2020).

Countryman: Relational term in Aboriginal English referring to fellow people of the land where we're from.

Dadirri: Refers to a specific way of thinking and doing from Daly River country, Northern Territory. Built from the work of leading First Nations educator Miriam Rose, Dadirri is a pattern and process of listening and reacting in response to country.

Dgagunbara: Barrungam relational term for 'country' – place of origins.

Djaukunde: Tribal reference to the clans neighbouring the Bunya Mountains.

Djirribal: Far north Queensland, specifically Tully area, Traditional Owners.

Durithunga: A Yugambeh translation for or on growth. Derived from the Wangerriburra clan's specific word of 'duranga'.

Elders: Relational term of and on experience and love for our older people and older knowledges.

Footprinted: Reference to the many paths, tracks, and walks of country.

Gaibarau:	The traditional Jinibara ngin Kabi name of a great countryman from Woodford now laid to rest in Brisbane. Gaibaru translate to 'scatterings'. His English name is Willie McKenzie.
Gamba ngindus:	Barrungam translation for 'thank you'.
Gamilaori:	On country reference to large First Nations group of New South Wales. Gamilaroi are freshwater people who carry the long storyline of the Murray cod and emu as major totemic ancestors.
Gari ina narmi	Davis, 2007, 2018; Bunya Mountains Elders, 2010): A Bunya Bunya song. This is a 'telling song', sharing where I am and where I come from. It has multiple translations now. For us as Barrungam- and Wakka Wakka–speaking people, it is sung at the start and end of corroborees as well as special gathering occasions. For the Kabi Kabi people, it is a 'telling story' song, where I am from, who I am. Its 'place' is within the Kabi ngma Wakka language–speaking groups.
Garma:	A festival of great import in Northern Territory, specifically of and for Yolngu self-determination as well as articulation of their needs. Created and layered through the Yothu Yindi Foundation, it is a regular yearly pilgrimage now, where Yolngu invite multiple national First Nations key stakeholders as well as non-Indigenous politicians and dignitaries.
Garmi:	Refers to a Barrungam relational translation that means 'aunty'.
Gundoos:	Barrungam and Wakka translation for children.
Gooreng:	Traditional Owners of the Bundaberg, saltwater country region of Queensland. They are northern neighbours to the Batchalla and Wakka and represent a change in Murri language from the southeast to central language areas of Queensland.
Gumungurru:	Barrungam and Jarrowair site of great import. This is reference and keeping place of an ancient

boul or duwur – closed stone arrangement, ceremonial circle. Our Bunya Murri Rangers are now caretakers of this important site. It is also a local language translation for the major river through dganbarra called the Condamine River, on Bunya country, in Queensland.

Gunya Meta: Murri and Torres Strait language translation for 'house' or 'home'. This is a reference to the long-standing Indigenous community–controlled organisation nested in the heart of Yuggera country in hometown of Logan City, specifically Woodridge, Logan Central.

Gurangadai: Barrungam translation for the Dreaming time, time before Migloos.

Guymbanjir: Refers to the Koori language group of the Central Coast of NSW. These are the saltwater people of the coastal and surrounding hinterlands.

Jarrowair: Barrungam and Wakka translation for 'giving' or the 'give-givers'.

Jinabara: Traditional Owners of the Kabi Kabi–speaking people of Woodford and surrounding regions. Jinibara means 'lawyer cane'.

Jinndi Mibunn: Language of the Yugambeh meaning 'eagle's nest'.

Jutja: A Barrungam relational term meaning 'father'.

Kabi Kabi: South-east Murri country people whose boundary starts north of the now Pine River in Queensland. Their saltwater boundary is the coastline from Bribie Island to Rainbow Beach.

Kap Mauris: Traditional cooking method of the Torres Strait and multiple saltwater people. It refers to 'earth ovens' or cooking beneath the earth.

Kgari: Very important Batchalla island. Kgari is the largest sand island in the world.

Kinnected: An Aboriginal English word for closer family kin, rather than or deeper relationally then 'connections'.

Koa: Traditional Owner group of north Queensland.

Kolab: IK relational term for equal, relational research.

Kultjas: Aboriginal English word for 'culture'.

Loreman: Refers to higher-learning principles and proto-cols of our people. Lore is an Indigenous Knowl-edge (IK) distinction of and between western ways – often referred to as 'law' and our ways, continuous cultural practice stemming from the oldest time as 'lore'. Lore relationally refers to story place, kin, and culture.

Makaratta: Yolngu translation for the 'coming together after a fight'. It has been gifted by the Yolngu people as a signifier and reference point for ways for-ward in up-and-coming national referendums in Australia on furthering First Nations rights. 'Makaratta' relates to the process of forming treaty and expanding truth-telling for healing in our nation. The Voice is the body of this recog-nition and expansion of further human rights for First Nations. A 'Voice', a new peak Indigenous federal body, ostensibly is what all Australians will vote for or against.

Mara: Barrungam for 'hand'.

Murries: As referenced in earlier definitions, Murri is the relational broader regional reference to Queensland Indigenous people of Australia.

Murriland: Broader social reference to our people of Queensland.

Migloos: Relationally means non-Indigenous (and refer-ences a whale in Australia – name gifted by the Batchalla).

Mimburi: A Jinibara relational reference to the source of energy, the site, time, place, and space.

Nahra Kati: Palawa, Tasmanian Traditional Owner, language for good numbers.

Ngada: A Barrungam relational term for 'grandmother'.

Noonthalli: Is Barrungam for 'teaches' or 'teacher'.

Nunukal: Traditional Owner groups of the saltwater region in and around Stradbroke Island. They are one of the only Traditional Owner groups on the east coast of Australia to procure Native title (ownership) closest to a capital city.

Nyumba bugir anga: Yugambeh translation for 'teaching clearly'.

Palawa: Tasmanian Aboriginal reference. The palawa demarcate their Traditional Ownership amongst First Nations by non-subscribing to Standard Australian English forms of their language. So very clearly and spirituality, palawa is not capitalised.

Practions: Expert 'Fire Country' lead Vic Steffenson's Aboriginal English reference to old people definition of practicing/mastering skills.

Quampie: A Nunukal reference to the saltwater mussel.

Quandamoopah: Written as well by Traditional Owners as *Quandamooka*; refers to the saltwater country surrounding now Stradbroke Island.

Relatedness: IK reference to the placement of self and country to knowledge and being. Lead Murri thinkers Professors Aileen Moreton Robinson as well as Karen Martin have been key at building out this place and theoretical refence for us in IK.

Riteways: Aboriginal English or pidgin creole play on combination of 'rites' – anthropological juxtaposition of our mobs lore, rites of passage. Directional path = right and way to go or follow or flow. Lingo also connects to 'proper way.'

Tjina: Markers of lore. Reference in Barrungam and Wakka to 'feet', also written as jinung.

Waanyi: Traditional Owners of outer west Mount Isa country. Boodjamla is a major site of significance and gathering for Waanyi Traditional Owners.

Wakka Wakka: Traditional Owners of the Burnett region, fellow carpet snake clans. From the Bunyas as a boundary line north till the Gooreng language group. Wakka Wakka is a broader regional language. Wakka Wakka's centre is Barambah, now named Cherbourg, the Aboriginal community–controlled base. It was historically the site where our people and multiple outside-of-region First Nations groups were sent to be 'protected' at the height of colonisation. Our Barrungam words and vocabs carry and kinnect to the base, shared language of the Wakka Wakka. Since we are a Bunya sunset clan, our language is often referred to in historical written records from early colonisation as a 'western Wakka Wakka' language.

Walpiri: Traditional Owners of the Central Australian region. Walpiri are renowned, internationally showcased artist. Their distinct desert art style is colloquially known as 'dot art'.

Wanjau: Barrungam and Wakka relational term for exchanges and relationships. A variation of wanjau is the 'place name' on country Bunya Bunyas called 'Warmga'. Warmga is the site our western Bunya Traditional Owners gathered on mass before heading up the range for Boobargun nguumonge.

Warra Warra: Barrungam (not Wikipedia-referenced) language term for the great water place. The place where carpet snake constricts, the 'fenced-in' place. My grandfather was born on country there. Originally, the 'place' was referred to as Cobble Cobble – water place. Cobble Cobble is an Australian Standard English variation of Carbal, our carpet snake.

Warril Yari Go Karulbo: Rivers yarning together, Ugarapul, Yugambeh, and Yuggera translation. Is a translation and reference point toward the Indigenous community collaborative, designed to create better voice and recognition of First Nations intellectual property.

Weave: First Nations languages translation on process and ways we work and yarn together.

Wiradjuri: One of the biggest Traditional Owner groups of New South Wales. Freshwater Kooris, their lands stretch west to the New South Wales border and over their great mountain ranges.

Yarning Circle:	A great scholarly approach to systems of learning and problem-solving – inquiry. It is an approach that purposefully places participants in relation of to and from an Indigenous cultural lens.
Yugambeh:	Traditional Owners of the south-east, specifically to the Logan River in the north to the Tweed River in the south and to the mountain ranges just outside of Beaudesert.
Yuggera:	Traditional Owners of the sandy region's creeks and waterways of their totemic ancestor, Yuggera, the sand goanna. The Yuggera's 'centre' is Ipswich.
Yothu Yindi:	Traditional Owner groups of the Yolngu formed a foundation for culture and life. They are hosts to the regular gathering circle Garms (mentioned earlier) as well as multiple First Nation school spaces. Yothu Yindi is a band and recorder of great national Australian songs and ancient chants as well as musical instruments. The music and foundation are a signpost for all First Nations to aim for and see what can be done in preserving and furthering the rights of us all as Indigenous Australian people.

~: Symbol used in text to connote kin ties to Australian tribal/Traditional Owner affiliations.

– -<: Symbol used to represent spirit.

References

Bunya Mountains Elders Council (Eds.). (2010). *Bonye Buru – Boobagun Ngumminge – Bunya Mountains Aboriginal aspirations and caring for country plan*. Bargara: Burnett Mary Regional Group.

Davis, J. (2018). *Durithunga: Growing, nurturing, challenging and supporting urban Indigenous leadership in education* (Unpublished PhD thesis). Queensland University of Technology, Brisbane.

Davis, W. (2007). *Spear making* (Unpublished master's thesis). University of Queensland, St. Lucia.

Steffenson, V. (2020). *Fire country – how Indigenous fire management could help save Australia*. Melbourne: Hardie Grant Publishing.

Intro to *Flow* Design

2

Strength-Based, Empowering, and Sustainable Indigenous Knowledges Education

◎ Strength-Based

The following is an abstraction of 20-plus years' work in the field of education and applying Indigenous expert knowledges in multiple learning spaces: K–12 (from the Preparatory year to Year 12, the final year of formal schooling), government and independent jurisdictions, and tertiary sites (specifically teacher training). Up front, I would like to acknowledge all the great communities I have worked with and alongside developing *Riteways flows*. Collectively through this book, the communities form part of the 'we' I refer to when writing. I have foregrounded these communities in the 'context'/place-based maps shown earlier. Within the Stronger Smarter Institute, where I have always operated as my authentic self, I thank Indigenous colleagues for sharpening *Riteways flows*; without their direct and indirect influence, I wouldn't be where I am, and we wouldn't have moved the dial and language of Indigenous education like we have. Now, working independently on Traditional Owner business (cultural and economic), I've found a new 'spiritual' home at the Indigenous Knowledge Systems (IKS) Lab's campfire based at home bases and kinnected to the bigger Deakin University campfire at NIKERI, on Waddawrung country.

A powerful piece of moving between great Indigenous-led First Nations–first institutes like Stronger Smarter (SSI), and now NIKERI, is that innovation and creation of safe space is at the core of the work they and we do. Working independently. Maintaining a rigour of interdependent systems, regular meetings, and check-in points to ensure we can work in home bases off 'main campus' locations is an amazing process our Indigenous-led Institutes have done and continue to lead in pre- and post-Covid work environs.

DOI: 10.4324/9781003298717-2

Symbiotically and, I guess, process-driven, both orgs heavily draw on our Indigenous Australian metaphors to resin/bolster the work and foci. SSI uses a 'Cultural Tree' metaphor quite extensively, drawing on knowledges from the Torres Strait Islands as well (*www.strongersmarter.com.au*), and NIKERI, specifically at the Labs, uses the 'Cultural Tree of life' and campfire as its signifier (*NIKERI Institute | Deakin*). Gamba ngindus ngin dir tu dir barras for the innovative systems thinking you bring to the relational table of having to work, sense-make, and 'be' as a Murri working within broader work systems and environs of education. Both campfire systems are exceptional in connecting the local to the global.

Shout-outs to campfire managers like Bandji Wayne Williams, ~Wakka Wakka. Wayne is an expert IK educator who bends our learnings into sandstone university medical and health education. As a cultural man, a family man, and an educator, Wayne provides for me the 'radar' to aim to be more like with his humility and strength. He is over 20 years' strong as Aboriginal Medical Service directorship, Carbal on our Downs, and was an original EATSIPS state-wide officer, making the program from good to great (sustainable) in his tenure. Wayne sits with me and us/all around the IKS Lab fires. Deadly Dyonne Anderson, ~Bandjalung, long-term Koori Principal's Chair of National Aboriginal and Torres Strait Islander Principals Association (NATSIPA) and fellow 2006 graduate of national SSLP. D and the NATSIPA families just invited and hosted the Te Akatea Maori principal's association to Australia, based in Sydney (2022). When you want to see *Riteways* in Indigenous leadership showcased, this biennial main event is a must see and do. Bandji Paul Bridge, Gidja man, Director of Kimberley education and long-time Director of Stronger Smarter Board, whose reputation as an Indigenous education expert precedes him and is patterned in the multiple national seats he holds, like former Australian Education Union offices. Thank you for 'seeing me' and always being a source of strength and practical Indigenous education delivery with your expertise in the Kimberley (the home of big boabs).

Tam Anderson, Principal of Briar Road Public School, a passionate western Sydney advocate and no better/best role model than this expert Koori educator. Tam represents the next-gen leadership styles – her footprint at the forefront of forums at NATSIPA. With her as Co/Chair of the SSI Board, there was and has been no better boss lady (previous); she has a calming and centring impact. Within Aurora (previously SSI), Jess King is another 'next gen' who is a leading research 'impact' officer and the research team's grounded-ness, as well as completing his Graduate Certificate of Education in hometown, Townsville, JCU. The Waanyi-type energy which is infectious is being mirrored now by Gungi Josh Waters, Gamilaroi. He is leading and building out IKS Lab processes, which is great to see seed, grow, and flow. Very proud to see the next gens naming and claiming their space and our IK place systematically – well done. And the deadliest SSI stalwart, Michal Purcell, Batchalla Yadgie. She and they have led the way over the last few years at the Institute, ensuring 'IK is all the way' and 'up front' at the beginning, middle, and all parts of Stronger Smarter. Mich has shown in the work she does and grown as an executive at SSI because of the sustainable leadership model we follow. She is now, and her work, in Service Delivery, led by Gamilaori lead officer Cass Ryan. A shout-out to Cass for her pragmatic approaches and always 'getting the work done'. I fly away from SSI successfully seeing the growth and ownership of 'transformative education' taken up by these leads.

Jutja Dr Merv Wilkinson, proud Nawu man, mentor, and leader in complexity and change management. Coming into SSI, you provided me the care and mentorship I needed to see the path of Masters, make sense of 'next steps' in higher ed, and gave me (as you do us all) the confidence to believe. With you still surfing at 70-plus, your pouri pouri is stronger than most, and your humbleness is something I aspire – we all need. You helped grow Stronger Smarter, and it's fitting that as I wove out, you pulled the threads tighter for the next leaders coming into the space of transformational change. Big esso bala, ~Jutja Merv.

Always a shout-out to mentor/Founder and fellow Co/Chair Dr Chris Sarra, ~Taribelang-Bunda, who has always allowed me and provided space for brothers and sisters like me and SSI teams above 'to be what we see'. A simple/technical foundation of all *Riteways flows*. Thank you, gamba ngindus, for seeing me.

And as I finish the writing here and what follows, new campfire knowledges I am assembling around, yarning with, and learning from. Founding IKS Lab creator at Deakin University, Dr Tyson Yunkaporta, ~Wik, is not one for, fanfare and yet he has such a strong following and support base – I enjoy and need our us/2 weaves = appreciated, Tys! And deadly 'founding fellow', the irrepressible spirit of Gumbaynggirr – such deep, rich knowledges and an integrity and respect on how you flow, deadly Dr Chels Marshall. A marine biologist by trade, a design thinker, mother, aunt, sister, partner – she is but one of the 'tall trees' that *Riteways* has affordance of and to share with and through. Thank

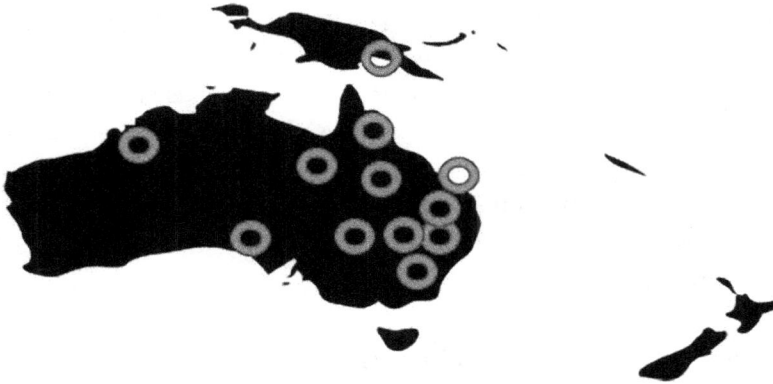

Figure 2.1 IK exchanges.

you for your invaluable insight and directions on our ways – regenerations. All Lab/ers and Ko/Lab/ers like Gungi Jack ('Jack is Back'), JMB AIME (Australian Indigenous Mentoring Experience) extraordinaire, it's been great getting to weave with you more, and, Sissy Fi, part of my/our Mackay family bases, look forward to hearing and seeing your 'face, place, and grace' have its space as it should in the early education field. The IKS Lab base at NIKERI in Deakin University, the support in different 'systems thinking' and 'space' to allow us to set circles and forge 'our ways', works. Respects to Director Prof Gabby Fletcher, ~Wiradjuri, for the 'time and space' for us all to ko/lab. Foremostly, now-time are Durithunga sisters B, Petah-Girl Hegarty and Faithy Green for me in current workflows. Both have been a part of my education journey and our community safe spaces for decades. B Wilson, ~Bandjalung; Petah-Girl Wakka Wakka ngin Cobble Cobble, Faith Green, ~Koa ngin Kabi, this is a shout-out for the persistent, consistent energies that you and other tiddas bring to our spaces – we continue to Durithunga.

As I write, it is remiss of me not to 'thank those before', so I reference and relocate these knowledge exchanges in honour and respect of 'them' and us who weave in more sustainable models.

Thank you all for leading as *Institutes* and taller trees to pattern a path for Indigenous-led thinking and leadership. Am so looking forward to seeing how far, long, and strong our campfires burn. And the end is our re/beginnings – fire sparks continued. Dir tu dir barras Gail Louise for all the strength around our home and campfires. I finished my PhD with you, which saw the birth of our baby daughter and now our first book. Never thought I could; you always say I should and would, my lady from another 'hood'. Love you. My mother, Nana Noonthalli Dawny Davis, and amazing siblings – my/ our signposts/markers. Gundoos, so proud of you all. It is you who take the sparks and remake the fire in ways, link ways, show new ways for the pattern to flow. Love doesn't translate well enough, or pride – dir tu dir barras does! Dir tu dir barras Cobble Cobble dgagunbaras Warra Warras.

A poem for us/all to share, *Riteways flow* to start:

BIUN BIUN . . .

Dgumge yonyung, dgumge yonyung,
Bianga bianga . . .
Look and can't see
Hear and no noise
Taste and no flavour
Smell and can't breathe
Stop, bianga
Feel – tingling, slow time;
Smoke
Eyes like nyal (eagle)
Binna like gooraman (kangaroo)
Mouth like yuggera (goanna)
Nose like barrunga (rat kangaroo, ~bandicoot)
Gujumba
Dgumge yonyung

Empowering: 'Biun Biun' in Barrungam[1] means 'dreams'. 'Dgumge' in Barrungam lingo means 'smoke'. This poem, and my reflections to come, relates to our storying from country through dreams which can be understood through the pattern and seeing of smoke. For myself making a kinnection[2] to what we do, I share wanjau,[3] writings/reflections of country, from country.

How does 'smoke' or fire story relate to *Riteways*? Because it is intrinsically linked, the two. I write from a carpet snake, freshwater story perspective, and fire is the antithesis, the opposite of water. Yet one and the same, fire needs water to work, and water needs fire 'to work'. When we 'smoke', repeat the pattern and energy of light from the fire, we must wet the leaves we burn to make a bigger smoke pattern. Not burn the fire out – too much water will do that. And good, fresh green leaves wet down then placed on hot embers make good smoke.

The preceding poem is one such reflection from country which is part of Cobble Cobble storying of the area. This is not a 'non-Indigenous historians or educators take and make of space and time' but our reflection, connection, voice. Further knowledge and insight on Cobble Cobble thinking and knowing kinnected to country can be found through IKS Lab podcast series and reshares of and on our 'think tank'[4] yarns through the 'Other Others' podcast (Yunkaporta & Davis, 2021) as well as 'Process & Protocols' section of our website. Further insights can be found in Cobble Cobble texts (Davis, 2017, 2018; Davis & Williams, 2021 and Cobble Cobble panels in our Native Lotus sculpture on Bunya Bunya painted 2022, Dolzan, T).

Sustaining: Within education in Australia at present, the overwhelming perspective is to work IK within the realm of Western education solely and create third cultural spaces (Bhabha, 2004; Chilisa, 2012; Davis, 2018) of learning where it can still be 'predominately non-Indigenous or Western parameters that give shape to the Indigenous knowledge discourse' (Nakata, 2007, p. 8). From that work, there has been a propensity to co-opt and self-select, copy, and design third cultural spaces, attempts to modelling practices which ultimately fail (Wright, in Packer, 2005). These 'copy/co-opted' models fail because the modelling is not developed *Riteways*.

This abstraction is about modelling our way – embedding Indigenous Knowledges through education spaces. To draw on the third spaces metaphor (see what follows), this is solely about IK with minimal attempt to Westernise the learning sphere.

The two larger circles above are the representation of Indigenous alongside Western knowledges. The arrows below indicate movement. As a 'cultural space', this is an area of constant flux.

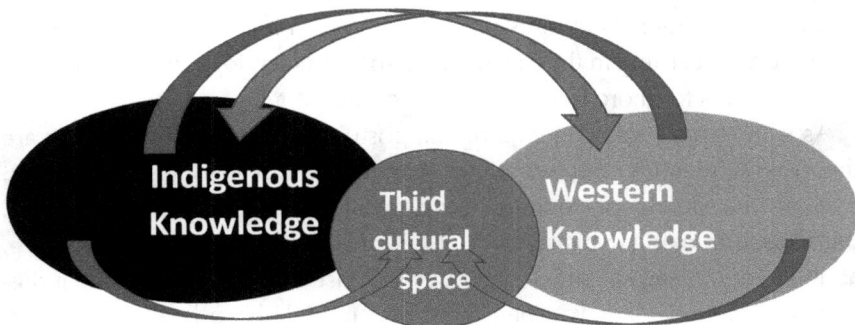

Figure 2.2 Third cultural spaces modelling.

A 'third space' is created when the two knowledge systems, ways of knowing, converge. Indigenous education programming can largely be understood in these spaces. Student wellbeing models deriving from Catholicism – Clontarf, mentoring models in Uni, AIME, and in sport, ARTIE – all work to position our identities within a broader mainstream picture. Even the 'latest' university-led research world imprinted Culturally responsive or 'cultural nourishment' programming coming from UNSW (Lowe et al., 2021).

Colleague Dr Tyson Yunkaporta advocated at a recent masterclass I ran in Melbourne, pre-Covid, on Indigenous research methodologies (IRMs), from his work (Yunkaporta, 2019), another view of the 'spaces' shared on the earlier diagram. His most recent provocations and experiences as an Indigenous scholar in the field is that the third space is further imbalanced. The Western sphere is shaped more like an oblong or oval sphere (much like the following diagram). And the 'cross-over' or third space between is much smaller. From his insight and centring of IK, the challenge for us as authentic Indigenous educators is to see that massive imbalance and work designs that are more sustainable and more reflexive of our practions (Steffenson, 2020) than trying to 'fit in' to the smaller prism created in third spaces.

And I use 'sustainability' as a concept here as a bridge. *Sustainability* is a very geo/political term of reference to the broader human rights goals and agendas of the United Nations. The United Nations Sustainable Development Goals cover 17 target areas for all areas of local and state governance to work on and, more collaboratively, with and for.

What I am learning (as the flow is always in motion), from expert IK practitioners like Dr Chels Marshall, is that regeneration is a more grounded, Indigenous-lensed view of sea and land management. For ease of translation here, I'll largely keep to 'sustainability', and I implore further *Riteways* thinking and learning in the regenerative spaces (keep logged on around IKS Lab campfires for more weaves and shares there).

As is the 'space' of academic rigour, postulation, and 'control', there are theorists, academics, and 'schools of thinking' who will contest, push back, attempt to 'redefine' or 'redirect' thinkings of and on cultural interface and third space thinking (Nakata, 2001; Dreamson, 2019). What I can and we, as Indigenous leaders and Indigenous-led Institutes collectively in Indigenous education, offer is a flag that these models have been practioned, tested, modelled, remodelled, and refracted. These models make sense to

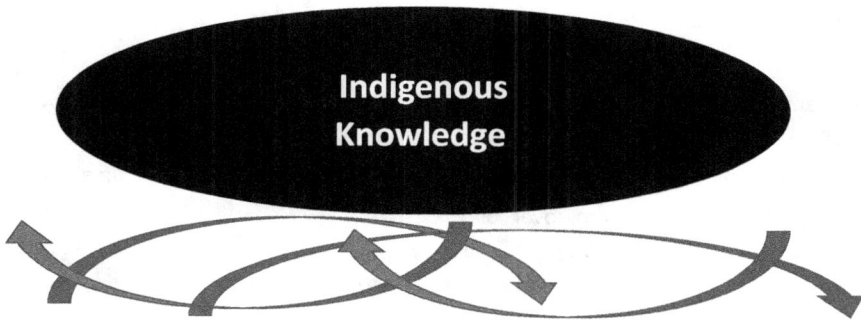

Figure 2.3 ***Riteways flow*** modelling.

our people and educators. And very openly, offer the 'in our space' academics in Australia a chance, as always, to yarn' 'with' rather than 'about' us. That is the way to continue to develop and broaden our impacts as educators, a role I traditionally hold in the highest esteem – noonthalli.

More to the point, and more to the challenge of sustainability, a humbling piece for me as a leading thinker and designer in this 'space', the modelling has been used to ground IK and develop more IRMs. A shout-out for more 'space being created' by leading Indigenous education practitioners like Wayne, Fi, and Gungi Jess King. Knowing your journeys intersect with mine and us/all knowledges of and from country, knowing that the models shared earlier and in what follow 'make most sense' to you, as Indigenous academics in situ, working so strongly in the field is enough of an academic war for me and hopefully us/all to engage in. Too much time has been 'paid' into a Western academic system which seems more fixated on 'understanding us' and situating us as a 'problem' than positioning us/all and our deep knowledges as 'solutions-focused'.

The following model goes some ways to showing what and where *Riteways* is best understood and where programmatic responses utilising *Riteways* should be grown from and grounded in.

This particular *Riteways flow* modelling foregrounds IK. IK is the centre of both the curriculum and pedagogical response, with the target to create better conditions for the flow of IK, not to 'respond' to cultural identity in curriculum and pedagogies; ultimately, *Riteways* aims at sustaining and regenerating knowledges.

Notes

1 Barrungam is the Western Downs, west of Bunyas language. This is the lingo of my Cobble Cobble people.

2 *Kinnection* (Davis, 2018) meaning relation to place and people – your kin and kith.

3 Wanjau translates to 'crossover' or 'exchanges'.

4 To match Figure 1 explanation of 'IKSL' to follow, we will use the full capitalisation 'THINK TANKS' from here on in through the paper.

References

Bhabha, H. (2004). *Bhabha: The location of culture*. London: Routledge Press.

Chilisa, B. (2012). *Indigenous research methodologies*. Thousand Oaks: SAGE.

Davis, J. (2017). *Binung Tjanga: Davis family storybook* (Limited ed., Family History book). Bunya.

Davis, J. (2018). *Durithunga: Growing, nurturing, challenging and supporting urban Indigenous leadership in education* (Unpublished PhD thesis). Queensland University of Technology, Brisbane.

Davis, M., & Williams, G. (2021). *Everything you need to know about the Uluru Statement from the heart*. Randwick: UNSW Press.

Dreamson, N. (2019). *Pedagogical alliances between Indigenous and non-dualistic cultures meta-cultural education*. New York: Routledge.

Lowe, K., Skrebneva, I., Burgess, C., Harrison, N., & Vass, G. (2021). Towards an Australian model of culturally nourishing schooling. *Journal of Curriculum Studies, 53*(4), 467–481. doi:10.1080/00220272.2020.1764111

Nakata, M. (2001). *Changing Indigenous perspectives in curriculum areas*. Paper presented at Aboriginal and Torres Strait Islander Education Symposium: Successful Futures, Cairns.

Nakata, M. (2007). *Disciplining the savages savaging the disciplines*. Canberra: Aboriginal Studies Press.

Packer, S. (2005). No common cents. *Australian Educators Magazine, 16*. Retrieved from www.aeufederal.org.au/Publications/AE/Spr05pp16-18.pdf

Steffenson, V. (2020). *Fire country – how Indigenous fire management could help save*. Melbourne: Hardie Grant Publishing.

Yunkaporta, C., Marshall, J., Davis, J., Waters, J., & Manning-Banningcroft, J. (Hosts) (2022, December 9). Increa$e. In *The Other Others* [Audio podcast]. Anchor. https://anchor.fm/tyson-yunkaporta

Yunkaporta, T. (2019). *Sand talk: How Indigenous thinking can save the world*. Melbourne: HarperOn.

Yunkaporta, T., & Davis, J. (Hosts). (2021, June 21). Research fellas. In *The Other Others* [Audio podcast]. Anchor. Retrieved from https://anchor.fm/tyson-yunkaporta

3   Understanding *Riteway* Flow in Context of Australia's Current Indigenous Education Landscape

The fore-fronting of IK as a base for pursuing improved teaching and learning outcomes for Indigenous students is a focus shared by Indigenous Australian academia. Aboriginal and Torres Strait Islander academics have begun to shape and map ways for us as learning communities to engage in an Indigenous Australian agenda. It's a process of valuing Australian holistic knowledge. This process is pursued through our own principles and practices and has the potential to transform education for Indigenous students into *Riteways flows*.

Our writers and thinkers in this realm are academics, including Professor Aileen Moreton-Robertson, ~Goenepul; Professor Martin Nakata, ~Torres Strait; Professor Irabinna Rigney, ~Kaurna; Professor Karen Martin, ~Goenepul; Professor Norm Sheehan, ~Wiradjuri; and Dr Mary Graham, ~Yugambeh. In defining this space further, Phillips et al. (2007) comment that the

> cultural interface today for Indigenous Knowledges and Indigenous Studies can be defined in four ways: Indigenous educators and Indigenous community; non-Indigenous educators and Indigenous community; Indigenous educators and non-Indigenous educators; and Indigenous Standpoint theory and pedagogy.
>
> (2007)

The work of Rigney, Nakata, Martin, Sheehan, and Robinson lay a foundation for the work that underpins *Riteways*, foregrounding Indigenous standpoint theory and pedagogies. In summarising the power of IK, Budin Yadga Will Davis reflects, 'Indigenous philosophy, principles of being, knowing

DOI: 10.4324/9781003298717-3

and learning are a necessary and integral core for authentic Indigenous education to occur' (Davis, 2007, p. 5). This is a powerful point. IK, through this process, as in Will Davis's 'Spear Making' curriculum, now being implemented in a broader community-controlled context, is essential if our ways are to be footprinted more heavily in education spaces. Martin achieves 'authentic Indigenous education' from her development of research from a Quandamoopah perspective, the theory of relatedness as told through the story of the Quampie, which defines ways of knowing, being, and doing (Martin, 2008). Sheehan achieves 'authentic indigenous education' through his principles of IK and learning through IK like art (2012). Nakata achieves 'authentic Indigenous education' through his focus on Torres Strait Islander identities and world views, reaching as he does for an Indigenous standpoint theory: an Indigenous standpoint that informs decision-making in all areas of transformational education (Nakata, 2007).

Generation 'now' – it's amazing to see the broader, mainstream influence of IK within education across every school. Daley River descendant, and 'off country' Logan local, Joe Sambono has been at the leading edge of curriculum writing and reforms from an IK perspective. Meticulously articulating IK perspectives through the prism of the national curriculum, ACARA. Joe's work culminated in 2018 with the publishing of over 90 elaborations of science. Back in the direct teaching and writing field, enabling university worlds to Indigenise curricula more, based at QUT, it'll be phenomenal to see what impacts occur through Joe's 'authentic Indigenous education' approach.

Joe's work can be coupled or juxtaposed amongst several other major influencers in the space and prism of education. Aforementioned Koori Principal D. Anderson has been at the helm of the IK-informed 'NATSIPA'. While holding posts as a principal foremostly, then as a manager within the Stronger Smarter Institute, D enacts in every interaction 'authentic Indigenous education'; she walks 'political is my perspective . . . my perspective is political' (hooks, 2003) style of education and fierce IK leadership.

Eagle-Eye Focus

Reflecting on my work at the Stronger Smarter Institute, IK, and Circle methodologies and sharing of praxis 'within circles' are central to how the Institute operates (Stronger Smarter Institute, 2017). The Institute's vision is to create transformational Indigenous education (*www.strongersmarter.com. au*). Through the Professional Learning space, SSI has run over:

- 200 leadership programs to over
- 4,000 alumni covering
- Every education context – urban, rural, remote – and
- Represents over 1,000 individual school and learning communities.

This is a significant footprint for an Independent Indigenous not-for-profit who weaves in 'third spaces' and negotiates programming across multiple states and jurisdictions.

SSI programs focus on Cultural Competence within the movement of transformational learning for educators (Stronger Smarter Institute, 2017). *Cultural Competency* in SSI refers to specific 'Behaviours, Filters, and Practices'. Curriculum and pedagogy are specific 'Behaviours, Filters, and Practices' school communities control. In curriculum and pedagogy, relating to Indigenous education, this has been 're-imagined' through a lens of 'cultural responsiveness' (Rigney, 2017; Perso, 2012; Lewthwaite et al., 2015). However, there is a lag in exemplars and models of and on sustaining cultural responsiveness. This book provides exemplars through metaphors on how to sustain and regenerate cultural responsiveness (Paris, 2012, NATSIPA Te Akatea Waitangi conference, personal communications, 2018).

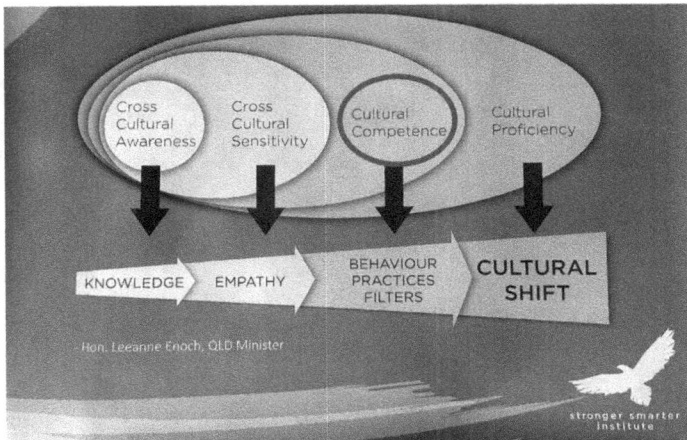

Figure 3.1 Cultural competence model (Stronger Smarter n.d.) – Stronger Smarter Institute's focus for professional learning currently.

Competence refers to the behaviours, attitudes, and actions of cultural approaches for learning for individuals, protocols, and practices to apply in 'cross-cultural', relating with other colleagues and community members (Gorringe & Spillman, 2008). SSI offers Australia's peak Indigenous education training, and this model (above) is a central learning for the Stronger Smarter Leadership Program © (SSLP©). I refer to it as 'peak' model because the SSLP© professional learnings have been internally evaluated on a consistency scale of 4.8/5 ratings for all participants (Stronger Smarter Institute, 2019) for over a decade!

Critique-wise, as a 'peak', the largest nationwide longitudinal study on Indigenous education in the country was conducted by Luke et al. (2013) on the early phases and impacts of the roll-out of the SSLP©. More recently, the SSLP© has been evaluated by the University of Canberra (2017) on its impacts as a regional professional learning model. The latest University of Canberra research found the 'scores . . . nothing short of exceptional . . . showing that the program fostered learning that was highly relevant to participants, epitomising quality professional development' (University of Canberra, 2017). The Cultural Competency model as flagged is a central learning acquired by participants through the SSLP©.

Riteways doesn't have Cultural Competency as its sole focus or driver. The *Riteways* model is focused on the Cultural Proficiency (see following) phase of cross-cultural relating. Cultural Proficiency for *Riteways* is the 'starting point' needed to enact Culturally Sustaining pedagogies and curriculums.

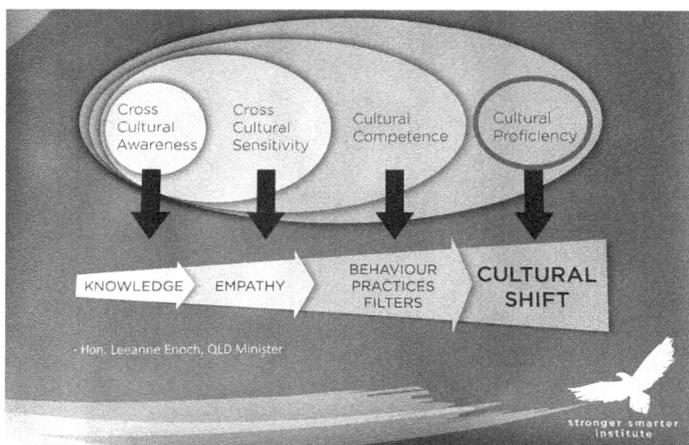

Figure 3.2 (Stronger Smarter n.d.) *Riteways flow* educator 'starting point'.

The provocation in this book is to ignite the fire needed for **Riteways** *directional learning; the highest standard of cross-cultural relating across all educational contexts must be applied.*

References

Davis, W. (2007). *Spear making* (Unpublished master's thesis). University of Queensland, St. Lucia.

Gorringe, S., & Spillman, D. (2008, December 7–11). *Creating stronger, smarter learning communities: The role of culturally competent leadership.* Paper presented at World Indigenous Peoples' Conference on Education, Indigenous Education in the 21st Century: Respecting Tradition, Shaping the Future, Victoria Aboriginal Education Association Inc. Retrieved from www.strongersmarter.com.au

Hooks, B. (2003). *Teaching community: A pedagogy of hope.* London: Routledge.

Lewthwaite, B. E., Osborne, B., Llyod, N., Boon, H., Llewellyn, L., Webber, T., Laffin, G., Harrison, M., Dat, C., Kemo, C., & Wills, J. (2015). Seeking a pedagogy of difference: What aboriginal students and their parents in North Queensland say about teaching and their learning. *Australian Journal of Teacher Education, 40*(5). doi:10.14221/ajte.2015v40n5.8

Luke, A., Cazden, C., Coopes, R., Klenowski, V., Ladwig, J., Lester, J., MacDonald, S., Phillips, J., Shield, P., Spina, N., Theroux, P., Tones, M., Villegas, M., & Woods, A. (2013). *A summative evaluation of the stronger smarter learning communities project: Vol. 1 and Vol. 2.* Brisbane: Queensland University of Technology.

Martin, K. (2008). *Please knock before you enter – Aboriginal regulation of outsiders and the implications for researchers.* Teneriffe: Post Pressed.

Nakata, M. (2007). *Disciplining the savages savaging the disciplines.* Canberra, ACT: Aboriginal.

Perso, T. F. (2012). *Cultural responsiveness and school education: With particular focus on Australia's first peoples: A review & synthesis of the literature.* Menzies School of Health Research, Centre for Child Development and Education, Darwin Northern Territory. Studies Press.

Phillips, S. R., Phillips, J., Whatman, S. L., & McLaughlin, J. M. (2007). Introduction: Issues in (re)contesting Indigenous knowledges and Indigenous studies. *The Australian Journal of Indigenous Education, 36S*(Supplement), 1–6.

Rigney, I. (2017). Decolonising Pacific Schools: Towards an Australian culturally responsive pedagogy (Inaugural David Unaipon lecture). London: Kings College. Retrieved from www.youtube.com/watch?v=bpqcU27kkWc

Sheehan, N. (2012). *Stolen generations education: Aboriginal cultural strengths and social and emotional well-being.* Woolloongabba: Link-Up Queensland.

Stronger Smarter Institute. (2017). *Implementing the stronger smarter approach.* Brisbane: Author.

Stronger Smarter Institute. (2019). *Stronger smarter field notes 2014–2019*. Brisbane: Author.

Stronger Smarter Institute. (n.d.). *Stronger smarter leadership © training posters on 'Cultural Competency'*. Brisbane.

University of Canberra. (2017). *Higher Education Participation and Partnerships Pro-gramme (HEPPP) Indigenous grants round 2013. Final report*. Stronger Smarter Schools Project, Submitted to Australian Government Department of Education and Training by University of Canberra, Bruce, Australian Capital Territory.

Patterning *Riteways*

4

Culturally Regenerative Pedagogies and Sustainable Curriculum Flows

Riteways hyper-extends current curriculum and pedagogical practices and filters. Yunkaporta refers to hyper-extensions and bending of space in time in his seminal piece, *Sand Talk* (2019). The hyper-extension comes from the movement away of blending or creating 'third spaces'. As Figure 2.2 shows, the focus of *Riteways* is not side-by-side recognition or reference to Western and IK systems. *Riteways* is IK-centric. With that as a directional path, the focus or output of *Riteways* is regenerative. Within the ACARA model, cross-curricula priorities represent a (notional/beginners) level of responsiveness to our Indigenous identities; however, it is not centred or aimed at sustaining IK practices. Learning maps and models from a national curriculum perspective are a 'tick in the box'. 'Many of the Aboriginal perspective's items, even in the most basic "processes" column, seemed to deal more with simple factual content rather than Aboriginal ways of thinking and doing' (Lowe & Yunkaporta, 2013, p. 5).

What's the impact or outcome of following the current 'lay of the land' only? What is the impact of only bridging a gap of cross-cultural relating to Cultural Competence? How can we generalise these outcomes currently? Even by looking at cohorts of Indigenous student Primary school data nationally gives some insight into generational impacts (Australian Productivity Commission, 2016a, 2016b). Indigenous young people within this cohort are overwhelmingly 'outscored' by non-Indigenous on national testing results. The Productivity Commission reports that 'Indigenous primary students have lower NAPLAN test scores on average than non-Indigenous' (Australian Productivity Commission, 2016a, pp. 51–52). Within Indigenous cohorts, the most important contributor to achievement within the observed data is still the socio-economic background of students (Australian Productivity Commission, 2016a).

DOI: 10.4324/9781003298717-4

Linking to further Indigenous education research, from the Productivity Commission, referencing the 'Close the Gap' targets, the Overcoming Indigenous Disadvantage report (2016) reinforced the Primary school data messages. Expanding to High School data, the Productivity Commission found that Year 1–10 attendance was not improving (Australian Productivity Commission, 2016b). What does this mean for the educational opportunities afforded our younger people? Lower attainment or disengagement in school-aged learning environs can lead to more social disadvantage like recidivism.

Indigenous young people represent disproportionate numbers in youth detention. Our young people made up more than half, 54%, of all those in detention on an average night in the June quarter in 2018 (Australian Institute of Health and Welfare, 2018, p. 11). In Northern Territory, Indigenous youth represent 100% of those held in youth detention centres (Allam, May 31, 2019). This represents a massive gap in learning potential. In lay terms, while *Murries* go 'in' (prison), *Migloos* go 'out' of schools in disproportionate numbers.

These lost opportunities continue to feed into 'the gap' data. Professionally and personally, this has been hard to stomach, especially when we know, grow, and seed our tall trees, all over the country, in all localised and complex community contexts (see Community Guarantee, p. 31–39). The Uluru Statement from the Heart speaks to this 'torment', the struggle in the 'gap', really well:

> Proportionally, we are the most incarcerated people on the planet. We are not an innately criminal people. Our children are aliened from their families at unprecedented rates. This cannot be because we have no love for them. . . . These dimensions of our crisis tell plainly the structural nature of our problem. This is the torment of our powerlessness.
> (Uluru Statement from the Heart in Davis & Williams, 2021)

Current 2020 educational trends highlight the importance of Science Technology Engineering, and Maths (STEM), raising the subject matter profile as a heightened learning opportunity. 'Reflecting the national discourse, most state and territory jurisdictions have identified education initiatives in STEM. A review of their respective education websites identifies numerous initiatives noting the importance of STEM fields to future careers' (Tynan, & Noon, 2017). What SSI research showed, backed by recent CSIRO Evaluation Reports on Indigenous programming, is that there is an internationally recognised 'high

Indigenous interest in Sciences' yet a low conversion rate for *gundoos* going through to Science, STEM, tertiary pathways in Australia (Tynan & Noon, 2017).

Even for young Indigenous people who are settled or survive in the current learning systems, there is a long-standing historical tendency to herd these young people jurisdictionally into lower-expectation, non-ATAR paths. Even when all attendance is followed, racism realities cause stress and torment for our young people, where they react and can become violent to the sense of 'powerlessness'. What does this mean? The opportunity which exists in the fastest-growing industry, STEM, education modelling currently is not equipping young Indigenous people with the skill sets to meet that opportunity. The inquiry model in the Sciences is a great example of what and how Indigenous learning potential could be converted into STEM career pathways (Tynan & Noon, 2017). *Riteways* does this.

Riteway flows provide a Culturally Sustaining and regenerative curriculum and pedagogical model for Culturally Proficient educators to enact. *Riteways flows* are predicated on teaching and learning methodologies which draw on the strengths of thousands of years of campfire knowledge, practices, and processes. And through educational practions (Steffenson), we, as Indigenous education learning communities, have developed a density of sustainable Indigenous education models (see 'Context Map', p. xiii). The greatest gifts our ancestors left and leave footprints to follow is sustainability. Marshall explains this well in a recent IK regen translation chapter:

> The purpose of providing platforms for Indigenous paradigms and traditional knowledge systems in modern humanity's sustainability is to provide pathways of innovative thinking and approaches by inserting this paradigm into the toolbox that advances evolution in adaptation and resilience in the face of human induced climate change.
> (Marshall, 2020)

Riteways by Design: Circle Methodologies, Patterns

This is not education 'to fit in'; this is education that 'fits'. The vision is to grow the next generation of cultural workers, healers, educators, and leaders who will be grounded in education modelling which not only nourishes their identity but also ultimately sustains its. *Riteways* focuses on circle methodologies. IK Senior Researcher and former Chief of Impact at SSI Jesse King reflected recently on IK connectivity with circle methods and inferences to Western ways of knowing:

> IK is observation. . . . IK favours longer term visioning, seeing patterns within the environment and interrelated links. . . . To me, IK, our way is all about how patterns and relationships between entities occur. We see the interrelating behaviours of certain animals or environs at certain times of the year and record that pattern. The patterns are learned through our links to country.
>
> (personal communication, 2019)

Bouls ngima dgagunbaras. All around country, there are permanent spaces/reminders and still flowing sites of circles and patterns of learning. The 'stone arrangements' speak to the antiquity of our land and also act as a 'more than' indicator to the process and enactment of circle work like Yarning circles in pedagogical and curriculum flows (Scott, 1988; Bunya Mountains Elders, 2010).

Flow forms in what movement? From which base? Flow as a concept draws on teachings from the south-eastern corner of Murriland, Queensland. Flow references deeper Indigenous thinking on the sites of greatest convergence. This, in the language of Kabi Kabi, based on Jinabara traditional knowledges (and shared, wanjaued, across Murriland and Australia), refers to mimburi (Gaiabrau, in Steele, 1984; Blair in Davis, 2018; Kite & Wurm, 2004). *Mimburi* is the source of energy, the site, time, place, and space of energy flows. Mimburi is everywhere, and it can be concentrated in certain places, time, and spaces. Areas of great mimburi are referenced as mating sites of certain animals, clusters of great trees, roosting sites of flocks of birds, concentration of fish in certain pools of water.

So areas of great convergence for totemic animals, like Barrungam and Wakka Wakka people, the Carbal, carpet snake, are sites of great significance. Areas include the great rock and sandstone areas at the foothills of the Bunya Bunya Mountains. Reflecting on areas which border Bunya Mountains, Gaiarbaru stated, 'Gugundair [just outside of current Cherbourg] is mimburi of the carpet snake. . . . This was fighting ground and corroboree place during bunyas' (Gaiarbaru, in Steele, 1984).

Mimburi as a concept was the first reference and recognition of Queensland Indigenous Knowledges in the land and was utilised by colonial forces (from

Patterned thinking is embracing the way of and for knowledge for this land.

How?? The design is a boul. A boul is a circle.

A boul:

And the boul is layered:

Within the bouls and between the bouls there is movement:

SPIRIT

SPIRIT

SPIRIT

Figure 4.1 Patterned thinking.

the late 1800s) to understand country and its people (Steele, 1984). Great sites of mimburi, over time, have become gazetted lands for national parks and nature reserves. In Queensland, the site of the great macadamia, gonbarra, for Yugmabeh and the site of the oldest Bunya Bunyas for Wakka, Barrungam Djakunde and Jarrowair, were the first national parks. Testament to our people and original Kabi thinkers and sharers of knowledge, the Kabi Kabi people refer regularly to and reference many times the site, space, and significance of mimburi (Hands, in Swan, 2017).

In concept and feeling, relationally to the environment, mimburi are spaces where there is concentration and articulation of life and energy. *Riteways flow* is a recognition that, for learning, *Riteways* are needed; response to conditions and indicators of flow are referenced to create better learning and knowledge transferral and dispersal of the pattern of knowledge on Indigenous identity curriculum, languages, and culture compared to other learning spaces (see *Riteways* indicators, p. 167 onwards).

The intricacies, detail, and augmentation of optimal learning, shaping, and responding to the surrounds have been elucidated in this country since time immemorial. There are patterns and paths and designs of thinking to learn and grow from that are not deeply understood in the articulation of 'what is education' and responses we have as a 21st-century Australian education system. Current systems are heavily predicated on Western models of centuries old and, in the Australian case, a century-old education system.

Riteway flows are a further recognition and articulation that our deeper learning, established through processes like wanjau, don't exactly 'fit in' and cannot be blended all the time. *Riteway flows*, more to the point of this piece, are modern adaptations and articulations on Indigenous Knowledges education 'that fit'. And if we, as an Indigenous polities, are to enjoy any of the freedoms and elucidations that come from education journeys, then creating better models of education flow must be paramount in all education design and thinking of and for an Indigenous polity.

The antithesis and reflection, refraction, retraction of *Riteway flows* models, be they home station learning, Independent Indigenous schools, Indigenous Knowledge units within schools, flexible school models, to continue the same propensity to sharpening or adapting or bending and blending our schooling models with a blind articulation of power and control, achieves one outcome, guarantees it. The 'gap'. A highly contested and 'known' space of and in the Australian Indigenous education field, the gap of educational advantage, the equity of education as a socially bridging ladder or course, the diaspora between Indigenous and non-Indigenous 'outcomes' on Western statistical indicators, will continue to grow (Walter & Anderson, 2013). In my last attempt to bridge a gap of knowledge or logical reasoning, I draw on a tried-and-true Western provocation from the Institute which applies to a range of impact thinking and education transformation: 'Isn't trying to solve the same problem with the same definition and design that created them the definition of madness?' (Einstein). And from our lens, as a palawa lead social statistician says in understanding 'good numbers' or nahra kati, Indigenous quantitative methodologies are methodologies within which the practices and the processes of the research are conceived and framed through an Indigenous standpoint (Walter & Anderson, 2013). Across first world colonizing settler nation states, Indigenous data largely conform to what Walter (Walter & Anderson, 2013; Walter, 2018) describes as 5D data. That is, mainstream Indigenous statistics focus almost exclusively on items related to Indigenous difference, disparity, disadvantage, dysfunction, and deprivation (Walter, 2018).

Situating the final call to arms through dgagunbara, specifically, Jutja Paddy Jerome (RIP), who, in his wise words and wisdom of 'getting back' country, tried to weave in multiple stakeholders like universities to support earlier IK work (Ross et al., 2013). When working up and developing a duwur – more closed circle process and rites-of-passage piece – he spoke and shared specifically on our Dreaming stories that influence our everyday environments – the space and time of now – which impact on us/all. The 'code', as Pa explained, related to the pattern of and on Cultural Indicator Species (Davis & Coopes, 2022), which 'may hold the key to further scientific advances' (Jerome & Wilkie, 2003, p. 3). Even when new bacteria or organisms grow and impact on contemporary life now, Jerome reinforces the power of Dreaming and story by stating, 'Our ancestors would expect that in the same locality as the organism appeared, will be found a plant extract that will keep this organism under control' (Jerome & Wilkie, 2003, p. 3).

The situational response or opportunity to learn our ways, deepen educational paths, sustain learning sequences more effectively and affectively is the macro-overlay design for *Riteways* – the flow pattern (Markers, p. 112). Steffenson, in his work, refers to the knowledge maps (Steffenson, 2020). Yunkaporta shares how 'we remember' through the share/study on Aboriginal memorisation techniques (Yunkaporta, 2019). And Marshall walks and applies regeneration through the national conceptualisation and praction of Regenerative story of country and songlines (Marshall, 2020). The situation is contextual and related to and must be grounded in the country where this learning takes place. Models we learn from and augment this approach in education now are Yothu Yindi Foundation, who leads the Garma Festival (going since 1990); Children's Ground, Central Australia, beginning in 2016; the Murri School, Australia's first Independent Indigenous school, begun in 1986; the latest and expansive Indigenous education model, Darkunjung Barker, opened in 2016 and expanding all around Australia, a First Nations–led school partnership model (coordinated by the Barker Institute); AIME's Imagination University, starting 'in the field' in 2005 and now diversifying to and through its own higher education and social entrepreneurship designs. This is not a one-size-fits-all approach but more of a way to interrelate and reposition our knowledge perspectives centrally and always weave our ways relationally.

This is *Riteways*, to lift and see our voices. And these ways, like the preceding modelling mentioned, are being shared through the practical reflection and refraction, inhale, and exhale of programmatic responses we have forged together in macro – whole of Australian/across states – and micro – specific Language program, Identity curriculums, lesson plans, and Strategic and Operational plan logics – levels. So even in the specific *Riteways* pattern and model designs to unfold in the following chapters, the essential elemental flow of and for the design to work is that it must be developed with wanjaus, exchanges, and reciprocal relationships at the forefront of mind and embodiment of praxis. The further reflections and articulations on specific *Riteways* patterns are not intended as a 'new' blind articulation and reticulation of power and power imbalances. In fact, even as I write now in real time, a storm bird – koel – is calling. That is the second distinct bird calling for me over the last few days. It signals shift and change, and I must make proper time and allocated time and space to being with and hearing from Bunya Barrahs (fellow countrymen and women kinnected to and around dgagunbaras). So respectfully I write this part here as a signal that to regenerate and make meaningful flows, you and we, as Indigenous educators, must take time to weave in and see the relational patterns that already exist, work at not discarding and distilling to binaries – either/or – but seek the sights of convergence and emergence. And to do that effectively, we/all must be in a 'safe space'. We must be coming from a strength base, not be caught in the Western adversarial design. Collaborations and kollaborators (Davis & Coopes, 2022; Fletcher et al., 2023) in all forms are important to see, define, and recognise.

Within our current Indigenous education design in Australia, the safest space (which I have most recently woven out of – again), which has been a 'space in the middle' as well as a liminal operator and provocateur for better systemic changes, is the Indigenous-led Stronger Smarter. In all my educational, personal, and professional learnings, it is the Stronger Smarter insight that has perpetually fuelled the fire in my belly – this point can't be understated. I would (and several 'us' do) go mad – literally throw our hands up, listen to our hearts, feel the strain, and leave (this is a phenomenon unfortunately in place and being experienced by Indigenous colleagues).

If it weren't for the Stronger Smarter Institute, I and we – and several of our colleagues have proclaimed this – would walk away in more droves as the continual realm of misinformation and disquiet from 'I didn't know' has a real and visceral impact on your wellbeing and overall mental health. Very succinctly, Koori Principal from outback New South Wales reflects on her re-engagement with Stronger Smarter training:

> [I]t was just the perfect time for me and it made me believe in myself again because I was starting to think that I couldn't do it. . . . I recon- nected with people who believed in me as well as making me see that I could do this and it was then that I decided that I want to be the next principal at Menindee Central School.
>
> (Kelly, 2019)

This 'challenge' in 'our space' of Indigenous education is reflected in the limited and limiting Human Resource (HR) data and opportunity that exist for our people. CIQ (Peek, 2023) is a newly formed Cultural Intelligence training space leading at specific corporate and organisational change (*learn more at culturaliq.com.au*). A current national HR study into the acquisition of perma- nent senior management positions for all of Indigenous Australia's working population, filtered by CIQ, found that an alarming 0.7% of all Indigenous employees made Senior Management positions. Surely, as a modern democ- racy offering a range of opportunities to 'all', we could aspire and achieve a better senior management positioning than this for First Nations Australians? Again, this is the 'torment' espoused in the Uluru Statement. Even when we 'make the cut' of regular workflow and positional authority, as well as oppor- tunity for more social mobility and stability, we are left with a roundabout of jobs or specialisations of roles which don't require our skill set or 'fit'.

And we, as its lead 'experts', Indigenous practitioners, continually are availed with the challenge that 'communities can't develop or sustain lead- ers'. That is bullshit. The current education systems we offer our communities overall can't develop or sustain our leaders. The leadership and intricate web of local knowledge and lead workers, practitioners, exist all around our communities. Urban, rural, and very remote, there exists an intricate mist net (Pascoe, 2014) of Indigenous leadership who are committed, who live, lead, and share in the fruits of their local community contexts. It is the system designs that continually miss the mark on propagating and providing the right conditions for that leadership to seed and grow (Sarra, 2011, 2012).

I share that insight earlier from the SSLP, Stronger Smarter Leadership, training circles. I have set circle with the Institute in all contexts of complexity and social diasporas. And in every challenging complex circle I have seen, worked with, and been exposed to, a similar strength and situational expertise exist in that microcosm. As Jutja Pa Paddy Jerome shared on the balance of culture on nature making balance, he surmises that the original Dreaming 'designed everything to be in harmony' (Jerome & Wilkie, 2003, p. 3), further lamenting, 'Unfortunately human beings tend to upset the harmony and balance of nature' (Jerome & Wilkie, 2003, p. 3).

My work in the Institute, our transformational lens, was to provide space and time for Migloo minds and eyes to see this leadership from cement sidewalks through to red dust plains. We have a national training model that guarantees participants will 'shift deficit thinking' and effectively build High-Expectations Relationships tools. Yet even in these contexts, reaching over 11% of all schools *in Australia (with 36% being the most 'complex'), we still have educators come in circle with base-level understandings about Indigenous people, histories, and cultures; we still have a significant number of educators who unconsciously subscribe to low expectations of our people. This is not the right condition or best position to be starting from as an educator*.

That is why, for *Riteways* to sustain and regenerate, we must move from the elemental levels of educator responsiveness and competency (see diagram, p. 22) of and on our people. Cultural Proficiency, in whatever theoretical form, the highest point of 'cross-cultural relating' in all its academic definitions, must be a benchmark for educators to engage in effective and affective teaching and learning and community weaving to enable sustainability and best traction and praction of programming. An attempt at this 'top-performing' model has been and is being rolled out in teacher education in Australia through 'Teach for Australia' type of models. In that space, what is not consistent is the organisational pivot, control, and contestation of and on 'space'. The actual Institutes that begin to grow and seed cycles within the Indigenous educational diaspora don't themselves enact a 'Culturally Proficient' stance or beginning. Anecdotally, I know, at community, state, and national levels, that 'new-forming' and 'space-taking' initiatives create a tension and frustration amongst us as fellow First Nations–led operators. I know from personal experiences, a frustration and voicelessness, a frustration and invisibility, I and we feel when 'new initiatives' are being drummed or messaged by politicians as the next 'Close the Gap' initiative. Again, this is our 'torment'.

What invariably happens in the 'current context' of Indigenous education currently in Australia that I see is the constant development of settler responses to Indigenous education without the base or proper *Riteways* principle of 'First Nations first' or Indigenous-led integration and instigation of relationship. So an independent, well-governed org like SSI, Indigenous-led is often overlooked or passed over for new 'Cultural Competency' models in the national training, the Indigenous education teacher training space. The independent not-for-profit is vying for 'space' and competing 'against' fellow Indigenous orgs or is pitted against the might of Australia's burgeoning sandstone university structures. Worse now is such organisations starting to coop our cultural symbiology, tagging their works as 'ochre' or 'Circle economies', to name a few from the national and international learning communities 'evolving' in our space.

What is empowering and exciting to see is, again, our community bases, our strengths, working out more weaves and wefts in bringing 'Voice' to the works and programmatic responses targeted at specific social determinants areas. What I allude to here (and is discussed in more detail from p. 96 onwards) is the Logan City context. Here, amongst Indigenous community–controlled collaboratives, our Indigenous polities and leadership have taken on the dominant social service modelling and proposed a more 'Culturally Proficient' position for largely non-Indigenous NGO and governmental departments. The funding model advocated for and won by the local Indigenous kolabs is 'Equity Partnerships' (EqPs). This model sets from the beginning of a programmatic relationship what monetary supports is wanted and then will be contributed to First Nations first thinking and leadership.

EqPs is not the norm for and of social services in education specifically. The mesh and melding of programs and share of resources is left up to the operators themselves, so often SSI and I, over the years, have led this brokerage independently. In the field and as a value proposition, SSI is 'too big to ignore' now, so a lot of the new models must come across or respond to SSI as an 'institute in the field'. This power relating is a good thing – a good position to be in as an Indigenous education, Indigenous-led Institute. And overall, a feeling of 'being too big to ignore' or, eventually, that new orgs 'need to respond'. Does that sound strength-based? Or supportive of Indigenous-led organisations/initiatives?

This, for me, speaks to the heart of lived and long models of discrimination and 'othering' which our people have had to endure, our 'torment'. This is the Institutional racism that exists, now in real time across our country. This is the moment in our history where we need to persist to resist and vote 'yes' for Voices in referendums of change. Because models like so-called independent models operating in systems of ASIC or CATSIAC, the national Indigenous registries of business and corporations, leaders like SSI or AIME all hold the same challenge. In fact, as I write, AIME Founder and Adjunct Scholar at IKS Lab JMB has led an innovative and culturally regenerative challenge of ending or weaving out of the Indigenous education diaspora. A breath of fresh air blown on the social impact fires. A breath of fresh air blown *Riteways* through jalnay, Bandjalung fire story, not led by profitable non-Indigenous-led university or corporation or 'big body' voices but led by the AIME charity.

An Indigenous-led response in Indigenous education, specifically gundoos pathways to university, is now, intentionally, on a path to ending in x10 years' time. The all-pervasive power of inequity and Institutional racism is such that a new (and country-informed) process of business trading is being designed and now actioned on a path to closure. A massive step of altruistic value which taps into the ancient principles of 'give-give', warmga, and is being fashioned by IK-led thinking and design. To end in x10 years' time for AIME, as I know it, is a path of potentiality infused in a system of open learning to be situated in an online university space and 'hand over the notes', as JMB requotes from Ray Charles (personal communications, 2022).

AIME is weaving out of the Indigenous education space, intentionally, to call in other, new regenerative practices and processes and call out the inequities of Institutional racism and inequitable market share of the so-called 'not-for-profit' sector. From the sandstone university sectors of Australia to the paved pathways of multiple schooling sites, tell me which educational institute has planned, and is actively planning, to 'weave out' of its space of operation – current wealth and industry lead? AIME is laying down a marker, providing a challenge for all who operate in our space (and operate at a high dollar value in every teaching and learning space – let's be honest), to look inwardly to project outwardly the positivity change and intentional change could bring because the insight an inspirational leader and leadership model JMBs AIME-rs show is, 'the system is too fucked – let's try and break it'.

New Reconciliation Action Plan (RAP) modelling is beginning to provide more national agreement-making and benchmark-setting of, and on, organisations to 'build more' Indigenous capacities and workplace capabilities. What a process like EqPs, shared earlier, shows is that in spite of 'baseline' RAP attainments and engagements, more testing and 'stretch of thinking' is needed in this bigger-org, non-Indigenous 'commitment' space. To clarify, RAP is good and 'culturally competent' needed work – like the base standard of flags and Welcome to and Acknowledgements of Country at major functions, baseline data Indigenous HR targets. And this is not *Riteways* 'beginning' or centralist point. If you apply *Riteways* and you're not at a Cultural higher level of Proficiency, **then the onus is on you to dig deeper and have more critical insight and design before you walk into our knowledge field**. This is a truth of and for educators wanting to flow in deep IK – 'authentic Indigenous education'. The 'gap' is in the training and translation points of and on Indigenous education and us as a polity. We are the most researched people in the world. To move further along the cross-cultural relating paradigm, this is the cognitive switch that must be hit to re-ignite the *Riteways* patterning and interrelating of and to country. Teaching is a privilege. And educators hold significant power in face-to-face delivery to the minds of generations. Our IK models of teaching and learning, in circles, transgenerational and transdisciplinary, are not congruent with the post-industrial 'factory' forms of Western schooling.

I was scared for being 'too cultural' in an Indigenous education role and in an Indigenous school. Several colleagues – majority non-Indigenous, some Indigenous – would warn of me being 'too cultural' throughout my career. The 'gap' data speaks to a truth that the current education offered to our young people and collective communities may not be 'cultural enough'. When young ones and older ones can't 'see a future' for themselves or in their identity, the most extreme and painful way to 'opt out', unfortunately, is self-harm. And all too often, our rates of suicide and self-harm are double than, triple than, others'.

That is why an HR reflection model (see the 'Mani model', Figure 5.1) and reflection on key questions are essential in deepening *Riteways flows*. How am I as an educator? Who am I in relation to the Indigenous community? What am I able to do and bring to the Cultural Proficiency challenge? And the ultimate question, Can I?

We all have a responsibility, Indigenous and non-Indigenous, to continue to shift the dial on educational opportunity. The weight of this responsibility as seen through a *Riteways* design is on Culturally Proficient educators – the other 97%. By sheer weight of numbers as 3% of the total population with lack of legal instruments like treaty, what *Riteways* offers in this position is not a systemic trademark or 'to-do' list. *Riteways* as a process offers educators the opportunity to enact with responsibility, equity, fairness.

I don't want Indigenous gundoos and families to be 'responded to'. I want, and we deserve, to be 'regenerated', revered in and through ways which link to the oldest human relationship patterning in the world. As a Culturally Proficient educator, I acknowledge that key questions emerge and develop responsibility in the privilege of facilitating learning for the oldest living, surviving culture.

When you have managed and developed the delivery of cross-cultural relating to the highest point, 'Cultural Proficiency', then come set pattern, sit in circle, and set ways which respond of and to us, guide the seen through the unseen, and know country will always look after us. When we come into relation at the highest point or parts of collaboration, then the success and longevity of programming are guaranteed. And our communities, in all our different context in all parts of Australia, guarantee that success – we are the strength, vibration, and rhythm that are the constant in everyone's context, rural, remote, regional, or urban.

References

Allam, L. (2019). *'System is broken': All children in NT detention are Aboriginal, officials say.* Retrieved from http://www.p.6w.theguardian.com/Australia-news/2019/may/31/system-is-broken-all-children-in-nt-detention-are-aboriginal-officials-say

Australian Institute of Health and Welfare. (2018). *Youth detention population in Australia 2018* (P11., Bulletin no. 145. Cat. no. JUV 128). Canberra: AIHW.

Australian Productivity Commission (2016a, June). *Indigenous primary school achievement, productivity commission research paper.* Retrieved from www.pc.gov.au

Australian Productivity Commission (2016b). *Overcoming Indigenous disadvantage – key indicators.* Retrieved from www.pc.gov.au

Bunya Mountains Elders Council (Eds.). (2010). *Bonye Buru – Boobagun Ngumminge – Bunya Mountains Aboriginal aspirations and caring for country plan.* Bargara: Burnett Mary Regional Group.

Davis, J., & Coopes, R. (2022). Our fire stories: Emergence through the circle work-process at the Indigenous knowledge systems lab. *Journal of Awareness-Based Systems Change, 2*(2), 85–108. doi:10.47061/jasc.v2i2.3892

Davis, M., & Williams, G. (2021). *Everything you need to know about the Uluru Statement from the heart.* Randwick: UNSW Press.

Fletcher, G., Waters, J., Yunkaporta, T., Marshall, C., Davis, J., & Manning Bancroft, J. (2023). Indigenous systems knowledge applied to protocols for governance and inquiry. *Systems Research and Behavioral Science,* 1–4. doi:10.1002/sres.2932

Jerome, P., & Wilkie, W. (2003). *The Jurrawa men's handbook: A description of Jurrawa culture and language.* Brisbane: W. Wilkie Psychologist.

Kelly, F. (2019). *"Every student podcast – episode 6"* transcribed by Scott, M. Retrieved from nsw.gov.au

Kite, S., & Wurm, S. (2004). *The Duunjidjawu language of southeast Queensalnd: Grammar, texts and vocab.* Canberra: Pacific Linguistics Research School, ANU.

Lowe, K., & Yunkaporta, T. (2013). The inclusion of Aboriginal and Torres Strait Islander content in the Australian national curriculum: A cultural, cognitive and socio-political evaluation. *Curriculum Perspectives, 33*(1), 1–14.

Marshall, C. A. (2020). The role of Indigenous paradigms and traditional knowledge systems in modern humanity's sustainability quest – future foundations from past knowledge's. In R. Roggema (Ed.), *Designing sustainable cities. Contemporary urban design thinking.* Cham: Springer. doi:10.1007/978-3-030-54686-1_2

Pascoe, B. (2014). *Dark Emu: Black Seeds: Agriculture or accident?* Broome, WA: Magabala Books.

Peek, C. (2023). CIQ. *Cultural IQ.* Retrieved from https://culturaliq.com.au/learn-more

Ross, A., Ulm, S., & Tobane, B. (2013). Gummingurru –A community archaeology knowledge journey. *Australian Archaeology, 76*(1), 62–68. doi:10.1080/031224 17.2013.11681966

Sarra, C. (2011). *Strong and smart – towards a pedagogy for emancipation: Education for first peoples.* New York: Routledge.

Sarra, C. (2012). *"Good morning Mr. Sarra" – my life working for a stronger, smarter future for our children.* St. Lucia: University of Queensland Press.

Scott, G. (Ed.). (1988). *Lake broadwater – the natural history of an inland lake and its environs.* Toowoomba: Darling Downs Institute Press.

Steele, J. G. (1984). *South East aboriginal pathways.* St. Lucia: UQP.

Steffenson, V. (2020). *Fire country – how Indigenous fire management could help save Australia.* Melbourne: Hardie Grant Publishing.

Swan, D. (2017). *Bunya Tukka tracks: Investigating traditional travelling routes of Eastern Australia* (Master's thesis). School of Architecture, Deakin University, Victoria.

Tynan, M., & Noon, K. (2017). *Indigenous STEM education project first evaluation report September 2014 – June 2016.* Canberra: CSIRO.

Walter, M. (2018). The voice of Indigenous data: Beyond the markers of disadvantage. *Griffith Review,* (60), 256–263. Retrieved from https://search.informit.org/doi/10.3316/ielapa.586241932732209

Walter, M., & Anderson, C. (2013). *Indigenous statistics: A quantitative research methodology.* Walnut Creek: Left Coast Press.

Yunkaporta, T. (2019). *Sand talk: How Indigenous thinking can save the world.* Melbourne: HarperOn.

5

Strength Base: Our Community Guarantees

With a meshwork of over 4,000 alumni across 1,000 different school/community contexts, can I unequivocally go on record in stating, in every context, no matter how complex, that there exist what I and the Institute call 'tall trees'? With kinnection to modelling Australia-wide, some of the insights I share are from direct involvement in service delivery – facilitating and participating in transformational training offered by Stronger Smarter. Other insights come from my research enactment, seeing the outcomes within circle transpire into what the Institute flags as 'Workplace Leadership Challenges' (Stronger Smarter, 2017). More sensemaking comes from the Stronger Smarter Approach, by our people. As the inaugural 2016 SSI head of research, I was exposed to hundreds of mixed-method case study data sets based on our alumni, which the Institute tags as 'field notes' (Stronger Smarter, 2017). There is engrained in every field note a link to the notion of pursuit of excellence and regrowing or sustaining the community-wide aspiration of Aboriginal excellence. And my people, in all my education and community organisational experiences, believe it. We know it. We look for it. This is the 'guarantee' and excitement working with a newly forming Institute, IKS Lab, brings.

No matter what workspace or project area I and we flow to, there is a great feeling across my home communities that our people have the ability, have the drive to 'do more', 'be more'. This strength exists all around Australia. My grounded-ness in my home community, off-country at Logan City, one of the most culturally diverse in Queensland, Australia, provided me with the base and teaching time and tools to seed and see these strengths grow. Mid-career, my PhD, Community Durithunga (Davis, 2018), was a way of 'paying back' and giving 'voice' to our people, especially our Indigenous

DOI: 10.4324/9781003298717-5

leaders, who, for a significant part of their working lives in education, fight against 'being heard'. Mantras like 'First Nations First' or new RAP commitments, with committee and overseeing structures, systemically, won't and don't shift a dial in Indigenous education if they're not seeded in the ground, alongside the Indigenous leadership that exists, the strength from within communities. Again, Founder Dr Chris Sarra quotes this best from his work and times at Cherbourg (the heartland of Stronger Smarter): 'We didn't go to Cherbourg and give the children a sense of being "Strong & Smart". . . . That was inside them already' (Sarra in Stronger Smarter, 2017). This point was raised well in the Durithunga PhD research where participants reflected on their challenges within 'good-meaning systems' as compared to the process and practice of setting Indigenous circle work *Riteways* – specifically, Durithunga way.

> One of the things that stands out to me is the equality of it all. . . . [N]o one person is dominant – is in charge. . . . [E]veryone's thoughts are respected. . . . Bring one another together . . . makes me feel strong.
> (Durithunga informant in Davis, 2018, p. 133)

At IKS Labs, we have the pattern of smoke from campfire hearths as our strategic IKS Lab plan – our guide. The premise here is, we draw strength from 60,000 years' worth of campfire knowledge, and now we can sustain these knowledges, apply our systems thinking to a complicated world, because we're not looking for tangible but relying on the tried-and-true method of seeing beyond and into the liminal (Fletcher et al., 2023; Davis & Coopes, 2022). ***Our communities, in all their unique contexts, guarantee success.*** There is a strength base, fertile soils, and definite pivot people and success pathways to learn from and gear more of our people towards (explored later through the *Riteways* amplification of 'Stories of Strength', p. 75 onwards).

This is the gap or lack of sight/vision of the current educational purview. A simple, culturally responsive mantra is chanted by Indigenous educationalist all over Australia (and is known around the world). The mantra is, 'You can't be what you can't see'. It is a powerful reflection of the value and the support Indigenous educators receive in education. A simple ask or applied task for bureaucracies working in Indigenous education context is, 'What is your Indigenous staffing level?' 'Where are Indigenous employees working in generally?' 'What streams of work?' 'What opportunities are being offered which grow the 0.7% Indigenous Senior employee index?'

In leading Indigenous programming work I have been a part of and coordinated, I have been actively involved in all stages of open and active recruitment of key Indigenous stakeholders and agents of change. In all my patterns of work, I look to increase Indigenous staffing and, in most cases, exceed Indigenous staffing levels. Part of the success to these models – a driving factor is IK our way, HR our way. The Mani model is a driving HR tool I designed, used, and adapted over multiple teaching and learning settings. A gift from this model is next-gen Indigenous leads (and non-Indigenous colleagues), referring or utilising the process in their own research and application of *Riteways* HR practices. The core tenant of the model is the 'more than' principle. The notion that relates to cross-'Cultural Proficiency' needed for *Riteways* enactment. And the core or driving tenant/position is 'self-reflection'. What more can (and then) will I be doing? Ultimately, I would, as a Traditional Owner of the western sides of the Bunyas, aim for the gift or 'give-give' of my people, who, as Bunya Barras, were also known as 'Warmgas' – the givers. Our roles collectively were to 'host', look after, bring visiting groups into country of bunya bunya – Boobargun nguumonge (this IK modelling is shared later via the Bunya Rangers model).

I'm no way near the feet of the embodiment of a 'give-giver', a warmga. However, I have the inclination and forethought to think higher than, aim to act better than, 'more than', because that is what was gifted in the land and who I am related to. And that is what was gifted to me by the carpet snake hugs and embraces of a Cobble Cobble mist net that stretches back to time immemorial. I aspire to warmga so the wanjau of *Riteways* in education is part of that process of sharing. If we, as Indigenous peoples, can't see ourselves teaching, leading, writing, principaling, board-of-directoring, then how can we invest in that field, that pathway? And if our trees across all communities are clumping or growing and regrowing in only certain areas, what does that say about the enrichment or fertility of the education pathway as a career choice if majority of our work is not in leadership?

The Mani model is one such example of Culturally Proficient First Nation learning tools. Operators like Cultural IQ, Peek's Bunaba and Yawuru, Watkin's (Torres Strait) 'Leadership Fit', Aboriginal Medical Services, and community-controlled orgs all have specific 'place-based' models of working and responding to specific cultural contexts. The Mani model works well as a macro-level tool of and for understanding own space within a broader Indigenous diaspora (or meshwork) connected to education. Some of these concepts are written specifically on and practiced through *Riteway flows* (specifically see 'Holism' and 'Identity' chapters to follow). In this instance, we will 'walk through' together the kinds of code-switching we must do as Indigenous polity and we need you to do as non-Indigenous colleagues while operating in this space. To centre our work or conceptualisations of and on a village 'way' or collective care and holism, we need to define how we relate and come into relation to others. Specifically, as educators, we need to be cognisant and doubly, triply aware of what we 'see, say and do' (Schein, 2010) in the Indigenous education and community space as well as place ourselves within a mindset that is strength-based: growths-focused, highly relational, and responsive to the continual change and shift of competing priorities, be they government- or system-wide. We used the Mani model to centre our practice and cut through the ideologically loaded and politically mined playing field of 'closing the gap', to see what we could co/create as a 'way' and tools of thinking then doing which centred our approach on the 'fire in the belly', our gundoos.

The Mani model (Davis, 2012) is based on our holistic views of teaching and learning – 'our' refers to our Indigenous Australian epistemology, ways of knowing, thinking, being, and doing (Martin, 2008[1]). *Mani* is a derivative word from Warra (Barrungam- and Wakka-speaking peoples); it connects to the word *Murri*, a word for 'human being'.

The human body overall is made up of separate but connected parts, each carrying out an important role. Our role as educators is to understand the sum of all parts of learning. Take time to sit, listen, smell, taste, and touch the learning of and for our community in ways that further strengthen our Aboriginal and Torres Strait Islander identities.

The Mani model provides a framework to create stronger cultures of learning based on our ways of knowing, being, and doing. This was the grounding tool or the 'way we wove' together foundationally at the Knowledge House at Loganlea (Davis & Grose, 2008), through Murri school works and EATSIPs. All programming and focus 'pieces' had to ignite our passions – we had to define what that drive, that 'fire in the belly', was.

The head, arms, belly, legs, and feet all form significant parts of our body. Durithunga[2] learning processes like these must be brought to our awareness if we are to build and strengthen our Aboriginal and Torres Strait Islander leadership in education. Frames like these draw strength from the teaching and learning of our ancestors, allow Indigenous education within a dominant Western system to reclaim our identity through the intellectualisation of our Aboriginality.

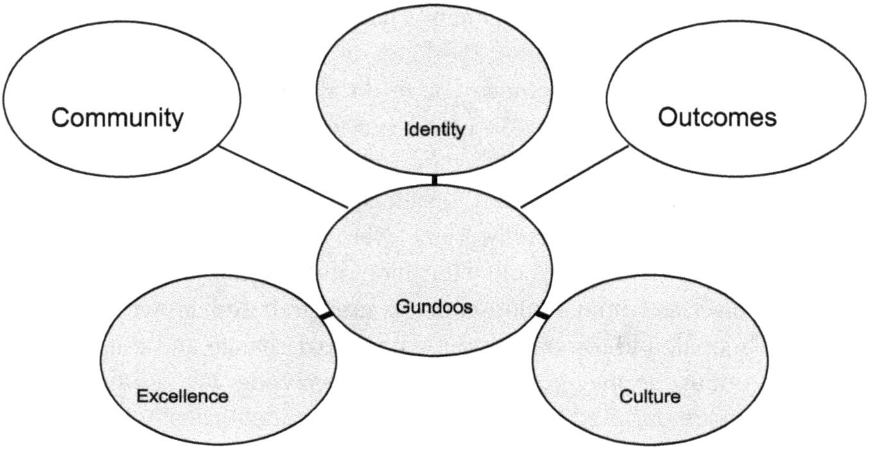

Figure 5.1 Mani model – human being.

The head is our Aboriginal identity, Traditional connections. This is the head, because our **connections to kin and country (identity)** must always be at the forefront of our mind, our awareness. The arms and hands form part of the processes of our programs – **community** and **outcomes**. These are our left–right combinations; community must be accessed and used as a guiding hand, and whatever processes we are involved in, we must evaluate for impact: was this a positive or negative experience? The belly represents our fire, our **gundoos**. This is the fire in the belly which keeps us balanced in our quest for building cultures of excellence. We cannot lose sight of our next generations. The feet, our grounding, is represented by **Excellence** and **Culture**. We are grounded in our culture and operate in other cultures like education which impact on how we do our business. We are grounded in the pursuit of excellence. Whatever we do, we have to strive for excellence; excellence is engrained in our identity, as shown through processes like Bunya, and it is this pursuit that we, as communities of learning, must pursue.

Ultimately, the reflection piece of and on the 'human body' was to lead to a personal reflection on where colleagues 'saw themselves' through a holistic lens. We utilised the Mani model as a way of deepening the Professional Development Planning experience of staff and colleagues in both state-wide offices and school spaces. So post-Loganlea, establishing the safe space model of Knowledge House, I then worked to weave the ways 'that worked' or had the highest impact on and for staff. Moving into other fields and roles of education, I and we utilised the Mani model as an essential HR mapping and tracking tool. Within all core leadership roles, I would, and teams, set specific yearly junctures to 'set up' discussions then 'plan for actions'. The second part, 'YOUR TASKs', is a key rhythm needed for Cultural Proficient education responses.

Your Task

We are to use the Mani model to reflect on our work thus far. How have we developed in the areas of the Mani model? Take time to sit back from the work you've been doing, you've planned, and reflect on the synergies and connections to holistic learning.

Some questions to consider while reflecting on your praxis are . . .

What has been my level and school levels of **community** engagement? Communities will sustain these processes long after we go. How are high-expectation relationships, **excellent** processes, being rolled out? What, to my awareness, has evolved in relation to the kinds of **cultures** our school communities engage with and promote? What are the **outcomes** of my work? How have these impacted on the school? Whom on country do I weave with? Who are the Traditional Owner groups and community Elderships and leaderships present? How has this **identity** been recognised, embraced, and encouraged in schools? Most importantly, what has been the **fire in my belly**? How has my work impacted on the young people and families we service? What are some tangible processes schooling communities have engaged with? What has been the benefit?

The purpose of a reflective HR process like Mani modelling is to move the power relational dynamics within the teaching and learning space. For culturally attuned and Culturally Proficient colleagues, this step of layering and knowing where we're coming from as educators would not be a challenging process. However, it is essential for further mist nesting and creating the right conditions of *Riteways flows* if all staff are responsive to this as a reflection and refraction point.

These baseline processes enable a further articulation of what and how we are modelling safe space creation and articulations. These regulatory steps of enactment, of looking and thinking, seeing and being, through different lenses, engender a better, more regenerative approach to the teaching and learning and community programming paradigm. 'Why?' you may ask. Because the process as an HR 'step' means the responsibility onus and proof of everyone 'doing' and modelling 'human-centred' or holistic ways of working is that we aim to care for all together, regularly, and will set these circles regularly to reflect, evaluate, and act. This is an individual reflection and articulation, not a tool learnt from guest speakers.

'Which way?' 'Who are you?' 'What's your mob?' 'Where are you from?' are questions of kith and kinship that place us as Indigenous people within the mist net of relationships and connections Australia-wide. More recently, I have embraced further our broader regional identity and have embraced the relationships and regulation of self amongst our collective Bunya Barras – countrymen and countrywomen of the Bunyas. The Bunya Bunya is our spirit tree. Bunya Bunyas are our sacred space – Boonbargaun Ngummonge. And here where I come, we come, I flow, we gather, the voices of country, deep time yarns from country, the songs of our birds, animals – howl of the dingoes and scurry of the bandicoots, as well as pathway movement of carbal – are heard, seen, and known. Sometimes our ways, Bunya Barras, come through the form of our tree – spikey. There is no intent of the tree to be spikey. Her leaves just are. The wider or broader pattern of Bunya Bunyas, though, is about giving; the fruits of the tree flower to produce cones of great size to share – bunya wanjaus.

When we are in pattern of Bunya Barras, we set circles, as has been done for thousands of years, over a longer time, then days and night, but stretch our connection through weeks and months. Tjanga culture impacts post-colonisation make this time away harder and harder. Forms of our communication like the long patterns established through Bunya Barras, named in country through place names like Warmga, symbolised through relationships across the Downs, via the signalling of smoke and then carrying of message sticks, are now chunked down to relation flows and questions of and on identity.

These quick questions now – 'Who are you?' 'Where are you from?' – place you and us in relation. We were blessed to grow up and around deep time orators. Leaders who mapped country and relationships with a seven generations' rigour and vigour through knowing and flowing relationships through names of families and family members. We do this still, a national code-switch placing us/all around country (urban, rural, remote, north, east, south, and west). The Mani model is part of the education code-switching and way for countrymen and countrywomen to know who educators are and what are their designs/connections/connectors to country.

The richness of modelling like the Mani model, patterned *Riteways*, means these enactments become highlights, signposts, or markers for good programming and sustainable practices. The practice of a process like Mani model becomes seen as part of the landscape of activity and enactment within the teaching and learning environment. The Mani model is a simple HR enactment which models strength-based approaches to its core. Activity and enactment that other ecological system design thinkers like Marshall refer to as 'the toolkits' (Marshall, 2020). The regeneration of programming and length of programming need this kind of practice and become readily recognisable amongst the regular teaching and learning spaces. The recognisability of processes like the Mani model, seeing strength bases through reflection of how I embody Cultural Proficiency, can be reflected in other activity designs. The next section on 'guarantees' will look at how IKs are reflected in the metaphor, literal and metaphysical, of trees – specifically, the conceptualisations of 'mother trees', which can be used to relate the strengths that exist within complex environs.

Kabi Kabi loreman and countryman Lyndon Davis speaks on the local areas that every environment in its peak condition has knowledge learnt and harboured by 'mother trees'. Mother trees, he explains, are the frontrunners and guides for all other elements in the local environ. He seeks these trees to read country more effectively (personal communication, 2019). SSI uses trees as metaphors and teaching tools. SSI purposefully utilises these deeper IK metaphors because we know and we believe intrinsically in our people. We know that for the Stronger Smarter Approach (Stronger Smarter, 2017) to work, all educators and all community members in all contexts, rural, urban, and remote, must be able to apply and must be able to see their success, draw on their strengths in their localised contexts. And our country, our communities, now guarantee it. There are fertile soils, fertile grounds; 'every community has a waterhole', as Michal Purcell, Chief of Operations at SSI, so eloquently states. The waterhole is the safe space, the springs and flowing waters where Indigenous communities naturally gravitate towards or signal as 'safe spaces'. The part that Stronger Smarter has centralised/essentialised in its work practice and the part that other education providers haven't mastered is seeing this landscape and continuing to lay action and activity, empower the local environ by responding to where the mother trees draw strength from.

This imagery and 'knowing' infused or embodied through metaphor and represented in our arts are an essential element of code-breaking and shifting the dominant Western pattern of thinking and doing. The simple yet powerful imagery of the 'gum tree' was and is chosen by Indigenous community members of Logan to represent Indigenous education leadership and advocacy:

> *Empowering culture, growth and learning through respect and Community to enhance the future of our jarjums.*
>
> (Davis, 2018)

This projecting and thinking of our community collective made me provide more safe space to 'look at' the mechanics of a higher-learning degree and seek other modalities to express the research journey. This power to Durithunga – grow other ways of showing the energy, the unseen and intangible, for the positive spirit of and on circle, the cycle of Yarning circles – was a safe space creator and significant contribution to the originality of research from a Logan context. The design, too, the preceding image of a gum – a native eucalypt – was chosen not just by Durithunga but locally by Aboriginal Community Health cooperatives to represent our Elders' safe space at Eagleby called 'Jimbelunga' (www.jimbelunga.org.au). Jimbelunga translates to 'friends' place' and is the site of our old people's home.

Figure 5.2 Community Durithunga.

Pushing further into the ways we reflect and refract knowledge in 'next step' IK research, I sort to kinnect to deeper yarns and ways of being that had been shown to me by our countrymen and countrywomen. Forever in a pattern of giving, myself, my family, my gundoos were gifted ways in and around the campfires to 'be' as Cobble Cobble. Singing and dancing were and are a live experience and visceral positive energy connect of 'doing and being'. In the mechanics of discipline of philosophies, I would argue, are all three – knowing, being, and doing.

The richness of our ways meant I wanted to utilise the closest space to our knowledge and research translation, so I looked at applying our singing and dance practices and patterns to this research space (still do).

As a higher-degree research piece, the space then made by my supervisory teams and then fought for in Western academic space and recognition was a better (for me and us) *Riteways* expression of the power and longevity IK engenders and our communities guarantee.

Nothing to me or for me and our group gets us closer to being than the songline and storylines taught then reshared. The energy transfer and deepening process that happens with learning is second to none in education. The pattern of the process is shared in more detail in the 'culture and languages' chapter.

There is an arrogance in Western culture and institutions like education whereby this lack of foresight and vision, the higher expectations Dr Sarra has advocated for decades, masks a deeper tension and deeper provocation. In the field of social or collective impact, where my current work roots my praxis, it never ceases to amaze me the tropes and archetypal

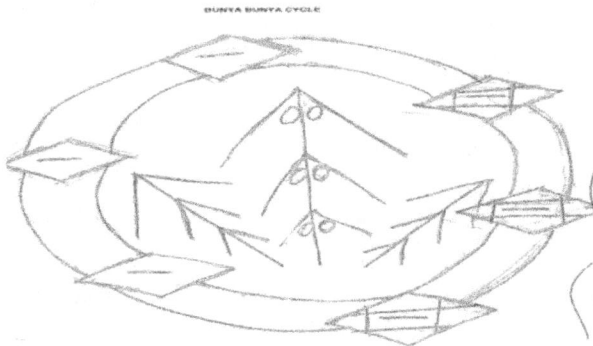

Figure 5.3 'Paint up' Bunya Bunya Cycle design.

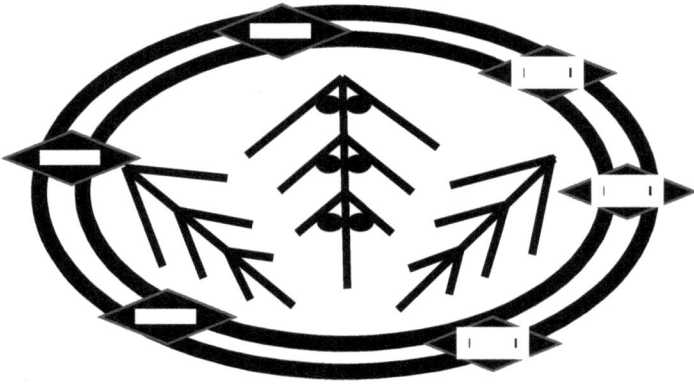

Figure 5.4 Bunya Bunya Cycle: '**to gather research**', Indigenous research methodologies design kolabbed with SSI.

language bigger Western systems provide in what organisational theorist Edgar Schein refers to as the 'see, say, and do' of work culture practice. The tropes I hear, I tune my binung to, now is the mantra of well-meaning systems to seek 'evidence bases'. This 'evidence base' is favoured or prefaced towards university or bigger NGO systems and organisations (not smaller community-controlled) and becomes a new code, for 'you, IK, First Nations places', aren't 'doing enough', don't have the capacity to 'research'.

This again is the 'torment' of us who want to work and weave in our field of and for social impact. The 'torment' and the question which will go to an Australian-wide referendum at time of publication of this book. The provocation remains: Do Migloos want to see us as equal partners, righting wrongs of previous racist legislation and power imbalances? Are the systems of education designed for Indigenous excellence, and do the practioners and broader non-Indigenous society want us to be successful? Henry Reynolds, in his groundbreaking research on unsettling Australian histories, defined this from Settler/Invader diaries as 'what is it the whispering in our hearts?' (Reynolds, 1998). The referendum to come will show if that 'whispering' was a murmur or will echo in our time, 2023, as a 'voice'. There is a continual power imbalance and power struggle that is at the heartbeat of our Indigenous–non-Indigenous relationships. Money is at the core of the 'gap' and current education logics. Our pain, our 'torment' from the hurts from our colonial past, have become a multi-million-dollar industry based on the pain and suffering of our people. Leading Indigenous educational-ist Dr Marnee Shay co-writes a telling piece on the funding discrepancies related to so-called 'Indigenous funding' (Shay et al., 2020). When new fed-eral 'programs' are announced as national 'models' for equity, where is the equity in process and projected outcomes? This all triggers thinking in the south-east to the base of our Indigenous names – Wakka, Kabi, Yugam all mean 'no' and form a way that represents who we are, the 'no-saying' peo-ple. There is struggle, hurt, and pain in this space. Our people have stepped up to the 'plate' and been chewed out and sometimes 'spat out' by the sys-tem both as practitioners and as participants.

There is a settlement of what has happened and continues to happen to our people – the gap that Migloos must come to terms with as a First Nation polity involved in a whole range of international forums and advocacies on human rights. The 'gap' is not *Riteways* position. Healing and moving for-ward on strengths are a priority for our people, the warmga proposition – 'to give and give' – and that is the potential *Riteways* modelling has.

Notes

1 '. . . Ways of Knowing, being and Doing . . .' 2008, Martin. K.

2 Durithunga refers to the Yarning circles woven by Indigenous educators in Logan. *Durithunga* is Yugmabeh language meaning 'to grow'.

References

Davis, J. (2012). Community connections in education: Community Durithungayarn-ing in circle on country, our way. In J. Phillips & J. Lampert (Eds.), *Introductory Indigenous studies in education* (pp. 164–177). French Forest: Pearson Australia.

Davis, J. (2018). *Durithunga: Growing, nurturing, challenging and supporting urban Indigenous leadership in education* (Unpublished PhD thesis). Queensland Uni-versity of Technology, Brisbane.

Davis, J., & Coopes, R. (2022). Our fire stories: Emergence through the circle work-process at the Indigenous knowledge systems lab. *Journal of Aware-ness-Based Systems Change, 2*(2), 85–108. doi:10.47061/jasc.v2i2.3892

Davis, J., & Grose, S. (2008, December 7–11). *Whichway? . . . What happens when embedding Aboriginal and Torres Strait Islander perspectives in schools meets the professional standards for teachers and an accountability matrix?* Paper presented at World Indigenous Peoples' Conference on Education, Indigenous Education in the 21st Century: Respecting Tradition, Shaping the Future, Victoria Aboriginal Education Association Inc. Retrieved from www.strongersmarter.com.au

Fletcher, G., Waters, J., Yunkaporta, T., Marshall, C., Davis, J., & Manning Bancroft, J. (2023). Indigenous systems knowledge applied to protocols for governance and inquiry. *Systems Research and Behavioral Science*, 1–4. doi:10.1002/sres.2932

Marshall, C. A. (2020). The role of Indigenous paradigms and traditional knowledge systems in modern humanity's sustainability quest – future foundations from past knowledge's. In R. Roggema (Ed.), *Designing sustainable cities. Contemporary urban design thinking.* Cham: Springer. doi:10.1007/978-3-030-54686-1_2

Martin, K. (2008). *Please knock before you enter – Aboriginal regulation of Outsiders and the implications for researchers.* Teneriffe: Post Pressed.

Reynolds, H. (1998). *The whispering in our hearts.* Sydney: Allen & Unwin.

Schein, E. (2010). *Organisational culture and leadership* (4th ed.). San Francisco, CA: Jossey-Bass Publishers.

Shay, M., Masden, B., & Creagh, S. (2020, October 13). The budget has more money for school programs for Indigenous boys than girls. *The Conversation.* Retrieved from https://theconversation.com/the-budget-has-more-money-for-school-programs-forindigenous-boys-than-girls-147746

Stronger Smarter Institute. (2017). *Implementing the stronger smarter approach.* Brisbane: Stronger Smarter Institute Limited.

6 'Riteways Flow Markings . . .'

⊙ SPIRIT-Duality . . .

Bianga bianga . . .

Look and can't see
Hear and no noise
Taste and no flavour
Smell and can't breathe

Stop, bianga
Feel – tingling, slow time;
Smoke

> *Uncle told me how those old people used to teach the little ones. This was the way a thousand generations had passed on vital knowledge with a love and gentleness. 'Look' they would say, and the children would gather around to look at a particular leaf, 'close your eyes, feel it' they would say. Rubbing the leaf quickly, they would say 'smell it', and breaking off a little of the leaf the children would taste. 'That's what that leaf is like in the early winter' the old women would say and then they would all move on laughing and playing . . .*
>
> (The Cocoon of Knowledge Djerripi Muraay's stories shared by Jutja Pa Paddy Jerome in Davis, 2018, p. 87)

I love walking country, feeling country, smelling country, responding to country. When walking in the forest with my wife (early on in our relationship),

DOI: 10.4324/9781003298717-6

we had to 'stop, bianga'. Different noises on country. Look up, see what's around. What can you see? Mark that tree; it's different from the others. What do we hear? Birds atop trees moving through the branches. Scurry feet and claws below, in the ferns. You can feel time – make it go slower.

When walking country, I love the quote from Jutjas ngima Ngadas, when our old people took him walking country: '[C]ome here Djeripi . . . they'd crush and rub the leaves . . . [s]mell.' The extra-sensory feeling, sensing, and making sense of the local environ are a time-honoured tradition of and for our people. The 'feeling country' also relates to the unseen – 'tingling, slow times, smoke'. This reference in the Biun Biun poem relates to spirit. When translating meaning of country, our people often refer to the tingling – goosebumps on skin, cold or dark feeling.

The spiritual realm and feelings associated with country are an integral part of making sense of *Riteways flows*. As Neidgie, a great Indigenous Australian thinker, designer, and philosopher, would say, based from his country in Northern Territory, 'spirit is all around you' (Neidgie et al., 1986).

Our countrywomen ngima mens understanding, 'knowing, being, and doing' in the spirit realm, is a kinnect as old as time in this country. Now tjanga, there are clear reference and regarded to the 'different' realm, time, and space of and on 'spirit world'. Such is the case in third space referencing that the Traditional Owner knowledges of the Anangu are revered within a Western, Australian medical frame. Ngangkari (Ngaanyatjara Pitjantjatjara Yankunytjatjara Women's Council Aboriginal Corporation, 2013) is Anangu, Western Desert language, meaning 'healers'. 'Ngangkari are men, women and children and we have ngangkari in our culture for untold ages. The knowledge of what we do remains with us' (Ngaanyatjara Pitjantjatjara Yankunytjatjara Women's Council Aboriginal Corporation, 2013, p. 21).

Travel my country, Bunya Barras; there are Aboriginal Medical Services who are designed or framed around knowledges connected to 'goondirs' or our 'sky people' – Goondir Aboriginal Medical Service (of the Darling Downs). Such relevance and reference to time and space now show a strong relational association our people have and share on spirit. All throughout country is and reference and reverence to Traditional Owner knowledges of and on healing and positive spirit directional path and flow.

Riteways flow, by design, tries to establish or recognise the segmentations or markings of great flows of learning, spaces to follow, and when enacting *Riteways* across multiple (see Figure 15.4, p. 167) markers, then when we create the right conditions for deeper design and patterned thinking to develop, grow, and sustain. Markers exists all on country, of country, and from country. Looking at education, specifically sustaining Indigenous Knowledges education, this way is far more attuned to the land than applying a Western theoretical lens which contains and controls knowledge. Our library books and canons of knowledge are buried, left on, or marked on the land, always for us to see, revere, hear, and see. And just like a modern-day ancient translation states from the Daley River, Dr Miriam Ungunmerr-Bauman refers to this being and responding to country as Dadirri. She explains that Dadirri 'renews us and brings us peace.' It's a process, a way of being, which is tuned into 65,000 years of knowledge as river people; 'we don't hurry the river we wait and become a part of the river' (2002). So Dadirri provides a powerful Indigenous thought process to ritualise and recreate in our learning spaces.

A metaphysic transcendence or symbiotic meshwork is created and can be maintained if the markers are seen and responded to. And the truths to tell, or direction of the flows of learning, are centred by the greatest wisdoms imparted, the concept of wanjau, ensuring that good spirits are seen and followed in the learning path. In these ways, *Riteway flows* can be visually seen or referred to as water flow, deep water, over rock, or swirls of smoke coming from fire. In all parts of setting conditions for sustainable flows of learning, responding, and reacting to those conditions is the need for enactment, praction (Steffenson, 2020). The enactment of flow, the activity of receiving and giving, is key for deeper *Riteway flows* to occur.

Spirit is marked so centrally in the flow design (p. 165), as spirit is a deeper reference to the unseen, the unknown (Sheehan, 2001, 2012; Neidgie et al., 1986). Recognising or referencing spirit enables a fuller definition and kinnection to Indigenous identity and weaves of us as an Indigenous polity. Spirit within current IKS Labs circle work is a built and out up to share ideas on our kinnection to specific animals and places of country. Specifically relating to the ecology of the land, in Labs, we are referring to this IK as 'Cultural Indicator Species' (CIS) (Davis & Coopes, 2022; Yunkaporta, 2021–present). All over country are a clear line and logics which grow, and flows are kinnected to specific plants and animals apart of the natural environ. Applying an Indigenous lens to this ecology, you begin to see, hear, and feel the reverence of country through the specific plants and animals endemic to country. The power of which, the significance of which, can be and is captured in the multiple group storying of the species as well as multiple names and references to species. The Bunya Bunya is a great example of this richness in diversity and 'telling' and sharing for story of and for bunyas. There is Bunya, Bonyi, Bonyi Buru, Boobargun Nguumonge, Yengee, Warmga ngima Jarrowairs. All words across the Bunya Mountains language areas – Bunya Barras refer to, relate, and signify 'place' and 'story' for our shared country.

There are, in all our cultural practices, situational meaning, countries, deep attachment to the metaphysical or spiritual worlds. The heightening or layering of this awareness – the metaphorical to the physical construct or enactment of learning – brings more contexts and thus lays the foundation for deeper learning and elasticity of knowledge. To arrive at a place of wanjau – cross over and exchange – is to have laid and relayed a deeper spiritual cognisance and connection to place and space. To quote a great Bunya Bunya Elder recently passed, the gift, as Elders of today explain, has been in the practice and ritualised process of sharing – how we relate, interact, and connect with others. 'Bunyas . . . is where we learn about sharing and caring about others . . . the Bunya festival – Aunty Beryl Gambril' (Bunya Mountain Elders Council, 2010, p. 6).

And the Bunya pattern, the mountain, Boobargun Nguumonge, is left on country for us to set circle, see, be on, and learn from. Such is the calling and spirit of wanjau on Bunya Bunya that our current Rangers and Bunya Peoples Association hold and set circles – all business and 'Caring for Country' around the collective image and metaphor of the bunya bunya – with our people sitting in circle, under the heading of 'healing Country, strengthening songlines, living and sharing culture'.

To quote the words of my beautiful lore woman (recently passed), Ngada Lily Belle, ~Jarrowair ngima Cobble Cobble):

> Let them know about their Dreamtime. We still got it. This – Uluru does it. That's a part of this. They're together, only we got herbs. We got food up here – Bunya nuts. . . . Let's do this right. For future generations.
>
> (Bunya Mountains Elders Council, 2010)

Spirit enlightens and provides a greater awareness and sensitivity to the fact that we are surrounded by paths of those past and in futures. To see spirit and raise spiritual awareness means we must act responsively and in the best interest of the local area and custodians who share the connections to country. Spirit learning reinforces the learning that we are not bigger than others.

We are a part of others and connected to many Dreamings. How we enact, behave, respond goes a long way to grounding us as learners and deepening our understandings of knowledges which have grown from 60,000 years of campfire intellect of country, from country. Within these cycles of knowing are reinforcements, too, of the important boul pattern of opening – exchanging or closing – holding information, learning, story, and song. Just because information is online – Wikipedia or Google – doesn't make it so. In fact, there is an innate bias and biases that come to the development and proliferation of new age/digital technologies that if they're going to be referred, revered, and signalled as potential learning enhancement tools, they, too, need to be grounded in *Riteways*. Previous Chief of Research at SSI, Jess King, reflected in his research portfolio that

> including a postcolonial computing lens in design provides a point of congruence to embrace cultural differences and move into a space of new hybrid practices, a third cultural space. . . . This provides Indigenous students the best opportunity to claim, create and administer their digital land rights now and into the future.
>
> (Stronger Smarter Institute, 2018)

Our IKS Lab is working on those kolabs now to inform better digital and country-informed designs.

Wanjau

Setting learning circles with wanjau as the core focus is the ultimate gift of and on *Riteways*: knowledge exchanges and flows. When inter-relations, knowledge exchanges, presentations, and practice care for country are enacted, the circle work can be magnified then trialled and re-practioned in other places. Wanjau, as a concept, must be the continual focus and drive and directional path for *Riteways* re/enactments. When bunya bunya was wanjaued on Boobargun Nguumonge, when Cobble Cobble clans of Barrungam, Wakka Wakka, and Jarrowair led exchanges, there were laws and principles, rights and obligations, taught, retaught, and known through the process of coming onto country. This is the greatest gift in our Island home. We can't survive and thrive in our country without open and honest, tested, and true, repeated, and reinforced wanjaus. So Bunya Bunya, for my peoples, was balanced, and wanjau occurred between our freshwater mobs in summer with the winter mullet, saltwater exchange of harvests in the west, the Kabbi Kabbi and Batchallas, Gorengs, and Noonocals.

So great and varied are these wanjau pathways that Aboriginal historians like Dr Dale Kirwin, ~Woirimi, have been able to map their routes, impacts, and routines through following the natural segmentation of the ridgeways now called 'great dividing ranges' (Kirwin, 2012).

In his mapping of country work on exchanges systems of knowledge and influence at contact times, Kirwin has been able to intricately show how these same systems have been used by colonial topographers and surveyors to follow roads and future builds in Australia.

In our fuller essence or 'being', the Kimberley spirit map of Mowaljarlai (Mowaljarlai & Malnic, 1993) is a great representation of IK on country. Of all these maps and recordings on country, there is a cleverness, an astuteness to show the importance of interconnectedness. There is a me/we dynamic that we always need to ground ourselves with and develop meaning of and for today (Fletcher et al., 2023). This provides insight on the macro design thinking on how *Riteways* as a knowledge and learning exchange fits within our systems of knowledge and being.

These layers are indicative of the flow markings of movement. The movement between is interchangeable, and the 'depth' or segmented nature and nurture of learning is not beholden to one learning 'time'. This is a continuous learning cycle. And in time, through constant practions, articulations, refractions, and reflections of IK in time builds its own energy and flow. *Riteways* is a process articulation.

Through *Riteways*, what I see and what we have practioned around Australia (to be explored in later 'Flowbook' chapters, p. 164 onward), as well as grounding in place bases (see maps from p. xiii onwards), are four distinct segmentations shown by the line markings in the outer circle. The 'seeing', now, of the intangible – earlier career weaves, and recording in a diagrammatical way for ease of translation – has been the regular rhythm set and felt of holding bouls, Yarning circle praxis in education. Planning, delivering, then reflection of programmatic activities and responses. Tools of the trade in my educational 'toolkit' bag have been the diarising and 'mapping' of ideas through concept maps, diagrams, art pieces as reflection and reflective pieces. A practice shown by my family groups then refined through educational practice post-university were 'free writes' (Freire, 1971). This praxis was woven as an activity as part of socially just education and learning.

Knowing what I do now and being the practitioner I am now, a better, more representative way of capturing that reflective practice would be 'free rites'. Using symbiology to 'chunk down' then refer to specific learning junctures and moments is an integral reflective practice and tool to use.

When I think, speak, write, and draw, I do so often in circles. The circle pattern is an important representation of and on my spirit and our ways of seeing the world. To 'look back' through the process of 'working up' this *Riteways* book, I have looked back on specific learning junctures and the tools used in mapping these circle stories. There is an intersectionality and duality that exists in the processes developed. And more so in my later career stages, I have sort to 'balance' more the 'on country' learning and privileging Bunya Barras more so than any other time in my career. So the distillation to come through this written text form comes from 'Barrungam Cultural and Languages Studies', alongside Nanna Noonthallis 'education story book'. This current praxis is woven or threaded from earlier YACCA (Youth Against Community Crime Action) group advocacy work (1990s) through to broader Indigenous community collaboratives: Warril Yari-Go Karulbo (now, 'Gnirigomindala' 2020s). The 'Knowledge House' experience (c. 2006–2023 and still flowing) at Loganlea SHS developed from the 'time-tabled' Indigenous lead teacher time allocated as an Indigenous Study Line (2000). Overarching Knowledge House policy developed for 'whole school PD and approaches' – Nyumba bugir Anga (Davis & Grose, 2008). Community Durithunga (c. 2000s–2023, still flowing today), Logan's Indigenous education collaborative, leading to broader design thinking on Yugambeh College, which led to my internship/Principalships as founding Indigenous Principal of Hymba Yumba (2010s, then an Indigenous Community Hub). All this work flows in and through Bunya Barras, specifically the Bunya Bush University, as a living, breathing learning space – noonthalli for our people's past and present (more research kolabs to come!). And to operate Riteway it must.

From this significant research base and space, coming from Murri country, there is 'sense made' and sense shown in the outputs of the regular project, processes earlier. The bouls that exist, shift, and change, the patterns of relationships that develop and, when done well, sustain and, in time, regenerate. All the processes reflect distinct ways of working and flowing. Again, to get to the best place of wanjau, we must work and weave ways that create an increase of activity (through enactments) that leads to multiple stories and demonstrations and illustrations of practice which form or can be pattered, like the bunya bunya in triennial harvest, take form of over-abundance. When fruits of our work and flows are abundant, then wanjaus is ultimately the gift; the gift of giving (the process) is the gift that country shows us.

In what follows we show some more detail on what the layers are, or signposts shown from these project and process flows. I use signposts as a signifier for the learning tools of country, the way-finders and directional trees and places which direct us around country. There is the physical or one layer, one dimension of 'setting a circle' in shape and in person. Then there is the exchange of relationships that happens between individuals in place of the circle as well as the change or impact of that pattern to the individual and place. Wanjuas are a 'place' like on our western bunyas – Warmga. And there is a distinct feeling, the intangible 'space' within. The space 'within' is what I refer to as the 'impact of that pattern'. You feel it. We can't always speak on or to it. And 'spirit', as I know it from all my years in education as well as on country flows, is the best English word translation for this.

The circle layers are connected and distinctive in *Riteways*. They are separate in their own individual meaning: what they represent or are meant to be and are. They are connected to all other parts through the movement of spirit, a flow which can be positive or negative, depending on each setting. And flows swirl and form in circle. To me through our works and, most importantly, modelled through sustainable and, ultimately, regenerative practions in local communities, place-based learnings, there are four segments of flow which set apart 'cultural responsiveness' to 'cultural sustainability'. Through *Riteways* circles and cycles of learning, these segmentations can be marked as:

HOLISM
IDENTITY
CULTURE & LANGUAGE
LORE

And how are these layers of boul known or understood? Through praction. Victor Steffenson, ~Tagalaka, is an IK expert in Indigenous fire knowledges. He is the co-creator and collaborator on 'Fire Stix', which is a cooperative Indigenous Australian effort to bring back Cultural Burning – IK our way. In his work, Victor utilises the knowledge systems and relationships with the land, referred to as connectedness, as the foundation of Cultural Burning

(Steffenson, 2020). In his model, in our layers of knowledge, doing is an important and living part of knowing. Knowledge is not defined through a static representation or gifting of doctorate or masters-level mastery of facts. Knowledges are best demonstrated through Cultural Burning, in the actions of applying and doing. Steffenson refers to this process as 'practions'.

The practions and actual activity motions reflected in the *Riteways* modelling to come reflect over 20 years' fieldwork within the spaces of education. I share this as I am, and our teaching brothers and sisters of Cobble Cobble heritage are, affectionately referred to as noonthalli. Our presence and enactment of IKs, utilising our ways, knowing our story and songlines, is referred to as 'teaching', and thus we are referred to as teacher – or knowledge shareholders.

In a range of educational contexts, all four indicators of *Riteways* modelling have been practioned. Respect must be recognised and given to the past footprints that have been laid in multiple third space contexts. The journeys before cannot be understated. There have been many 'gifts' at the cross-cultural interface. This is *Riteway*s point of difference. The deepening of *Riteways*, the enactment of *Riteways* through practions, is a continual process of birth, death, and renewal. *Riteways*, in their greatest sense and strength to grow positive Indigenous education energies, are in application of the boul – circle patterns – to ensure all parts are in flow and one doesn't dominate the others and parts are connected, not disjointed or refigured into separate compartmentalised Western knowledge systems or productions.

References

Bunya Mountains Elders Council (Eds.). (2010). *Bonye Buru – Boobagun Ngumminge – Bunya Mountains Aboriginal aspirations and caring for country plan*. Bargara: Burnett Mary Regional Group.

Davis, J. (2018). *Durithunga: Growing, nurturing, challenging and supporting urban Indigenous leadership in education* (Unpublished PhD thesis). Queensland University of Technology, Brisbane.

Davis, J., & Coopes, R. (2022). Our fire stories: Emergence through the circle work-process at the Indigenous knowledge systems lab. *Journal of Awareness-Based Systems Change, 2*(2), 85–108. doi:10.47061/jasc.v2i2.3892

Davis, J., & Grose, S. (2008, December 7–11). *Which way? . . . What happens when embedding Aboriginal and Torres Strait Islander perspectives in schools meets the professional standards for teachers and an accountability matrix?* Paper presented at World Indigenous Peoples' Conference on Education, Indigenous Education in the 21st Century: Respecting Tradition, Shaping the Future, Victoria Aboriginal Education Association Inc. Retrieved from www.strongersmarter.com.au

Fletcher, G., Waters, J., Yunkaporta, T., Marshall, C., Davis, J., & Manning Bancroft, J. (2023). Indigenous systems knowledge applied to protocols for governance and inquiry. *Systems Research and Behavioral Science*, 1–4. doi:10.1002/sres.2932

Freire, P. (1971). *Pedagogy of the oppressed*. New York: Seabury Press.

Kirwin, D. (2012). *Aboriginal dreaming paths and trading routes: The colonisation of the Australian economic landscape*. Brighton: Sussex Academic Press.

Mowaljarlai, D., & Malnic, J. (1993). *Yorro Yorro*. Broome: Magabala Books.

Neidgie, B., Davis, S., & Fox, A. (1986). *Australia's Kakadu man bill neidge*. Darwin: Resource Managers Darwin.

Ngaanyatjara Pitjantjatjara Yankunytatjara Women's Council Aboriginal Corporation. (2013). *Traditional healers of Central Australia: Ngangkari*. Broome: Magabala Books.

Sheehan, N. (2012). *Stolen generations education: Aboriginal cultural strengths and social and emotional well-being*. Woolloongabba: Link-Up Queensland.

Sheehan, N., & Walker, P. (2001). The Purga project: Indigenous knowledge research. *The Australian Journal of Indigenous Education*, *25*(1), 23–29.

Steffenson, V. (2020). *Fire country – how Indigenous fire management could help save Australia*. Melbourne: Hardie Grant Publishing,

Stronger Smarter Institute. (2018). *Reading review: "Postcolonial computing: A lens on design and development"*. Brisbane.

Ungunmerr-Baumann, M. (2002). *Dadirri inner deep listening and quiet still awareness*. Emmaus Productions. Retrieved from http://nextwave.org.au/wp-content/uploads/Dadirri-Inner-Deep-Listening-M-R-Ungunmerr-Bauman-Refl.pdf

Yunkaporta, T. (Host). (2021–present). *The other others* [Audio podcast]. Anchor. https://anchor.fm/tyson-yunkaporta

7 | Seeing *Riteways* Through a Third Cultural Space

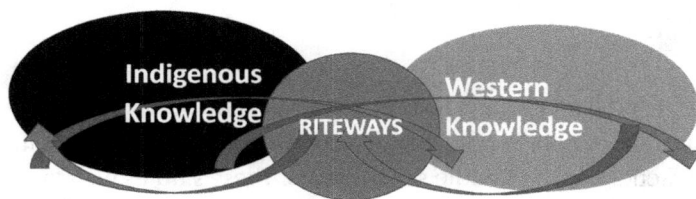

Figure 7.1 Seeing *Riteways* in a third cultural space.

Deepening understanding and applying *Riteways* in educational praction requires insight on how *Riteways* modelling is enacted currently (discussed briefly in 'Context' chapter). *Riteways flows* in no way denies the existence, persistence, and articulation points of IK in education praxis and education settings now. To enable deeper and sustained *Riteways* (explored in later chapters), it is important to 'step back', look, and reflect on examples of how *Riteways flows* are practised in the field:

> *Look and can't see*
> *Hear and no noise*
> *Taste and no flavour*
> *Smell and can't breathe*

In circle patterning *Riteways*, we can view the segmentations or marking patterns seen through a lens of current practice or third space applications (Davis, 2008, 2018; Chilisa, 2012). The brief descriptors that follow provide more context on 'third space' articulation and direction of current praxis. This in no way is an exhaustive or fully representative 'list'. This is a 'glance'

DOI: 10.4324/9781003298717-7

at what the mainstream modelling and current third space practices 'look, feel, and sound' (Schein) like.

Holism

For example, there have been and are enacted now attempts, actions, and activities on deepening holistic understanding – mainscream/mainstream adaptation of holistic learning (Exley & Bliss, 2004). Proliferations of '8 ways' holistic teaching and learning are good examples of current exposures and show the length of time in which a third space process of holistic learning can 'look like' in schooling contexts now.

Lore

Weaving in and lead IK specialists in areas of expertise. Blessed to co-create Indigenous and South Pacific Island curriculums in Mackay, specifically '3 Kultjas' practions in the middle school years. These studies were augmented by specific 'learning on country' trips for Indigenous-only students. The current 90-plus elaborations of IK in national curricula ACARA for all school settings is a great example of our knowledges in third spaces (ACARA, 2019). I choose these models of interface as they are good targets and movement of our IK into Western 'sacred' realms of so-called scientific objectivity. Expert weavers like Joe Sambono, Dr Jodie Edwards, and Dr Chels Marshall have all worked with collective energy and integrity in the 'shared space' to have our IK recognised and weighted the same as Western science.

Languages

Lead models in south-east Queensland, operationalisation of latest Australian Indigenous language syllabus. Important to layer these knowledges in context. The right balance to create more educational rites and freedoms for our people is to not have languages stylised and referred through Western academic lenses only. An example of this is simple practice on who teaches, why we teach, and what path is laid for community. The nesting of language is a great praction that works for sustainability – exemplified through Yugmabeh Museum works, now captured through YRACA (Yugambeh Regional Aboriginal Corporation Alliance) and partnership and lead Koori work of Wiradjuri, Barkandji, and Bandjalung language nests and learning (Stronger Smarter Institute, 2017). In nesting, this is the opportunity that avails itself, the additional overlay or symbiotic overlay of cultural practice. Languages have been so well-embedded in the south and southeast because of other praction of song, dance, and setting circle together. And the language nests of Yugambeh and now regrowing Wakka Wakka, for example, in school contexts, have the challenges of not being mainstreamed too much – power of the state education system becoming the 'controlling body', hiring and firing their 'language experts'. The local Jinndi Mibunn language nest, Murriland, operating after-school, nested in Yugambeh, is a great example or *Riteways* point of difference in praction. Murriland operates across school jurisdictional sectors, across age groups, with Elders and jarjums side by side, run by a community-controlled organisation. The challenge here is languages being co-opted by the Western education systems and not being fully grounded in community context, therefore without responding to this local environment, if this pattern continues, won't ultimately be sustainable.

Identity

Identity is or could be seen in a range of aspects around educational settings now. Our Indigenous flags are in virtually every school. The new 'First Languages' website email tags that several non-Indigenous colleagues use (*First Languages Australia*). Every school acknowledging and providing Welcome to Country spaces. Such to the point is identity reclamation or articulations in a third space, that every Indigenous-specific program within school spaces reflects what Indigenous community–controlled orgs have done for years – assert own identities through own Indigenous shirt designs, customised uniforms, or stylised outfits.

The articulation and plying third cultural spaces in mainstream identities must be acknowledged. It is where the majority of our Indigenous education work is based. It is central to all *Riteways* programming to develop, grow, and nurture a strong sense of self and belonging. We can't get to a space of and on centring practices from a Culturally Proficient way unless we begin the journey of enactments through Cultural Competence, Cultural Empathy, and at the very least, Cultural Awareness (see Figure 3.1). These positions have been expertly delivered and programs completed by lead agencies advocating on the 'third space' like Stronger Smarter, for over a decade.

Tapping into the roots, the strength of over 60,000 years' worth of camp-fire knowledges, the oldest-living, surviving culture is something all Murries and Torres Strait Islanders should be immensely proud of. The gap is a Western colonial construct of identity. The gap as modelling like *Riteways*, like Yunkaporta's Sand Talk and Steffensen's praction model show, is a fault of the education system, not a fault of identity, not a gap of who we are. And in this space, it should always be balanced with the imbalances of other gap data.

What does the system of Indigenous youth population represent in youth detention centres? Does it represent a criminal people or a criminal system? 'Proportionally, we are the most incarcerated people on the planet. We are not an innately criminal people' (Uluru Statement from the Heart, in Davis & Williams, 2021). How can a Territorian citizen, a non-Indigenous youth, be 100% more likely not to be affronted by the law, sent to juvenile justice systems, then Indigenous? What identity bias is at play which keeps growing this as a lived reality of our people? Further study and analysis are needed in the non-Indigenous steps in recidivism. Non-Indigenous school-aged children get suspended and excluded. Yet in a reality like Northern Territory (can be replicated across the country now), a non-Indigenous path away from current education systems is less likely than Indigenous to be locked up and detained. 'Just us' or 'justice'?

'As a matter of fact: answering the myths and misconceptions about Indigenous Australians' (ATSIC, 1998). Some systems of education still use this resource to provide further understanding for non-Indigenous workers on the degrees of difference and equity we are exposed to as Indigenous polities. The aforementioned challenges of Aboriginal and Torres Strait Islander identity within a Western construct/lens are so well spoken and shared by mainstream that even populist mythologies develop whereby federal governments have to counteract those negative perceptions and constructs of deficits to create anti-racist tools! Organisations like Reconciliation Australia established now follow these processes up with a regular snapshot or 'barometer check' on the thoughts/feelings/understandings out in Australian society on Indigenous issues, history, and culture (Reconciliation Australia, 2022).

This is the opportunity and difference *Riteways* models offer in more reflective Indigenous identity and strength. It is our community right to know and feel and practice education that solidifies a positive sense of Aboriginal and Torres Strait Islander identity – not continually ask and render it to bend. This is our human right!

That is why in the space of teaching and learning, we would advocate that *Riteways* always begins from a 'starting point' of cross-cultural 'Culturally Proficient Relating'. *Riteways flow* or **Riteways focus is on IK-centric teaching and learning**, not positioned (as most culturally responsive education is now), on third spaces.

References

ACARA. (2019). *F-10 Australian Curriculum: Science Elaborations for the Aboriginal and Torres Strait Islander Cross-curriculum priority*. Retrieved from www.new-content-elaborations-for-the-australian-curriculum-science-f-10.pdf (australiancurriculum.edu.au)

ATSIC. (1998). *As a Matter of Fact*. Retrieved from www. atsic temp (pbworks.com)

Chilisa, B. (2012). *Indigenous research methodologies*. Thousand Oaks: SAGE.

Davis, J. (2018). *Durithunga: Growing, nurturing, challenging and supporting urban Indigenous leadership in education* (Unpublished PhD thesis). Queensland University of Technology, Brisbane.

Davis, J., & Grose, S. (2008, December 7–11). *Whichway? . . . What happens when embedding Aboriginal and Torres Strait Islander perspectives in schools meets the professional standards for teachers and an accountability matrix?* Paper presented at World Indigenous Peoples' Conference on Education, Indigenous Education in the 21st Century: Respecting Tradition, Shaping the Future, Victoria Aboriginal Education Association Inc. Retrieved from www.strongersmarter.com.au

Davis, M., & Williams, G. (2021). *Everything you need to know about the Uluru Statement from the heart*. Randwick: UNSW Press.

Exley, B., & Bliss, J. (2004). Using culturally relevant texts and Grant's Holistic Framework to connect Indigenous early readers to SAE print-based texts. *Practically Primary*, 9(3), 11–15.

Reconciliation Australia. (2022). *2022 Australian reconciliation barometer*. Retrieved from www.Australian-Reconciliation-Barometer-2022.pdf

Stronger Smarter Institute. (2017). *Implementing the stronger smarter approach*. Brisbane: Stronger Smarter Institute Limited.

8 *Riteways* Focus

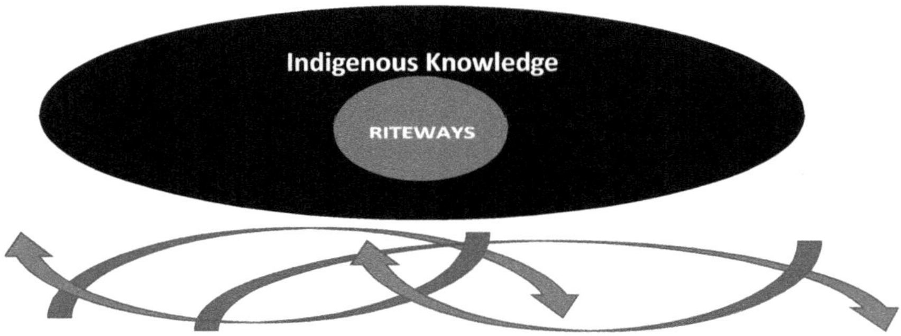

Figure 8.1 Riteways IK-centric flow.

With these thoughts and current cultural interface and cross-cultural relating (Dreamson, 2019) provocations and practices in mind, *Riteways* as a flow should always be referred to in its original design, as a circle. *Riteways* focus should always be seen as IK-centric. It is the intended learning and higher-order conceptualisation to provide a learning path which is responsive to the circle. This is the pattern, more aptly the markers, we will follow and for deeper places of *Riteways flows* have followed.

We must recognise and be responsive to the swirls and woosh of energy spirit (represented in Figure 15.3 onwards as arrows) provided on our learning paths and know that each teaching and learning moment is directed by this. In the truest form of noonthalli praxis, we are facilitators of learning because there are knowledge holders, across all four layers and within the inner flow, that lead in deep knowledge lore connected to spirit and exchange that must be called on, that must be referred to, or the flow will not sustain and deeper learning enactment will not be achieved. This teaching

DOI: 10.4324/9781003298717-8

tool, or reference point, gives kudos or recognition of key learnings I have taken and Stronger Smarter. As discussed earlier, no matter how complex, how remote, how impoverished in Western forms of economics a community may be, how deeply entrenched in 'gap' data about them, what exist in all our communities are tall trees. I draw on analogies from my own spirit trees in the south-east (which are the tallest), the Bunya Bunya, and it refers to all our trees across the lands, be they gums or brigalow, coconut or ti tree. In every community, there are reflections of those community strengths. In all my travels across all works and walks of life in education, a blessing gifted through the Institute, this is one pattern that remains truest (Stronger Smarter Institute, 2017).

Riteways flows can be understood in this reference point, that like the age-old Murri concept ngima wanjau, there are deeper ways to learn and knowledge-exchange and respond to local learning environs which can actually propagate and grow more tall trees. The strength to flow, then, is not in the individual growth of the tree but the connected communities and links that are created. The shade and organisational factor of warmth and sustenance is the gift of giving. To have any conceptualisation of knowing the greatest that was our culture, as referred so eloquently through recent historical accounts like Pascoe's 'Dark Emu' (2014), is to know and believe that Indigenous excellence is in all our communities, knowing that it exists now, as Yunkaporta articulates through his Sandtalk. Understand how 'Indigenous thinking can save our world' (Yunkaporta, 2019). The power of *Riteways*, as is articulated so poignantly through 'Sandtalks', is that Indigenous authority, capacity, and capability come in multiple forms and are alive now, not defined through a Western lens. 'In Aboriginal Australia, our Elders tell us stories, ancient narratives to show us that if you don't move with the land, the land will move you' (Yunkaporta, 2019, p. 3).

Empowered Through Knowing, Relating Through Being, Living Through Strengths: Ember-Blowing Education

Knowing the signs before doing; living and breathing the markings. Seeing and being in Circle: Cycles.

Grandfather bought land at the Bay, which he gifted to Dad and was sold by our cousins, then regifted – smaller portion to grandsons (who still own a parcel of the land at Urangan). He always showed and taught us through his gundoos a reverence to 'old Wakka Wakka – carpet snake'. We had many carpet snakes at the Urangan property, which weren't allowed to be touched or killed. Grandfather passed on his land at Urangan in 1978 (Davis, J, 'Binung Tjanga', 2017).

Nana Cynthia Gorham (née Riley, RIP), Mary Davis line of our carpet snake clans, niece to Grandfather Fred, said at a recent 2010 gas line meeting in Toowoomba:

> '[M]y Hervey Bay Davis – how are you? How is the land?' . . . We (the Davis brothers), replied, 'Good Nana we still have some of the land left.'
>
> 'Orrggh good. . . . You tell him to build on the land . . . [b]uild a home on the land . . . [b]ring ol Carpet Snake back. . . .' [W]ith that she motioned with her hand the snake.
>
> (Binung Tjanga extract)

Garmi Lilybelle Colonel (née Jerome, RIP), Alice Davis line of our carpet snake clans, great-niece of Grandfather Fred, retold her Granny's (Granny Alice) stories of movement on and of country.

> Towards the end of her life, Granny went blind. She was always talking about her country, and she wanted to go home. So, we organised some trips back for her. She showed me where some of the important camping places had been – near Warra, near Bell, a meeting place on Cooranga Creek. . . . The last trip was in an old car. We needed to get water for its radiator, around the part of Gowrie Creek. . . . When we stopped for water, we decided to have a camp. . . . We saw a big gum tree with markings carved on it, so we told Granny about it. She went to the place, and when she came back, she quickly made us put out the fire, cover it over, and go away. At the time, she wouldn't talk about it. About a week later, Granny told me that we should not have been there.
>
> (Binung Tjanga extract)

Just like the knowing and reverence afforded deep time Cultural Indicator Species like carbal, 'carpet snakes', referenced to Jutja Grandfather Fred. Just like the extra-sensory motion and movement between spaces his eldest sister, 'Granny' Budin Garmi, Alice showed and shared. Feeling and experiencing country through her deep time memory and sensory perception of land. The indicators to follow next form part of that tracking, ways of understanding flow. Identifying and belief in the patterns which either aren't seen or could be there, feeling and knowing they are without fully receiving the details. *Riteways* indicators are an outline, a way to know the flows to come will take shape when discipline is applied to the enactment of regular activities – the discipline of our circle work.

Riteways indicators for enactment:

Riteways flow model = SPIRIT -< HOLISM: CULTURE and LANGUAGE: LORE: IDENTITY = *Wanjau* (expanded modelling from p. 164 onwards).

Understanding the Enactment of Riteways *Flows*

Before enacting *Riteways flows*, we must define how IK layers/markers circle work link or are related in the model. Each is an important individual space, and each is connected to the other in full circle. Enacting these spaces (ember blowing) builds legacy and provides conditions for sustainability and, in best practice, regeneration (Marshall, 2020). In the Durithunga original PhD research, I sort to define the energy and express the 'feelings felt' by our Indigenous leaders in circles, to demonstrate and show 'safe space' in action. *Riteways*, in a lot of sense, is a 'building out' of the Durithunga original research and articulation of the 'how to', direct pedagogy, and enact circle work that is regenerative. A key part of the Durithunga thread of research is on the 'Circle: Cycle' definition, action, and activity. When doing 'circle work' now in professional development workshops, offering keynote or guest panellist discussion, I use the praction of Durithunga as a guide: 'rule of three', no one bigger than me (Davis, 2018).

To understand or be proficient in circle work is to know that circle work cannot be 'directed' or 'taught' or 'led' by one. In the practice of regular Durithunga Yarning circles, whenever decision points or propositions were raised at the then monthly yarning process, the 'Seedling' process of 'rule of three' was applied. 'Rule of three' became a way and remains a signpost in Durithunga and SSI-trained circles on what is a base premise of circle work translation. When ideas, provocations, or pieces of work need to carry between the 'cycle' of the monthly yarns, then consultation of 'bigger than

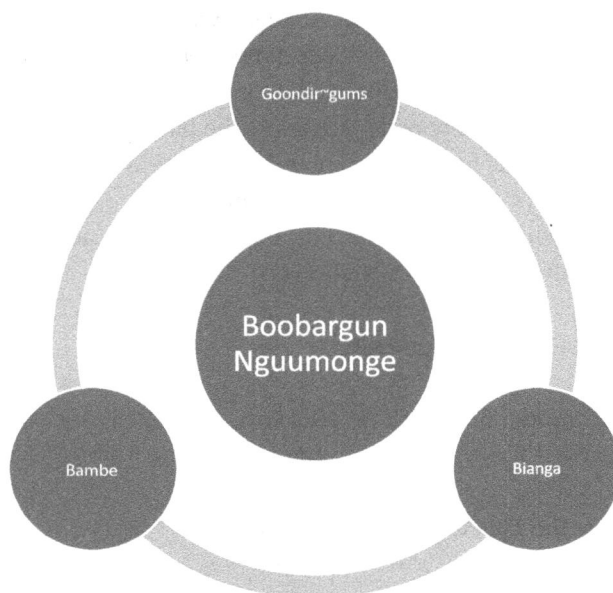

Figure 8.2 Leadership as we are taught.

me', at least three other Durithunga voices were and are essential in the development and delivery of *Riteways* circle pedagogy. Three becomes the base line reference point of and on community work and actions. And this three-part way of doing and enacting learning is part of our Bunya Barra rhythms.

Figure 8.2 is always bigger than me and, on country, specifically Cobble Cobble, west of Bunyas, is a clear articulation of 'voice' being diplomatic, voice being fierce, voice being healing. So very much so, we seek and define leaders and the best leadership in this way, made up of our teachers, noonthallis, who listen and learn and share; bianga, our fighters; bamas, who protect and 'stand up'; and our healers, goondirs. And these leadership styles are both male and female spirit and energies. We need this more; we seek this more. And this is a practice currently which sits at the core of IKS Lab campfire work. The conceptualization of 'more than one' is used to design and show *Riteways flows* in different IK contexts as well. The 'Circle: Cycle' has been developed into a specific case study structure to show how enactments can grow and what 'bigger than me' flows look like.

Seeing this deeper duwur way, expanding to a broader teaching application, using 'circle' work, the other significant truth from the Durithunga research was the signal of movement. So the Durithunga process as a community of practice was based on regular movement of circles. This is the reference to 'cycles'. When the circles were set, to ensure movement of ideas, headspace, centrality, we moved around different strength bases. 'The Circle: Cycle creates a set base and the cycle ensures a flow of new ideas and identities. . . . The Circle: Cycle creates fluidity and movement – not staying stagnant – a process of rippling in action' (Davis, 2018, p. 111).

Central to the creation of a flow in *Riteways* is the pedagogic concept or kinship reference to wanjau (explained earlier). Wanjau in Barrungam refers to 'exchange'. Central to exchange is the process of reciprocity (Davis, 2018; Bunya Mountains Elders Council, 2010; Kirwin, 2007). Wanjau is what grounds and sustains the *Riteways flow*. For *Riteways* models to work and take shape, it must interrelate with and between different knowledge systems, curriculums, and activities. This grounding principle, the centre of flow, provides the conditions for the circles of knowledge to expand and contract, leaving distinct layers or markers to follow (see Figures 15.3 and 15.4). Wanjau is our 'how' . . . why? Is spirit . . . as a relational people, we have moved far too along and away from the centre of spirit and kinnection. An inversion of the so-called Australian 'Close the Gap' targets and numbers is an indication/directional path, dare I say it; 'correlation' of decreased 'wellnesses'. Upcoming studies like 'Mayi Kuwaya', the National Study of Aboriginal and Torres Strait Islander Wellbeing, are further examples in time of the rich data 'on us', 'for us', 'by us' which will help further program knowledge and implementations of what works and is in the best interest of Indigenous peoples.

I was shocked to learn recently that in thriving Murri or larger Indigenous communities, there exists, 'linguistically', ×2 'highly functioning' language–speaking areas (personal communication, Des Crump, 2022, Indigenous Linguist, ~Gamilaroi). This is juxtaposed or can be 'compared' linguistically to many Queensland Indigenous communities, well into the hundreds, of 'Language Revitalisation' (LR) linguistically rated groups. Yet in this same length and breadth of Murri country, I know, and we see flow as kinnected communities, a multitude of strong cultural, spiritual, and country-centred 'still-on-country' language groups. Within the microcosm of south-east Queensland, for example, where colonisation, and thus language, impacts have been heaviest, there is a recent explosion of Indigenous dance troupes and expressions of individual and linguistically different Traditional Owner knowledges.

When you are outwardly expressing your story, your people, through song and dance, you are expertly weaving our languages. This has always been the truest and best referred sensemaking to me. Rather than 'place' our languages within another domain of colonial reference and, ultimately, control, linguistics, be sure to refer to and see our cultural practices now – like the singers and dancers of today equally and more reverently.

These 'identities' and expressions of positive and distinct Traditional Owner 'centres' and sense of selves bely the 'linguistic statistical evidence' of/on Language Revitalisation. To start from these baselines of 'knowing', the colonial gaze always puts us as an Indigenous polity at a 'less than' position. If you believed everything you read or was framed in migloo written word, I wouldn't be; my people's identity doesn't exist. Barrungam as a language (than by research default, our people) is, according to Wikipedia, 'extinct' (n.d. *Barunggam language, Wikipedia*). If the power of migloo word and researcher 'facts' is correct, then I am not here writing to you in my human form. I send this book through the spirit realm, which reinforces the *Riteways* modelling – centrality on relationships and, specifically, spirit. Which if true should make this a 'bestseller'.

In relation to 'identity' and doing more programming '*Riteways*', what the preceding paragraph does show as an example, reinforces, is the pattern that despite invasion and the 'heaviness' colonisation has brought and still brings, the challenge for Culturally Proficient educators is to look out, seek to find our 'tall trees'. They exist in every context, are a part of or are referenced in every community in all contexts, urban, rural, remote.

At a recent 'on country' Barrungam Languages and Cultural Studies Teachers professional development (held at Chinchilla, 2022), there were great yarns on nuance. To do Language Revitalisation work, in context of where sites of invasion, taking children and families off country, new implications of Native title legislations, and the very real bad spirit of colonized 'acting', which can re-form as a process of lateral violence, there is a significant space and strong expression of loss, strained and pained identities, perceived gaps of educators in 'knowledge and understanding' of self. And as an Aboriginal linguist working with our Barrungam languages says, '[N]o matter where I go . . . whenever we're at places like here, I always remind community, educators, Elders, language is never lost it is asleep' (personal communications, Des Crump, 2022). This is the nuance of having a Culturally Proficient Aboriginal linguist.

In a social construct of absolutism, so-called scientific 'objectivity', it is essential to build more balance in an education and learning cycle that has favoured the preceding 'language is extinct' thinking, at the detriment of new and emerging forms of strength and representations now of 'culture', 'identity', and 'language'. This is a real struggle of identity of and for us, not just as Indigenous peoples, but as an Australian nation, which pushes and struggles with the strength bases our communities produce and our own educational ability to name and 'make space' for contemporary culture and identity. For myself, previously working as a lead Stronger Smarter officer, this was and is the most consistent struggle. Observationally, it is quite abhorrent how many barriers and walls are placed in front of the Riteway operators, workers, and do-ers in all our community spaces. Institutionally, this is done with sometimes 'not knowing' and, as a continued pattern of repeated behavioural action and activity, reflects 'Institutional racism'.

It's why I'm enjoying and focusing on the kinds of works IKS Lab promotes. We have time and headspace to look at the broader pattern of relationships and drill into the 'hows' and 'whys'. Adjunct scholar JMB must be highlighted again here. His work through the Indigenous not-for-profit space is a clear 'way in' for non-Indigenous into third cultural spaces, namely, at university level, to see our mob aim and aspire to achieve higher learning goals. His and AIME's[1] latest iterations, and his sharings within Labs, have been focused on the international stretch of equity of education. From 'doing the work' for nigh on 20 years as well, JMB sees the broader implications and impediments of systemic racism as a need to 'overcome'. The balance or tension I flag is that, alongside being the most 'researched' people in the world, when we get to innovation spaces, sites of new and renewed energy and focus, operators may still apply a colonial gaze, an academic eye or lens to 'who we are' and 'what we do' as Indigenous polities.

Our struggles and positionality in our countries (dgagunbarras) are the concept/construction around 'Traditional Owners'. Great Indigenous Professors before my teaching times wrote and led many new innovative programs regionally and around the country. I refer to bough breakers like Dr Eve Fesl, Mandawuy Yunipingu, and Elders like our Cobble Cobble ancestors, Jutja Tony Davis, Garmi Dec Angeles (née Davis), and Jutja Merv Riley (née Davis). 'Colonial power brokers' like Bilin Bilin in Logan, Yugambeh; Barak on Koori country (Attwood, 2021); or Dundalli and Bussmamari more closely related to my kin. There is a 'trick' we're made to think on, feel less about our current identity. Dr Fesl wrote 'Conned' (Fesl, 1993). By current standards, this text can be quite jarring, and in a lot of contemporary speak today, significant parts are now politically incorrect. Yet in its construction is also hemmed in by linguistic absolutism and heuristics of and on colonial racial power relations – her commentary is not representative of significant number of 'mixed-race' Murries today (this li'l black duck is one of them). More recently, an esteemed colleague/friend/ally, Jutja Prof Norm Sheehan, ~Wiradjuri, has continued to test and push the academic boundaries around the reflection and refraction of 'us' and our identity. The power of the work from the 2000s onwards, which Sheehan represents, is a naming and claiming on how we learn through Indigenous principles, processes, and practices and 'not about' (Sheehan & Walker, 2001; Sheehan, 2012).

As our academics as Indigenous polities has progressed and become more nuanced and representative of and on our identities, 'now' as a contemporary culture, still dealing with the tensions remonstrated in Fesl's piece, redesigned in Martin's piece (2008), and refined in Sheehan's (2012) pieces. Now, scholars like Yunkaporta (2019) and Marshall (2020) provide further insights today on how to embrace and learn through Indigenous Knowledges. The next chapter is a further extrapolation of this progression. Simply placed in 'context' of the broader education diaspora and political impacts and interfaces of learning our histories and cultures. For the Culturally Proficient educators, this way of seeing and being and experiencing good educational flows is called 'doing it *Riteways*'.

Note

1 Australian Indigenous Mentoring Experience.

References

Attwood, B. (2021). *William Cooper – An Aboriginal life story*. Melbourne: The Miegunyah Press.

Bunya Mountains Elders Council (Eds.). (2010). *Bonye Buru – Boobagun Ngumminge – Bunya Mountains Aboriginal aspirations and caring for country plan*. Bargara: Burnett Mary Regional Group.

Davis, J. (2017). *Binung Tjanga: Davis family storybook* (Limited ed., Family History Book). Bunya Mountains.

Davis, J. (2018). *Durithunga: Growing, nurturing, challenging and supporting urban Indigenous leadership in education* (Unpublished PhD thesis). Queensland University of Technology, Brisbane.

Dreamson, N. (2019). *Pedagogical alliances between Indigenous and non-dualistic cultures meta-cultural education*. New York: Routledge.

Fesl, E. (1993). *Conned!* St Lucia: UQP.

Kirwin, D. (2007). *Aboriginal heroes: Dundalli a "Turrwan" an Aboriginal leader: 1842–1854*. Nathan: Griffith Institute for Educational Research, Griffith University.

Marshall, C. A. (2020). The role of Indigenous paradigms and traditional knowledge systems in modern humanity's sustainability quest – future foundations from past knowledge's. In R. Roggema (Ed.), *Designing sustainable cities. Contemporary urban design thinking*. Cham: Springer. doi:10.1007/978-3-030-54686-1_2

Martin, K. (2008). *Please knock before you enter – Aboriginal regulation of outsiders and the implications for researchers*. Teneriffe: Post Pressed.

Pascoe, B. (2014). *Dark emu: Black seeds: Agriculture or accident?* Broome, WA: Magabala Books.

Sheehan, N. (2012). *Stolen generations education: Aboriginal cultural strengths and social and emotional well-being*. Woolloongabba: Link-Up Queensland.

Sheehan, N., & Walker, P. (2001). The Purga project: Indigenous knowledge research. *The Australian Journal of Indigenous Education, 25*(1), 23–29.

Stronger Smarter Institute. (2017). *Implementing the stronger smarter approach*. Brisbane: Author.

Wikipedia (n.d.). *Barrungam*. Retrieved from https://en.wikipedia.org/wiki/baru%c5%8bgam#History

Yunkaporta, T. (2019). *Sand talk: How Indigenous thinking can save the world*. Melbourne: HarperOn.

9 'Doing It *Riteways*'

Riteways takes form or makes shapes in its design like other IK-rich processes. As explained earlier, the Durithunga research, for example, Indigenous practitioners, referred to their 'form', 'shapes', their 'circle layers', as 'Seedlings' (Davis, 2018). To yarn effectively in Durithunga Yarning circles, all Indigenous practitioners had a guiding frame or book to work from – 'The Durithunga Seedlings' (Durithunga, 2006). From doing the Yarning circles regularly and cycling each one in different localities, it became obvious to more senior Indigenous education operators, the founders of the Durithunga yarning process, that there were Indigenous members who were not as 'tuned in' or adept (education experience–wise) or confident in stretching the third spaces paradigms. To promote the us/all concept of holding and patterning circle work, we created structures to support new members in circle as well as guide praxis of senior members, have a baseline expectation to direct the Durithunga energies and flow of circles. The aim from the 'Seedlings' formation work was (and remains) to guide our people in circle, not prescribe or dictate how business should be done. Durithunga circles over their formative years were able to effectively build responses to the 'torment' felt within education structures. The safe space work, coming together on regular intervals to hear each other's voices and share experiences, make sense of the Western structures. This core work of 'being' together was augmented by the process of understanding and 'knowing' how to behave and interact in circles. The 'Seedlings' were designed and then shared amongst Durithunga membership to aid in the continuation of Durithunga safe space and voice as well as ensure new members were able to come into relation with others with some grounding and direction as to how Durithunga functioned.

DOI: 10.4324/9781003298717-9

The four layers in *Riteways* modelling are like this 'rulebook' or guiding structure – shape. The four outer layers are a macro part of the design. These macro parts need to be followed to ensure elasticity of knowledge and functionality and action of proper way, *Riteways* learning flows. The four main markers of the *Riteways* model can't exist or be taught separately without reference or deepening in action and activity which is kinnected to the others. A significant condition to create more flow and build strength in programming is spirit. I refer to spirit through an IK lens (Neidgie et al., 1986; Ungunmerr-Baumann, 2002; Bunya Mountains Elders Council, 2010).

SPIRIT -< . . . Understanding Flow

Spirit is everywhere. As defined in an earlier chapter (p. 53), spirit and spirituality are an essential flow indicator. We've chosen to code-switch or coop the words of social impact and quantitative evidence design in research to place *Riteways* within the current plethora of theory-of-change logics as well as constant Western stream and call for 'evidence bases'. The indicator model choice is important because they should guide *Riteways flows*. The most important practions to occur, though, are from within individual teaching and learning spaces. For eternity, as it has been since time immemorial, this is the most *Riteways* place to begin – a country-centric logic model.

The Dreaming has provided (and still does) a kinnection to spirit world and story. Understanding reference and reverence of spirit is the overarching connection for *Riteways flows* in education. Elders and cultural leaders within our communities consistently espouse the centre of spirit worlds – referencing country and the old people.

On Bunya Bunya country, Garmi Lilybelle (RIP) would share yarns up on country on the importance and reverence of place (Yunkaporta & Davis, 2021). 'Look at this place bub. . . . Look all around . . . beautiful. . . . Look at the birds, their colours. . . . That's the Dreaming. . . . Beautiful' (personal communication, 2010). Spirit is all around us. When this is said and known, there is kinnection to understand loved ones ancient and recently passed are all around us. They go to a special spirit world, and entities live in spirit places as well. '[T]he Rainbow Spirit may reside in certain pools in creeks and rivers and may appear in our dreams as a snake or as light. . . . The Rainbow Spirits' solid form is represented by the carpet snake' (Jerome & Wilkie, 2003, p. 7).

Within south-east country, learning on the spirit world is often learnt/ taught, known, and retold through the lenses of contact and colonisation. Native title records refer a lot to the first-hand accounts of Elders like Gaiabarau (Steele, 1984) or Garmis in recording studies or testimonials (Parker & Lambert, 1993). And for us as 'live' and 'living entities', we carry, as we always have, the connection and kinnection to country, to the areas Australian law courts and Australian (mostly white Australian) lawyers fight for in Native title. We carry these deep kinnections through our tjina, through our hands, na, in our dir, in our baluans. When Elders like Jutja Pa Paddy shared those knowledge transferrals, '[L]ook djeripi . . . smell . . . taste . . .' (Jerome in Davis, 2018), that was, and still is, a living connection to the world today. Bunya Barras still do those practices today – tjanga.

And the 'keeping' or the 'code' of that language on deeper spiritual informatics is in country, the snap of the tree, the crack of the wood, the placement of these parts on our hearths. Lighting around the circles of our fires then sharing the yarns which place them – the elements for the fire and us, the kinnections we share to the stories being told. 'Ember blowing' is a great visual reference for spirit. The metaphor of fire has multiple meanings and learnings. Fire burns bright; flames are visible, visually striking – heat you can see. Smoke rises and billows into the air. The wood that burns down, the tinder, and the kindling, it all forms part of the fire message. From the embers fire can be re-fired. From the embers there is fuel for next fires. Spirit is smoke; it can't be seen like flames. Smoke is a smell and taste.

To blow on these flames, creating a flow for spirit, is a *Riteways* method. Spirit is the 'connecting' element that cuts across all *Riteways* layers (shown in Figures 15.3 and 15.4). Spirit is feeling. Spirit is recognising and seeing mimburi (Gaiarbaru in Steele, 1984) – flow. That is why, in the *Riteway* modelling, 'SPIRIT' is represented by arrows which show movement. As the great IK philosopher Neidgie says, 'I feel it with my body, with my blood. Feeling all these trees, all this country, When this wind blow you can feel it. . . . You can look, but feeling . . . that make you' (Neidgie et al., 1986, p. 51).

Spirit is setting circle, then tightening circle so we can see each other, can hear and listen to each other: it is the 'experiential tuning in' (Jerome in Davis, 2018). Other cultures speak on mindfulness (Lama & Jacobs, 2011). IK mindfulness is reverence of and for spirit. IK mindfulness is recognition and reverence for Eldership. It is the understanding, too, that the embodiment of spirit may be good and bad. Neidgie and Compass (Neidgie et al., 2020) both provided turn-of-the-century IK translations on the story of 'spirit', darker and shadier sides. Batchalla texts from Moonie Jarl and Wandi (Jarl & Wandi, 2014) are great earlier translation pieces also (from the south-east).

The recording and reflection of enactment is an important interrogative and deeper analytic process to engage through the 'doing' of each layer. In all parts of *Riteways*, and especially as an establishment phase, *Culturally Proficient educators must build into routines processes of reflection and articulation, especially important to make judgement on how good energy is flowing.* To regenerate and rejuvenate praxis of Cultural Proficiency requires the expected junctures of and action towards rules and directional flows. How this transpires and develops can be individuated. And making the time and space for review and response is an essential element to ensure sustainability becomes a part of the norm. What we ensure when we reflect, write/ speak, and share is a systemic development of knowledge and markers on how we do business and continue processes that work effectively. The process becomes a marker, a guide on the pedagogy. This links to next extrapolations on the 'discipline of circle work'.

Reflection processes can come in multiple forms, as stated. A continual reflection log, whether it be specific journaling or 'free rites', is one such way of recording. Capturing story through lens and sharing reflections on outputs is another. These have been the most successful 'Mani model' maps, visual reinterpretations, and 'showing' the circle work in action. Open discussion and articulation points on programmatic evaluations are another. Within the Stronger Smarter Institute, they have developed a rigour and integrity when it comes to professional learning outputs and outcomes post–program training. These regular outputs are enshrined within the culture of the organisation, a part of its flow, through the continual practice and discipline of the Stronger Smarter educators, known broadly as Facilitators, who must gather, as a regular practice, the evaluation feedback sheets from participants on the program outputs (Stronger Smarter Institute, 2017). When this develops as habit and then becomes a norm, there develops a robustness and elasticity of design which propagates more robust or further streams of learning. *The signal here is, practitioners, teachers, facilitators must be involved in a constant process of evaluation, reflection, and discussion* (explored further in 'identity' curriculum and pedagogical chapters).

The Discipline of Circle Work

There is a staunchness built in the Institute that is a part of its way and DNA. Founder, Dr Chris Sarra, has articulated this, and it is benchmarked quantitively within the Institute as 'High Expectations Relationships Index' (Sarra et al., 2020). The spirit of the people, the learning of the ways and maintaining significant relationships with and to the spaces where the Stronger Smarter Approach grew and flows, Wakka Wakka on Cherbourg, is part of the inbuilt nature. To nurture all new and beginning members into a Stronger Smarter circle is to flow within the meaning and deepening of IK through this way – High-Expectations Relationships.

As I wove effectively in and out of the Institute over the last two decades from my perspective and experience, it remains as a core part of the 'bringing together' of all programs, research, board delivery. What the Institute has done is build a belief then through practions-maintained actions which ensure any new Stronger Smarter Approaches continue to build on the original designs and make it relevant today (Stronger Smarter Institute, 2017). And we believe that. When the founder says, 'We now expect dramatically improved results will be delivered and Indigenous students will enjoy' (Sarra, 2012, p. x), he knows it. The refinement, development, and articulation of *Riteways* has been a part of our ways since time immemorial. We could not grow and thrive on one of the most inhabitable climates without process for higher-order social and personal developments as well as wellness indicators. That's what circle work is. A constant striving for excellence and articulation through multiple perspectives, bigger than me – us/all.

So rulebooks, like set in Durithunga contexts, the evaluations of participant experiences from within Stronger Smarter training, are part of an IK pattern which looks to not just being a community of practice but seeks to regenerate and grow a bigger meshwork of IK-informed practitioners. From these Indigenous-led contexts, there is more learning to flow and understand.

Case in point is, the regional, external review of Stronger Smarter training in Canberra (University of Canberra, 2017). Here the University of Canberra analysed the outputs of educators who came to Stronger Smarter training. Internally, the Institute knows, through proof of its concepts, through the regular, expected discipline of tracking and responding to participant feedbacks, that Stronger Smarter Leadership facilitation generally scores and is rated by participants very highly, 4.5/5 (Stronger Smarter, 2017). When an independent assessor worked side by side with the Stronger Smarter facilitators in the latter part of the 2010s, the scores recorded on program 'transferral', the core elemental learning of High-Expectation Relationships, University of Canberra scored facilitation outputs at 6.7/7. 'The report suggested that the positive changes and strategies would continue beyond the life of the project, and the outcomes would "ripple outwards" as teachers and principals shared knowledge and strategies to improve educational outcomes for Indigenous students' (University of Canberra, 2017, p. 3).

What the preceding case study shows is, the lead indicator or tracker of success for the outcome of Stronger Smarter training, wasn't the 'point in time' reference of a study from an external provider vis-à-vis Canberra University. No, what Stronger Smarter has developed is a great discipline of efficacy. This is the singularity of belief and message of the Stronger Smarter Approach. The key cornerstone of the approach is 'High-Expectation Relationships'. For the Institute to achieve its higher expectations in education relationships, part of the teaching and learning sequence was and continues to be 'achieving high results' for teacher professional learning experiences (Jackson, 2019).

So the outcomes which now are reflected in a number of discrete and broad longitudinal studies on the externality of the research of and on the impact of Stronger Smarter training are not the critical learning or success factor. The critical success in Stronger Smarter is in its attention to detail and discipline through High-Expectation Relationships. To achieve transformational change as part of the theory-of-change logic for SSI is to ensure SSI Facilitators are providing the right conditions and delivering the SSI leadership training in the same rhythms and patterns of original designs mapped and scored according to the participant feedbacks (Jackson, 2019 and Stronger Smarter Institute, 2017).

This is a core tenet of what founder, Dr Chris Sarra, refers to as bringing 'rhetoric to reality' (Sarra et al., 2020). This reality of Stronger Smarter ideation, design, and then delivery means new programs from and for Educators in a range of contexts; there is a service guarantee that when participants set circles, based on the evaluation processes well-established, reflection and recording journeys of over a decade's worth of programmatic response for largely teacher training, *what the Institute can guarantee through its evaluative process and discipline is a highly regarded and sort-after learning experience; it offers its own 'golden eagle' standard of 4.5/5 participant experience rating for trainings delivered.* This rings true to what Dr Sarra, as Founder of the Stronger Smarter Approach, espouses:

'the Stronger Smarter Approach doesn't leave anybody at the margins, it's about taking everybody with us on the journey' (Sarra, in Jackson, 2019, p. 5). And this marker alone is the baseline all programmatic responses in the field of Indigenous education must start with at the Institute. The Institute doesn't just espouse 'High Expectations' for educators; the Institutes applies 'High Expectations' service delivery to itself as a peak Indigenous teacher training institute.

As a living or live model of Indigenous entrepreneurship in education and IK translation, what *Stronger Smarter sets through this 'golden eagle' standard is a benchmark of and for sustainability*. These reflection points are Culturally Sustaining and are an essential process in reviewing and then renewing Stronger Smarter Approaches in the current field.

Part of this formulaic response is grounding on country where circles are set, having community voices speak and lead. Part of the *Riteways formulaic response is being grounded on country where circles are set, having community voices speak and lead everything*.

This is a significant Cultural Proficiency – having country guide everything, having community voices speak and lead – which is the opposite of social impact and social research agendas currently. 'Evidence base' (as discussed earlier) is a new wildfire being used and bandied by university and big NGO structures within our Indigenous education and social services fields. I want to share what our IKS Labs calls 'cautionary tales' for context and final summation of and on the articulation and praxis of any spirit-type curricula. Too often, our dimensions of learning and articulation of the knowledges of 'self' are defined by the coloniser. When Australian writers and researchers wrote and recorded in anthropology our history in the 1900s – for example, Harney and Elkin (1968) – or recorded songs and stories of the south-east, they did so with the lens of patriarchy and male-dominated gaze in research. They did so in reference to a time and space when Indigenous leaders were practicing cultural lore (less contact) in the 1900s. What I love from my own Native title experiences is my peoples' collective agency and 'knowing' still alive and vibrant and distinctly different from the coloniser's voice. In spite of carrying some of the longest lived-on country experiences in south-east and now representing leaders within a multitude of fields – Indigenous Health, Law, Education – our people, the Cobble Cobble people of the Barrungam speakers, west of Bunya Mountains, still have not 'won' or been shown a way forward to the Native title process in spite of our Elders and leaders organising since 1997! What I am signalling here is that although we retain rich knowledges and deep time kinnection to country, our identity or polity, it would seem, is 'not enough' for recognition of our Native title. Moreover, the new systems in place to supposedly support and enable us to claim our Native title exist and manoeuvre in a malaise of old systemic structure and inability of systems which are predicated on the coloniser, not grown from the root of the oldest-living, surviving cultures and campfire knowledges. Real time now, I am waiting as a Native title applicant to receive any correspondence, written, mailed, or otherwise, on our latest Native title meetings held in December 2022. In fairness to our Elders past, I contacted our 'organising' department to register for meetings and provide contact details for replies. Theirs, it would seem, are not disciplined circle works. These Native title systems might prescribe more fulsomely to the Wikipedia-type definitions and constructions of and on my Barrungam identity, mentioned earlier. This, again, is the real 'torment' that exists.

In these Native title sessions, when our broader western plains groups come together, I love, as an IK researcher, to sit and listen to my countrymen and countrywomen speak and lead the floor. The 'Elkins' of the past I was shown through Western research and anthropological knowledge shares are balanced by my mob's recognition and articulation of female researchers and doers in the anthropological fields who were, in Australian mainstream research streams, 'forgotten', as well as clear articulation of researcher bias and how state Native title body reps allow parts of research 'into' our connection reports without full acknowledgement of the different relationships migloo scholars like Elkin and Tindale (Tindale, 1940, 1974) for us on country and Winterbottom's (in Fesl, 1993) of the world had within the southeast. Female researchers like Tennant-Kelly (1935), who spent and wrote specifically about our peoples, gathered at the government reserve of Cherbourg. Her research at the turn of the 1900s was 'lost' to own family estates and never seen in the sandstone structures on anthropology. This linkage was denied because of her gender. There is a real gender bias and further equity issues that processes like *Riteways* bring better flow to.

When referencing spirit ways, our people don't rely on the 'one way' yarns, the one knowledge keeper and speaker of story recorded by the male anthropologist or ethnologist. Our people speak of two. Our people speak of goondir ngin goondirgums, male and female spirit healers. Earlier Australian research bias can be heavily weighted to males and not the female strength, which we know is central to the heartbeat and flows of tribal lore. The earlier recordings, though, did record a 'standard' of living and being, which in Elkin's title is defined as 'high distinction' (a thwarted university point score refence), as well as a regal, greater than, principle. What 'tall tree' conceptualisation does now is show that those patterns of relationships are fed and regrown through the living pattern of relations to country now. What Stronger Smarter's 'golden eagle' standard does is guarantee that when practitioners enter a third space training which uses Yarning circle methods as its main pedagogical tool, the regular discipline and outputs of effort in training guarantee knowledge transferral to a 'high degree', translation and transferral of knowledge, to a high standard. How Stronger Smarter differentiates from mainstream teacher training spaces is, it deeply dives into the concept of bias through assumptions and looks to unpack the invisible knapsacks educators carry into all education spaces. It does this 'circle work' by having two Facilitators lead in together, support each other in the development of and enfoldment of 'circle work'. To 'do' and enact these aforementioned *Riteways apply a discipline* and *standard to practices* ensures programs are sustainable.

Currently, in re/searching IK translations of the south-east, we are working to build more knowledge and understanding of the Indigenous female voices as part of the anthropological recordings which are foundational for sandstone universities yet whose voices have remained silenced or not upfronted, as non-Indigenous translations of the day could not and did not support such reference or regard to our female leaders. Prof Aileen Moreton-Robinson positions our female voices best in her reflections on 'Whiteness Matters' (Moreton-Robinson, 2000, p. 254). In surmising her groundbreaking work on 'calling out' racist and deeply seated colonial power imbalances, Robinson flags:

> [I]t is not Indigenous women's anger that oppresses. It is not the anger of Indigenous women that locks children up in detention centres . . . or produces racist policies of mutual obligation or denies people their human rights. . . . [I]t is not the anger of Indigenous women that manufactures white race privilege and power.
>
> (Moreton-Robinson, 2000, p. 254)

Our old people, our strength base, are built on a backbone of learned and sustained practice and articulation of *Riteways* across the country. The rich diversity of Indigenous languages and individual polities is a great example of this rich strength. Over 250 distinct language groups. From this baseline, our people created and recreated, responded to, and articulated shared and sustained ways that ensured our people flourished and could then see the test of time, now tjanga. This is the sustained living and giving in a natural environment which valued human diversity and provided ways and processes which enabled our people to work individually and collectively. Yunkaporta articulates this well when discussing the governance protocols we use currently in IKS Lab work: 'Our governance is based on protocols from the huge multitribal gatherings that occur in the Bunya Mountains on Wakka Wakka and Barrungam Country every 3 years (Bunya Mountains Elders Council, 2010), as they have done forever' (Yunkaporta in Fletcher et al., 2023). The use of our ways protects and enrichens knowledge practice and articulation of and on our processes. Yunkaporta reflects further on the power of dgagunbaras, Boobargun Ngummonge, and the setting of broader circles like the Bunya Bunya gatherings, which he poetically refers to as our embassy.

> These are embassy protocols that allow Lab members ('labbers') with diverse tribal or clan affiliations to self-regulate within a framework of Aboriginal Law, enabling individual self-determination while also binding us in networks of relational obligation that extend throughout a 'deep-time' ontology encompassing both ancestors and descendants as stakeholders.
>
> (Yunkaporta in Fletcher et al., 2023, p. 2)

It's not that our ways aren't there or are totally foreign. The challenge for education in Australia now is that these ways have never been given the fuller space to flow, make, and respond to challenges, unabatedly and unashamedly Indigenous.

Riteways means tapping into and privileging these ways and this story. Foregrounding telling and retelling until our learners are active participants in a knowledge fabric which reconnects and doesn't disconnect from the longest-living, surviving culture. This knowledge 'deepening', over time, should be part of a normative process. This is *Riteways* challenge, and that is what the opportunity *Riteways flows* offer. To achieve this kind of educational enactment requires Indigenous community control and leads – upfront and clearly articulated and simulated. If we are non-Indigenous educators, this requires 'beyond Cultural Competence'. The responsibility is for 'Cultural-Proficient' praction as an educator being able to walk alongside and, sometimes, behind our people.

Recognising these right conditions, the 'indicators', provides the right pre-conditions for deeper IK learning to occur. What the model of SSI training or place-based models like Durithunga Seedlings show is that there's a need to effectively follow program activity – a set curricula – and then review and regulate the behaviours to form a habitat that becomes a part of the process of delivery. The two facilitator teams holding SSI leadership programs, the guide or 'rulebook' on expected behaviours, all form way finders, markers to enact positive social impacts. *Riteways* applies similar logics in its more fulsome enactments. These right conditions provide the space and kinnection to enable enactment of *Riteways flow*. Enactment of *Riteways* comes through activity, listening, and learning through ->

/HOLISIM/LORE/CULTURE and LANGUAGE/IDENTITY/

We will now deepen observations further on what activities can be enacted through each learning layer opportunity. This is mapping and sharing educational maps through doing. What we wanjau here are specific reflection and action points of over 20 years in the education field working in and through micro – specific curriculum developments – and macro – policy and 'train the trainer' models – be they state or nationwide.

Again, the explicit nature of sharing *Riteways* designs and activities is about enacting, responding, and referring to learning opportunities which will ultimately lead to sustainability – so once off NAIDOC, Welcome to Country or guest speaker 'events' are not the focal points of proficient *Riteways* enactment. Community brokerage, recognition of intellectual property, parents as first teachers, then pathways to teaching and leadership programs are examples of more sustainable, regenerative, and strategic enactment of *Riteways*.

To track and understand one's part in *Riteways* enactments is an essential discipline to master. We use the circle model of 'fullness' to map the depth of activity and enactments across the markers. This activity then creates a rhythm and flow of circle work which layers knowledge. Seeing and recognising the markers like 'HOLISM' is different again to the activity and enactments within each segment. Spirit is the constant flow, a part of all *Riteways flows*. Then, through enactment of learning layers, the 'doing' of *Riteways* activities and discipline to reflect, review, and enact creates a deeper understanding of the program activity and feeling of movement and energy within the space.

In the next part of the text will be each individual marker's enactments and activity examples. If embedded and embodied well, the learning and praxis can become sustainable. The exemplars to follow act as a guide on how to 'do' *Riteways*. Each Culturally Proficient educator will develop and have current strength-based approaches to draw from and relate. These next chapter definitions provide some signposts on what *Riteways* looks like and feels like. At the end of each marker chapter will be examples of the deepening of learning shown through the *Riteways flow* indicators.

References

Bunya Mountains Elders Council (Eds.). (2010). *Bonye Buru – Boobagun Ngumminge – Bunya Mountains Aboriginal aspirations and caring for country plan*. Bargara: Burnett Mary Regional Group.

Davis, J. (2018). *Durithunga: Growing, nurturing, challenging and supporting urban Indigenous leadership in education* (Unpublished PhD thesis). Queensland University of Technology, Brisbane.

Durithunga. (2006). *Durithunga seedlings, protocols principles: A working document derived from Durithunga* (Unpublished Manuscript). Logan City.

Fesl, E. (1993). *Conned!* St Lucia: UQP.

Fletcher, G., Waters, J., Yunkaporta, T., Marshall, C., Davis, J., & Manning Bancroft, J. (2023). Indigenous systems knowledge applied to protocols for governance and inquiry. *Systems Research and Behavioral Science*, 1–4. doi:10.1002/sres.2932

Harney, B., & Elkin, A. (1968). *Songs of the songmen*. Adelaide: Rigby Limited.

Jackson, C. (2019). *A mindset change: How the Stronger Smarter Leadership Program supports educators to enact high expectations in Indigenous education*. Brisbane: Stronger Smarter Institute Limited. Retrieved from REP_SSLP_changing-mindsets_final-1.pdf (strongersmarter.com.au)

Jarl & Wandi. (2014). *The legends of Moonie Jarl*. Ultimo: The Indigenous Literacy Foundation.

Jerome, P., & Wilkie, W. (2003). *The Jurrawa men's handbook: A description of Jurrawa culture and language*. Brisbane: Publisher W. Wilkie Psychologist.

Lama, D., & Jacobs, A. (2011). *His holiness the Dalai Lama – infinite compassion for an imperfect world*. London: Watkins Publishing.

Moreton-Robinson, A. (2000). *Talkin' up to the white women*. St Lucia: University of Queensland Press.

Neidgie, B., Davis, S., & Fox, A. (1986). *Australia's Kakadu man bill neidge*. Darwin: Resource Managers Darwin.

Neidgie, B., Ilkgirr, B., Nayinggul, J., Wauchope, J., Williams, J., Cooper, R., Yuludjiri, T., & White, W. (2020). *Clever man – the life of paddy compass namadbara*. Canberra, A.C.T.: Aboriginal Studies Press.

Parker, L., & Lambert, J. (1993). *Wise women of the dreamtime: Aboriginal tales of the ancestral powers*. Cammeray: Park Street Press.

Sarra, C. (2012). *"Good morning Mr. Sarra" – my life working for a stronger, smarter future for our children*. St. Lucia: University of Queensland Press.

Sarra, C., Spillman, D., Jackson, C., Davis, J., & Bray, J. (2020). High expectation relationships – a foundation for enacting high expectations relationships in all Australian schools. *The Australian Journal of Indigenous Education, 49*(1), 32–45. doi:10.1017/jie.2018.10

Steele, J. G. (1984). *South East Aboriginal pathways*. St. Lucia: UQP.

Stronger Smarter Institute. (2017). *Implementing the stronger smarter approach*. Brisbane: Author.

Tennant-Kelly, C. (1935). Tribes on Cherburg settlement, Queensland. *Oceania, 5*(4), 461–473.

Tindale, N. B. (1940). *Distribution of Australian Aboriginal tribes: A field survey*. Adelaide: Royal Society of South Australia.

Tindale, N. B. (1974) *Aboriginal tribes of Australia: Their terrain, environmental controls, distribution, limits, and proper names*. Berkeley, CA: University of California Press.

Ungunmerr-Baumann, M. (2002). *Dadirri inner deep listening and quiet still awareness*. Emmaus Productions. Retrieved from http://nextwave.org.au/wp-content/uploads/Dadirri-Inner-Deep-Listening-M-R-Ungunmerr-Bauman-Refl.pdf

University of Canberra. (2017). *Higher Education Participation and Partnerships Programme (HEPPP) Indigenous grants round 2013. Final report*. Stronger Smarter Schools Project, Submitted to Australian Government Department of Education and Training by University of Canberra, Bruce, Australian Capital Territory.

Yunkaporta, T., & Davis, J. (Hosts). (2021, June 21). Research fellas. In *The Other Others* [Audio podcast]. Anchor. Retrieved from https://anchor.fm/tyson-yunkaporta

10 | Holism

o **HOLISM:**

Bunya Bunya Cycle image

Figure 10.1 Holism.

Holistic nurture and nature of being is not a foreign concept for us or mainstream educators. Within the cultural interface (Nakata, 2007; Davis, 2018), holistic 'attempts' to learn and deepen IK learning include bilingual education (Hunter in Singh, 2001), Holistic Learning Framework (Grant in QSA, 2000), and Eight Ways Learning (Yunkaporta, n.d.) frame. Essentially, these tools provide a 'balance' and can 'ignite the spirit' and strengthen the motivation to 'learn' through Aboriginal culture. Now in education we even have

DOI: 10.4324/9781003298717-10

national Indigenous education learning tools and places like Reconciliation Australia's Ngarragunnawalli.

Notions of holistic learning are integral to the conceptualisation of Indigenous education. Holistic models of learning and pedagogy are engrained in the teaching and learning of our Indigenous culture from family to family member. Holistic learning is no better shown than in the definition of Quandamoopah ontology as shared by Karen Martin (2008). Holistic learning is a comprehensive tool which impacts on all areas of education. Holistic models and concepts are based on Indigenous ways of knowing, being, and doing.

Djirribal Elder Uncle Ernie Grant has been a front-runner in the education field from K to Year 12, in developing and articulating a unique holistic framework through a Djirribal perspective. His learning frame, the 'Holistic Planner' (Grant, in QSA, 2000), had significant impacts on learning communities nationwide and is widely used in preservice teacher training.

The holistic framework is a Djirribal tool based on the land and families connected to Djirribal. In schools, there is exposure to and use of holistic tools and models from different Murri perspectives. The planner is used as a way of synthesis and analysis of complex issues, viewed from an Indigenous perspective. This Djirribal frame provides a strong footprint to unpack or begin to work through complex Indigenous study topics, where reference points are connected to the whole, not as separate and compartmentalised.

The enfoldment of the Holistic Planner is the Djirribal Local Area Studies tool, another great place-based method to utilise. I preface the usage as great as it has been the foundation for further Queensland-based Indigenous education expansion spaces. In Queensland, what I refer to specifically is the previous ATAR Senior School subject Aboriginal and Torres Strait Islander Studies, as well as the formation of (Australia's last) Queensland Indigenous Language Syllabuses (in the mid to 2000s). These curriculum tools enabled us as Indigenous educators to push for more voice and space within mainstream curricula designs if our communities lobbied for and wanted 'more space'. These tools and articulations of our way of programming were a catalytic agent for change within Indigenous school–specific teaching and learning spaces. Experiential learning within the context of the local community, storying, and language of the land all provide a deep learning tradition to draw from. This is the 'deep well' Ungunmerr-Baumen refers to when she says, 'Dadirri recognises the deep spring that is inside us' (Ungunmerr-Baumann, 2002, p. 1).

Riteways enactment through layers like 'holism' is about remembering this strength (deep springs) and tapping into our way of doing business. Holistic tools or use of analysis only works when holistic practices are practioned and heightened. So in every interaction, every step of education response, there must be a deep connection and practice or reference and articulation of how 'the work', the 'learning', impacts and interrelates to our holistic learning as holistic beings. Current Indigenous community work, language, and practice around 'cradle-to-the-grave' approaches for localised programming are a good reference point. Two models of holistic learning we share as cases in point are on country, our Bunya Bunya Murri Rangers. And living off country, the Community Development work of Gunya Meta on Yuggera-speaking country.

Local Area Stories: How to Enact

Bunya Bunya Rangers[1] were collectively worked and grown from the on-country work of Indigenous facilitators working and walking side by side with us as Traditional Owners. Through the 'Caring for Country' program, we built a joint Traditional Owner guide for working on country, 'Bonye Buru – Boobargun Nguumonge'(Bunya Mountain Elders Council, 2010). We held Yarning circles on the mountain to situate Traditional Owners (a lot of whom are involved in Native title and cultural heritage negotiations with gas companies – for-profit work). A telling driver or connector to country, a point of difference of and on this process, was the clear demarcation from Native title business and cultural heritage, which Traditional Owners refer to as 'gas line' business or 'walking the line'.

The demarcation agreed by us was to have no 'sitting fee' structure (unlike Native title, cultural heritage works, which is renumerated). Then to sustain the good work and enact our Caring for Country plan, we dreamed – aspirations – and had x4 ranger positions created, the Bunya Mountains Rangers. This was 2010. The Rangers have sustained on country through Bunya Peoples Aboriginal Council management for a decade. Our Traditional Owner groups, like mine, the Cobble Cobble people, maintained gas line (cultural heritage) work and kinnection to the Bunya Peoples Aboriginal Corp (BPAC). Our Traditional Owner groups of the west (without Native title) even became anachronized by big business (called the BCJWY). While BPAC brokered a 'no fee for service' model, with the main aim of co/management and safe

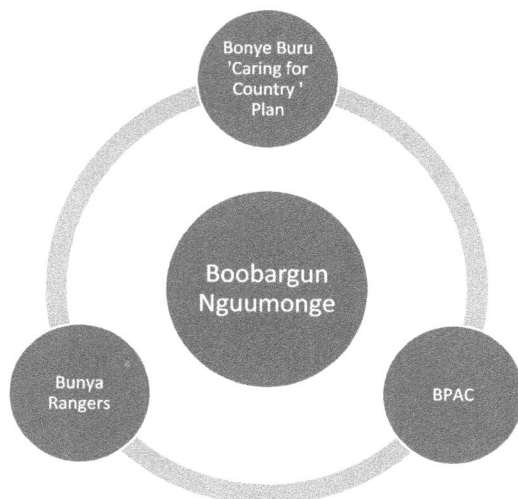

Figure 10.2 Local area story: Bunya Bunya Rangers.

space developed through more Murri Rangers programs (paid roles), we had (and have), as Traditional Owners, paid-for service work through gas line–type commitments and have been grouped as Barrungam, Cobble Cobble, Jarowair, Western Wakka, and Yiman (BCJWY) peoples.

I don't make the gas line reference lightly in text here. There are several countrymen and countrywomen who are opposed to the continual extraction of our lands. The gas line process I have disengaged from. However, several of my countrymen and countrywomen as well as multiple Traditional Owners across the Downs have engaged in this work. This is complex, and Tys and I yarn on this complexity of country on our 'Research Fellas' episode (Yunkaporta & Davis, 2021). A piece I'd like to flag here is, I see my people choosing work on gas lines because there is no other economic benefit afforded them or us without this gas line work. Without full Native title rights, a fight my people have been engaged in since 1997, we hold no other negotiating rights or powers with State government or Mining industries. Several of my countrymen and countrywomen choose this work as it literally puts food on the table for families. The Rangers work and collective 'Caring for Country' business afforded me and fellow Traditional Owners with another space to be, feel, and advocate for country.

The Bunya Mountain Murri Rangers have sustained on country and continued to have an impact on the cultural heritage, knowledge, story, and sharing by providing a clearer Murri history and knowledge maps to country. All around the mountain, which my people refer to as Boobargun Ngummonge, there are stone boras and cave sites of great significance. As well as on country, Bunya Mountains specific heritage trail and maintenance work is the regular upkeep and GPS recording and maintenance of bora and cave sites.

During the time of writing, our Rangers celebrated and opened space for reconnection and healing at the opening of the Bunya Bush University. As Cobble Cobble people, we got to sing for country and have a major contribution to the artistic panels now based on country as part of the permanent Bunya Bush Uni site. It is a great honour and privilege to be a part of that reclamation and healing process.

The great work of the Bunya Murri Rangers is now galvanised and grounded at the Gumungurru cultural heritage site of the Jarrowar, a significant bora ground. Work is able to be sustained and grown on country further through the invitation and continued setting of circle process opened up to multiple Traditional Owner groups. This process opens further safe spaces and renews cultural ties to the area in that the Bunya Murri Rangers are seen as a joint collective, a joint group who we, as Traditional Owners, can collectively, through BPAC, or individually, through our own Care for Country trips or program designs, engage back on country with.

The most important enactment of the circle cycle design ensures Bunya Bunya business, in spite of the messiness and conflicts occurring through Native title process, continues to regenerate and provide new streams and pathways opportunities for us as a collective of Traditional Owners. And for this countryman, it has been a needed balance post–messy Native title business. The Bunya Mountains 'Local Story' has been healing.

Living off country, the local Indigenous-controlled organisations like Jinndi Mibunn and Gunya Meta hubs in Logan City, Yugambeh and Yuggera country specifically, are great reference points on community-led design and sensemaking. They both are models on how safe spaces are wedded and will always need to be there for Indigenous community members. As a local community member associated with Jinndi Mibunn, I fondly recall in the 1990s, and remember our Annual General Meetings, where all our Cooperative members would get a chance to speak and make sense on what the organisation was 'doing' for us. Lively discussion and debates were held, and questions asked on program integrity by all members and listened to by the 'Board', nominated and 'voted' reps of the organisation. The fiery or spikey conversations, after airing, would always end with a good community meal –

breaking bread after to seek closure. 'Leadership can change by the hour or minute in Aboriginal community meetings according to the subject discussed. Aboriginal people find it easy to adapt but often people outside the community find this very confusing' (Anderson, in Bunya Mountain Elders Council, 2010, pp. 11–12). At those earlier times, it was the important cooperative work centred on Aboriginal housing. Now it has transitioned to further 'community services' portfolios (still with the cooperative membership at its core).

Gunya Meta is a long-term research and community development partner. From the 'other side' of the Logan River, it exists as a localised, place-based area of study and deepening learning. The Hub exists or has grown out of the need for more focused urban support for our Indigenous families in and around Woodridge, Logan City. Generationally, I was a previous board member in my early career teaching times from early 2000s. I now weave back in a consultancy support role. Gunya Meta has, over 20 years, taken and remade its circle in accordance with the local environ and remains one of the few First Nations community–controlled entities within Logan City (only to be surpassed by Jinndi Mibunn on the south sides of the Logan and Albert Rivers).

Gunya Meta acts as a good signpost on local area knowledge and studies as it is respectfully nested and responsive to Traditional Owner footprints, and it has a responsiveness and connection to the diverse Indigenous communities who call Logan City home now – mostly living off country. *Gunya Meta* means 'house' in Murri as well as Torres Strait.

The Hub is exceptional in that through its strategic Indigenous leadership model and concepting around the traditional 'home', it has grown its community outreach work through philanthropic and strategic partnering. Into 2023, Indigenous community membership of Gunya Meta has grown an outward focus, to grow to scale and sustain its programming well into the future (captured earlier as GM25). Its chief architect and CEO, Aunty Faith Green, ~Kabi Kabi, has built an amazing meshwork of supports and place-based her and Gunya Meta programming within the heart of her expertise, which is education (Prep–Year 12).

The circles below go some ways to showing what Gunya Meta's social impact flow looks like. Focused on education, Gunya's programs flow from the Early Years, through to Middle and Senior Schools. GM25 is Gunya Meta's Strategic Plan to 2025 and targeting aimed at equipping staff to build towards more sustainable practice and functions as Indigenous education

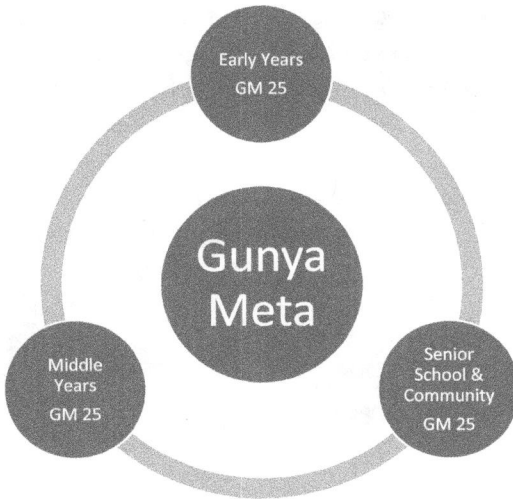

Figure 10.3 Local area story: Gunya Meta.

experts. Within the Early Years are 'Healthy Jarjums' and 'Bullang Jarjums' programs. This work is being developed side by side with bigger institute research kolabs. Moving into the Primary and Secondary Schooling sectors, Gunya can deliver specific place-based programming to the Middle Years, through 'Deadly Teens', and to Senior School ages through 'Transitions to Work' program.

To support the 'house' and 'homely' context, Gunya Meta provides in all its community program deliveries; the HQ hub also offers TAFE qual training for adult learners wanting to re-engage and contribute to their own education or broader community services. Gunya Meta expertly operationalises these program works by being steely focused on its role as a First Nations community safe space. Over the years, both strategically impact them economically; they have said no to program offers like in child protection, which may cause more harm for local families and lessen the opportunity for broader engagement in the lifelong learning opportunity Gunya Meta's education programs provide. Just like the Bunya Murri Rangers, Bonye Buru Caring for Country guide, just like the Djirribal holistic planning model, there is a clear map and reference point on how to enact holistic care that Gunya Meta leads in a First Nations community–controlled context.

With programmatic staff, a regular stream of TAFE cert trainees, and a board which oversees the strategic operationalisation of its GM25 plan,

Gunya Meta is well poised to see further growth and sustainability of its praxis. What would work even better amongst the third spaces of education (where its programming is mostly based) is a fuller investment of expansion of this model so the mist nets created and regenerated can flow through all parts of our First Nations community and not just be based or centralised on the one HQ locale on Mayes Avenue in Woodridge (which it is soon to move from based on current real estate booms and crash on our local area).

Note

1 Bunya Mountains Murri Rangers.

References

Bunya Mountains Elders Council (Eds.). (2010). *Bonye Buru – Boobagun Ngumminge – Bunya Mountains Aboriginal aspirations and caring for country plan.* Bargara: Burnett Mary Regional Group.

Davis, J. (2018). *Durithunga: Growing, nurturing, challenging and supporting urban Indigenous leadership in education* (Unpublished PhD thesis). Queensland University of Technology, Brisbane.

Martin, K. (2008). *Please knock before you enter – Aboriginal regulation of outsiders and the implications for researchers.* Teneriffe: Post Pressed.

Nakata, M. (2007). *Disciplining the savages savaging the disciplines.* Canberra: Aboriginal Studies Press.

Queensland Studies Authority – QSA. (2000). *Aboriginal and Torres Strait Islander senior studies senior syllabus.* Brisbane: QCAA.

Singh, S. (Ed.). (2001). *Aboriginal Australia & the Torres Strait Islands: Guide to Indigenous Australia.* Footscray: Lonely Planet.

Ungunmerr-Baumann, M. (2002). *Dadirri inner deep listening and quiet still awareness.* Emmaus Productions. Retrieved from http://nextwave.org.au/wp-content/uploads/Dadirri-Inner-Deep-Listening-M-R-Ungunmerr-Bauman-Refl.pdf

Yunkaporta, T. (n.d.). *Aboriginal concepts of synergy and interface.* Retrieved from http://8ways.com/Interface+theory

Yunkaporta, T., & Davis, J. (Hosts). (2021, June 21). Research fellas. In *The Other Others* [Audio podcast]. Anchor. Retrieved from https://anchor.fm/tyson-yunkaporta

11 | Lore

Lore refers to traditional Aboriginal and Torres Strait Islander Knowledges (Hunter in Singh, 2001). As stated earlier, IKS Labs expands further by applying Aboriginal Lore and governance systems to our current, contemporary research field. 'Our governance is based on protocols from the huge multi-tribal gatherings that occur in the Bunya Mountains on Wakka Wakka and Barrungam Country every 3 years' (Fletcher et al., 2023, p. 2). This is part of the IK weaves that have grown as part of the vernacular, speaking about our tools and ways of knowing. Lore also relates to beliefs, doctrine, experiences, folk wisdom, teaching, and scholarship. It is the 'ways of being' as we interact with our worlds, both physical and spiritual.

In practicing sustainable third spaces of education, we have developed a south-east model based on 'na' and 'tjina' – the hand and the footprints. Basically put, the IK leadership journey can be best mapped through 'na' knowledge and practice of 'the hand', which is about 'knowing' your own identity. And 'tjina' – footprints – is about sustaining relationships (to be explored more in depth in later chapters on 'identity').

Relational weaving oneself, individual self in flow is the key. Developing the Cultural Proficiency (Stronger Smarter Institute, n.d.) of all our teaching teams. Cultural Proficiency as a sociological model refers to understanding more about yourself – what I can do as an individual, respect of self, my identity in relation to the flow of IKs.

So Cultural Proficiency is, in this context, woven in the application of IKs. By applying 'relationality theory' (Martin, 2008) and using an 'embedded' approach, we create a space of learning which enables the development of greater Cultural Proficiency. The na ngima tjina process shows again the applicability of learning through our cultural metaphors and not 'about'.

DOI: 10.4324/9781003298717-11

Application of this *Riteways* modelling is an essential element of building more culturally safe practices and spaces.

The layers of activities or actions within 'lore' work are signposts or forms to follow. The Yarning circle is a great scholarly approach to systems of learning and problem-solving – inquiry. It is an approach that purposefully invites all to participate in knowledge making, allows the 'silences' that are part of our traditional mode of communication, and is grounded firmly in the values of respect and reciprocity. Knowing the form of a Yarning circle is important, and then applying Yarning circle in multiple ways is essential to grow deeper learning experiences. *Riteway* principles for yarning and actioning of Yarning circles work on connecting to those knowledges and processes as the best practice proper way for our gundoos. 'Circles are important because there is no beginning or no end and therefore no completion but continuous cycles' (Martin, 2008, p. 80).

For all Yarning circles to maximise learning, all must follow a process for deeper engagement. Listening is essential in circle. Circle participation requires silence and reflection. When yarns are developing, whether through message sticks or stones, it's important to acknowledge who is talking – everyone can see everyone in circle. It is essential not to talk over others: this is how we are talking, listening, and communicating. No shouting is an exemplar of Yarning circle processes. Dadirri – deep listening (Ungunmerr-Baumann, 2002) – as explained earlier, is described as 'a time'. The time is symbolised by the great rivers of the Daley region. To quote Ungunmerr-Baumann: 'We cannot hurry the river. We have to move with its current and understand its ways'. In this is a lesson on perceptions of time: 'There is nothing more important than what we are attending to. There is nothing more urgent that we must hurry away for' (p. 2).

This simple signal/sign of a Yarning circle is a good learning tool and way to tune in. We have used this symbology to hold hundreds of open Yarning circles in professional development delivery as well as in education and community org bases and contexts.

So how can we centre ourselves in circle today, post–Migloo contact? We develop a knowledge system and response process which is not predicated on 'how we're seen', but we share yarns on 'how we relate'. What are the strengths we share? This is a powerful flip on the Western triangular/ hierarchical model of knowledge. Our lore, our identity, speaks on Warriors and Providers who have societal strength: 'sharing' as a core value. We didn't meet politically over violence or come together for 'Holy Wars'.

o **LORE:**

Figure 11.1 Lore image.

Our political identities, our construct as a polity, have been predicated on the notion of responding to the habitat we have been gifted and sharing the natural resources in a systemised and deeply refined way (Pascoe, 2014; Kirwin, 2012). Coming together, sharing, and being with large groups in a shared space is all about political acumen and sustainable, regenerative growth. We refer to this process as embassy (Davis & Coopes, 2022; Fletcher et al., 2023). To collectively gather and maintain meaningful and deep relationships wedded to the land is a continual gift and inspiration patterned on country. As Pascoe (2014, p. 229) states in his conclusion of 'Dark Emu', denial of that collective, systematic, and deeply refined relationship with the land is 'the single greatest impediment to intercultural understanding'. *Bunya Bunya* Elder *Aunty* Beryl Gamble (RIP) shared how this collective relationship, the sense of embassy – 'bigger than me' – was based on 'sharing and caring'. She noted, '*Bunyas . . . is where we learn about sharing and caring about others . . . the Bunya festival*' (Aunty Beryl Gambril; Bunya Mountain Elders Council, 2010, p. 6). Pa Paddy Jerome, our Jutja, extrapolates the notion of embassy further, citing our country's references to time and space: 'This land is our mother' (Jerome in Bunya Mountain Elders Council, 2010, p. 12). 'We are part of a spiritual structure. That's Aboriginal culture. That is Boobarran Ngummin, the Bunya Mountains, our Mother'.

The nuance or ability to set circles for better pedagogical alignment is a telling piece as part of regenerative curriculum design. 'Doing' circle work is as important as 'setting' circles and, like all pedagogical tools, requires constant refinement to enable the best outcomes. In this next section, I will detail in part 'how' the circle work can be practised and what signposts are needed for setting 'safe' and 'strong' circles. Foremostly is the reference to the spiritual elements of bouls. It is an important place and space to slow down yarns/activities and actions and be present in the moment with relations and relational exchanges. The setting of circle refers to the 'coming into' bouls. Here, respect is enacted or can be through several layers or markers – seated in circle, not far from each other. Being able to see the person next to you and thusly be able to hear. The sound of silence is essential.

Within current knowledge systems and structures, it is essential, then, to build blocks and forms where our people show and grow strength and be recognised for this. Why? Because our weaknesses or 'gaps' have already been reported on ad nauseum by people representing many Western knowledge paradigms. Our people are defined outside of IK circle in deficits (Walter & Anderson, 2013). Political discourse in Australia (as explained earlier) is all around 'closing the gap'. *Stories of Strength* provide the process to lay further foundations of learning based on what has been achieved by our people, through our people's footprints. That's the way we have been taught and make connections today. Our people, including our precious gundoos, can see themselves through these Stories of Strength and can see themselves enacting their own Stories of Strength – you can't be what you can't see.

Stories of Strength get to the heart of the challenge of education in current forms. Stories of Strength, as a Yarning circle practice, are ways on how to embed a strength-based approach. Moreover, the enactment of Stories of Strength is a cognoscitive effort and skill to look for and see the strengths of our people all around us, the strength of country.

Why is this important in the current-day relationship knowing and doing in education? Because the educational context or microcosm, for example, is 'all purveying'. The dominant hegemonic discourse is framed around nationalistic Indigenous approach 'Close the Gap'. From the outset, in any social programming, health, and wellbeing, our people, as a polity, as a living entity now, are dominantly defined as 'a gap', a negative distance in statistical data. Which, when challenged (more often by Indigenous people), it becomes clear, as Indigenous Social Statistician, Dr Maggie Walter has shown regularly, that the aggregated data will always show statistical impoverishment, deficit, and construct, a 'less then' position of and for our people based largely around the population size of our people and impacts of colonization. The core challenge Dr Walter purports is for statistical spaces to be more discerning of data and dis-aggregate so the richer and more Indigenous profile-specific, strength-based story can be shown, quantitatively. She explains 'how' this can be achieved, statistically, through her data share on the 5Ds of Indigenous Australian data (Walter & Anderson, 2013, p. 86; Walter, 2018).

Dr Walter, ~palawa, describes the 5Ds of data as: disparity, deprivation, disadvantage, dysfunction, and difference. These 5Ds of mainstream

Australian data research 'on us' 'do not, and will never, meet the data requirements of negotiating a fair and truthful relationship or information an Aboriginal and Torres Strait Islander voice' (Walter & Anderson, 2013, p. 86; Walter, 2018). The key research challenge, as Walter reflects, is to centre strengths on narratives of 'who we are as peoples', reject the Migloo value systems as the unacknowledged norm, and privilege Indigenous voices, knowledges, and understandings. The way forward and past 5D data is application of further Indigenous statistical design, which Waters calls 'nahra kati – in palawa meaning 'good numbers'.

Stories of Strength form part of the data 'narratives' of who we are as a people. Enacting Stories of Strength means 'we can be what we can hear and see', visualise moments of time, peoples' past footprints, and management of complex environments to grow positivity, ensure *Riteways* good spirit flows. These stories enable us within circle to see what steps our ancestors have taken, which inform our steps now and into the future. Prof Aileen Moreton-Robinson has detailed this process well over the past decades (2000).

Lore in higher learning – the research field – is an important area to establish lore connects and kinnections. When these aren't deeply grounded or applied, there is a space where other models, more blended or off country models, are used or referenced. This is vacuous and unsustainable. Because, as lore dictates, there are story places in all parts of the country. The story places are reflective of the distinct and unique identities we all share as Indigenous Australians. Our dganganbarra Australian map of country has multiple – over 200 – pieces of Indigenous identity, separate and unique to the local lay of the land.

Within my PhD research, I had to place the Durithunga learning model in context and pattern of the country it is based (Davis, 2018, p. 28). Our people refer to these unique places as 'country'. To expand on contemporary context of Indigenous identity, we must always define the 'roots on country', then move to how we 'share' or 'come into' country. So always in our being and doing, praxis and activity, we are reflective of the pattern of relationships and difference of experience as Indigenous people.

This process takes a responsive and reflective approach which moves from 5D (Walter & Anderson, 2013) data thinking and shifts research to the relational context on which we live and are based. On reflection of PhD-level research on collaborative community of practices, centring IK from country was a core component of this IK research (Davis, 2018). Centring

IK from country through lore is what was achieved through Durithunga research specifically. Tumba Tjina was the relational weave, the lore that was created in the research process of and on our Indigenous communities of Logan (Davis, 2018). To even begin the research process, Traditional Owner permissions were needed and sort for ethics 'sign-offs'. And before this, Durithunga, as a community of practice, already had several leading Logan Traditional Owners who were a regular part of Durithunga Yarning circles. What the research focus on Durithunga as a community of practice did was afford more opportunity and evidence bases to define and articulate, ultimately translate and transmit, how IK was researched and reciprocated within the education spaces. Just like the pattern of 'Seedlings' documentations to 'guide' Durithunga members, I was tasked through Durithunga research to co-design and kolab on what 'research protocols' were needed before any research began (see protocol table, pp. 101–102, Davis, 2018). The protocol process provides researchers with directional way finders to keep a directional path – true north on 'what can be shared', 'what should not be shared', and 'how to share' further safely and ways that aren't about the individual.

And the storying of country – explanation of boundary lines, citation of sources, and centring of Durithunga context within a balaun nyumba yarn – open, shared story of Keehandahn (Barlow & Best, 1997), provides a good solid grounding for all future works within the Logan field on markers and ways to see the IK in the land. Ultimately, the intellectual property rests with the Yugambeh people today and as Elders inform. YRACA is the new way of knowing and being and referring to IK within the local area and for future education works in and around the Logan City diaspora. This storying and this reference material – the localised storying of the area – is essential and is still referenced (as it should) for future Yugambeh and Yuggera studies and Language Revitalisation programs. What it does or provides as a teaching tool is a way to see the world from Yugambeh perspective – time and place as well as time everlasting.

Lore should be well-established, living, and breathing Scopus of works. Lore through enactment is easily defined and referenced. When there is no specific kinnection to lore, there is a gap in the elasticity and potential sustainability, then regeneration of programming. A great educational example of this, a 'non-lore' benchmark, is the stylised or non-referenced/refereed co-option of art or Indigenous artistic styles. The intricate knowledge and design of Walpiri 'dot art' is a great example of this. The contestation of the right to Aboriginal flag representation was another 'point of time' when lores of country intersected or ran 'up against' Western laws on intellectual property.

Lore work refers to the experiential exceptionalism our people wove and weave as part of sensemaking of our countries. Already in this text I have shared 'Stories of Strength', particularly in relation to language speakers of my extended family groups. Now we will expand on this some more through specific reflection and connection to higher-degree research. In the PhD work, I shared the archetypal Story of Strength (SOS) from our country on the importance of listening, called 'the cocoon of knowledge'.

SOS: The Cocoon of Knowledge

The cocoon of knowledge, as told to/by Peter Djerripi Mulchay (personal communication, May 2008):

He (Jutja Pa Jerome) would tell me of his first years, years of love and contentment. It was as if you were cocooned, warm in the embrace of that loving family structure. I think his most treasured memories go back to times he spent with the family he loved. The time spent with his grandfather, Old Uncle Jerry Jerome, stayed with him the whole of his life. The Old Man would call him over and they sat together. 'Djerripi' he would say, 'close your eyes', and he would begin to speak. Uncle told me that his words, that old language was like poetry. Every word would fill your mind, and he spoke so gently that you would hang on every word. With his words you were taken to the exact place the exact moment to feel the exact experience that the old man wished to share with you. Uncle told me how those old people used to teach the little ones. This was the way a thousand generations had passed on vital knowledge with a love and gentleness. 'Look' they would say and the children would gather around to look at a particular leaf, 'close your eyes, feel it' they would say. Rubbing the leaf quickly, they would say 'smell it', and breaking off a little of the leaf the children would taste. 'That's what that leaf is like in the early winter' the old women would say and then they would all move on laughing and playing.

(extract from Davis, 2018)

Just like the embassy protocol discussed earlier relates to broader IK systems research, so too is the need-to-know place-based Traditional Owner stories and knowledge as well as draw on own strengths and stories of and on place. To not be able to place oneself within the broader map of own country means there's a piece of work we need to do and achieve in this space so the story of us is as clear and concise as the rays of sun which hit all our country places or the winds that blow over the land. To not place oneself or identity to country means the mist nest which tightens and binds us is looser and needs more thread and story to capture the yarns connected to one's individual identity. And we have these spaces now, like Reconciliation Australia, more aptly the Healing Foundation and Link Up, which all provide an expertise and discipline in rethreading and reweaving our collective stories. I flag this because colonisation and colonial experience (the 5Ds) impact is real; our mobs were taken from country and placed on missions or reserves. That is our responsibility as an Indigenous person, identifying and claiming space to ensure the Stories of Strength place-base us and we can kinnect to them.

After sharing this example of 'deeper listening' technique mobilised through Stories of Strength, we will share other examples as models on 'how' to build or maintain knowledge strength. Pulling on Djeripi's thread and shares from Pa Paddy Jerome, we'll go out to the broader relational weave to my people of country – specifically, the six lines of carpet snake (the mothers and fathers of Pa Paddy's generation) who 'make up' the Traditional Owner group of the Cobble Cobble people.

This Cobble Cobble story is a story of great resilience and resistance. As I write and type this education piece here, the local birds starting to break the daylight morn, singing it in, I have nested, next to me a prized picture of Jutja Grandfather Fred Davis on my left. This is a photo of him in his later years, with a beautiful mop of white hair, and it is taken at the prized Davis stronghold of Urangan, on the land he bought as one of the first Indigenous landholders of the local area. This land and Grandfather's, as well as Grandmother's, stories play an important part of our knowing and retelling of the Settler/Invader story of and for our people. With strong links back to country – we are still referred to our line of the x6 'lines of carpet snake' – we, as an extended Davis family, are known as 'Hervey Bay' Davis. That folklore, that story, is central in grounding us as well as taking us to the times when and where Grandfathers and Grandmothers would have faced an extremely different, brutal, and always confronting colonisation space, time, and history in the early 1900s.

SOS: Jutja Grandfather Fred

Grandfather Fred (is Pa Paddy's Great Uncle), he grew us up on Batchalla Country from freshwater to salt water and in Hervey Bay we maintained strong connections with our families on Country, on Cherbourg and in Hervey Bay . . . Grandfather and Grandmother as well as Great Uncle Harry (his brother) and Aunty Annie are buried at the bay – we go to Point Vernon to pay our respects. . . .

Grandfather Fred's tumba connects us to Warra; Barrungam speaking country, the lands bordering the Bunya mountains and stretching out along the Condamine River (Gummanguru) and creeks of Barrunga (Dalby). Our freshwater grandfather settled and set up our family on the salt water of the Batchalla, Hervey Bay. Grandfather and Great Uncle Harry Davis bought land there, at Urangan, to raise our families upon and effectively escape the restrictions of the Protection Act[1], which had split many parts of our extended family.

As a young fellah we were brought up on the salt water – knowing we had strong connections to Wakka Wakka (carpet snake peoples). Grandfather's sisters were forced with their families to live on the reserve at Cherbourg as part of the Protection Act. These families connected to our Davis line include the Jerome, Riley, Blair, Bligh and Bond families. Grandfather always made space for our families in Cherbourg on our land. They could break away from the reserve and holiday in Hervey Bay. This story and this land play a big part in our family history. Our father, Alfred Davis Snr RIP, shared our strong connections with the land, kin and country by sharing songs like Guren ina narmi and Island songs like Black Swan, which imbued in all of us a strong pride and sense of self and connection to our heritage.

'Binung Tjanga . . .' extract (Davis, 2017)

This Story of Strength places us as a Cobble Cobble clan member within the context of the wider historical impacts of colonisation at that time. Take a moment to sit with the yarn and reflect on what the story is telling us about the time and places Grandfather is kinnected to. How are these times and places referred to? What do you feel when you think on this yarn, our storying?

What I love – and I know because I live and we feel it every day, blessed to be grown from such a strong familial base with the loving embrace of carbal, the carpet snake, forming such a strong social and emotional bond – is the transferral of that love, that positivity, that energy from time and space. There is country referred as well as specific places and people – relations to see and 'be' with, kinnect. Expertly, over the years, the Elders ngin noonthallis shared multiple stories and wove constant yarns of love and respect and feeling to create a connective tissue, the mist nets, as referred to earlier, to capture the time and place and bring us/all in relation to the stories. Just like the onus for *Riteways flow* is to be Culturally Proficient, as educators, when developing and deepening the praction on Storying of Strength, we must implore the notion of responsibility to listen and tune into the deeper story of love and kinnection – that is how you now show respect.

The storying is a multiple-layered process. Relationally, it is a Story of Strength because it is 'archetypal', is a particular story, has its own identity; to pay it homage, it must be highlighted as a significant piece to share, not a run-on activity or footnoted reference. That is why the process of sharing is a way to bind Yarning circles – create a distinct energy and flow. And when shared, their next part (what is later referred to in the 'identity' chapter as 'whole-part-whole') of knowing and doing is 'deep listening' then 'reflecting' and, ultimately, retelling or referring elements of the story which speak to you/us as individuals. The knowing of the storying is only as powerful as the retelling and recontextualising of self in relation.

When we deepen our reflections, pivot pieces to build on, and capture further strengths, then we move some ways in creating more positive *Riteways flow* and energies. These are campfire yarns, from our hearths and connected to our hearts. The 'pattern in which we gather and sit around these campfires as Indigenous researchers is a circle. And the circle pattern creates a distinct flow of energy, time, and knowledge transfer' (Davis & Coopes, 2022, p. 86).

SOS: Bunya Bunya Yarning

This yarn is written and shared for my deadly sister Budin Yadgie, Megsy Jane. She is a fearless leader, teacher, carer, aunty, advocate of her people, and representative for our people as Indigenous Australians.

This is a Bunya Bunya yarn kinnected to her Country, her spirit, her ancestors, her heritage as a Cobble Cobble woman.

The Bunya Bunya is the special nut grown, harvested, and shared by my people on Booburrgan Ngummunge (boo-bar-gun num-ooonge). Booburrgan Ngummunge is the spiritual name for Bunya Bunya. Booburrgan Ngummunge means 'mother's milk'. In the words of one of my elders past, Jutja Uncle Paddy Jerome: 'We belong to this land, the land is our Mother. We are part of a spiritual structure. That's Aboriginal culture. That is Boobarran Ngummin, the Bunya Mountains, our Mother' (Jerome, in Bunya Mountain Elders Council, 2010, p. 12).

Every three years, the Bunya Bunya has a bumper crop. On the third year, at Bunya Bunya Mountains, the gathering place of my people, we would (and still do) invite others from all over Queensland and far south into New South Wales to join in the ritual feasting. The Bunya Bunya Festival is part of Booburrgan Ngummunge. Traditionally, this kinnection Country to spirit would last from two to three months of the Bunya Bunya season and longer.

The fruiting Bunya Bunya produces a large cone, bigger than a pineapple, shaped like a ball. Within this cone are Bunya Bunya nuts. There can be 50–100 nuts in a cone. My people used these nuts in many ways. We'd roast and boil them; my family still puts them in campfires – we grind them up to make our special damper. And as we gather as groups to eat, we hold ceremony; we sit, listen, share, and learn.

As a proud Traditional Owner of the Bunya Bunya Mountains, I bring the bunya nut collected on Country. This bunya nut is from Bunya Bunya Mountain – Booburrgan Ngummunge. It has been gathered by my family at the time of the Bunya Bunya harvest (December–February) this year. I bring it as a kinnections to Country and representation of gathering and sharing.

Yanande (yin –un-dee), Megan Davis

Budin Yadgie, Prof Megan Davis is an inspirational leader and Indigenous community advocate. Within her next steps career development, movement through the United Nations, she asks for more of her Bunya Bunya story to steer and focus the Indigenous portfolio within the international human rights community.

Through this knowledge transfer, Megan uses the story and physically had bunyas – gifted from country to share, as has been our pattern for thousands of years with a broader international campfire. She is the granddaughter of Jutja Grandfather Fred. She is a 'next generation' of the Cobble Cobble storyline. A traditional owner and diplomat born from the rich storying and embassy of Boobargun Ngummunge.

What the preceding examples of lore show is the need to build up and out strong banks of Stories of Strength. The story becomes a part of the lore of the group and *Riteway flows* because the learning comes through not just learning about the rich stories shared. In the example of the Bunya Rangers piece, learning through the model of setting circle vis-à-vis a 'way to gather' now, in contemporary times reflected in the 'Caring for Country' doc. When tuning into other yarns and Stories of Strength from Bunya Bunyas, the international model example of Prof Megan Davis to the United Nations is a rich way of understanding and juxtaposes two very significant sites of gathering from time immemorial – the Bunya Bunya to contemporary United Nations diplomacy/embassy base in New York.

In all aspects of *Riteways*, there is a need to employ, refer, and enact deeper educational relationships with lore holders – Indigenous Knowledge holders. The Traditional Owner footprint provides the most fertile ground to grow out programmatic responses/enactments. The Traditional Owner footprints must be at the forefront of any enactment of *Riteways*. And what I have found over the decades of *Riteways* enactments, this forefront and lead process is accessible through all educational contexts, be that remote, rural, or urban.

Despite colonisation and the continued gap education being enacted, there exists a steeliness and a readiness across all Indigenous contexts to refer to, revere, and respond to the Traditional Owners of local areas. And working with my people, alongside my people, we have never found this a hard thing to articulate or access. What is hard and representative of the gap data in all contexts, urban areas in Australia, I would say more so, that the quality engagement and articulation of Traditional Owner relationships is least sort after and least accented in the areas where Migloo populations dominate. Colonisation is used to 'blame' by Migloo practitioners as to the reason we don't deepen engagement: *'It's hard to know who to refer to?'*

What came to us in learning at a recent IK masterclass on the Durithinga PhD research was, the biggest 'gap to close' is the relational gap, the distance of non-Indigenous research when it comes to the deeper notions of lore, country, and kinnections. Physically, we could see the movement of yarns and patterns of discussions which flowed from individual Indigenous researchers to national and international think tanks present (personal communications, April, 2022). When it came to 'check in' points and reflections of participants, feedback loops became sharper and focused on more need for 'time and pace' of research, as well as the absolute need for researcher authenticity, relationality. So negative has researcher footprint been on and the impact it has had on Indigenous representation today vis-à-vis the pervasiveness of 'the gap' that so much more work needs to go into pre/relational build, time, and energy for positive, meaningful, and sustainable researcher practions.

The Durithunga protocols (explained earlier) are one such way of seeking and attaining active community research participation (Davis, 2018). How does this fit within a process of 'lore' or articulation of circle flows? Well, just like our thinking is patterned, longer-termed, the relationality and connection we share across communities and strengths we can build collectively is a systems instrument for change and better way for social change organisations to 'be' in the field. We share this following 'way' as a marker on the deeper meaning and articulation when it comes to an IK translation of and on 'circle work'. It is more than just setting a shape of a circle. It is the space and distance between. It is the kinnection and heartbeat. It is the silence. And for us as Indigenous polity, it is *Riteways* to collaborate and design in circle – in collectives. A lot of Indigenous brothers and sisters and many 'people of colour' colleagues who weave in and out of this text will see and hear the skins they speak (Delpit & Dowdy, 2002). This is a 'learning' well picked up from Stronger Smarter. By far, the majority who were 'shocked' or had 'aha' moments in the Stronger Smarter leadership training were non-Indigenous colleagues (Stronger Smarter Institute, 2017). For a lot of the Indigenous colleagues, these processes were and are reaffirming. I write this way so non-Indigenous see the skin we speak and know that the processes translated here are more than just simple patterns of and on design but intricate webs of relational weaves and wefts that need to be 'seen' in and as a pattern first, then the thread pulled, the mist net tighter, to capture the deeper relational way and weave that makes those in circle accountable to each other to promote good spirit/good will. The lore translations to follow are ways, based in PhD research and academic peer review, for 'evidence-based' researchers to cite and grow processes from (they need all the help they can get . . . as long as they cite the work where it came from . . . please . . . gamba ngindus).

The people, situated 'within' the IK leadership circle Community Durithunga, have gifted us the principles and ways of working – circle work – to learn from. What the PhD forced for me and us (alongside multiple 'authentic Indigenous education' research) is the establishment of clear relational lines of reciprocity. And reciprocity is not just a simple 'exchange'; it can happen in multiple ways and rhythms. A telling piece from the research was keeping 'in principle' or aligned to what the Durithunga circle work was based and offer and be open to multiple forms of reciprocity or 'ask' and 'tasks' needed by Community Durithunga at that time. So although an agreement is made, as a researcher, a community's power is always to ask for more – if needed.

Moving from relationship readings/reference of the 'principles' of our people and circle work is establishing clear protocol to mark and fence in research relationship. This is important, nay essential, as a lot of ethnographical and anthropological as well as educational research has been premised in Australia on the 'othering' of my people and placing Indigenous identity within a narrow lens of 'culture' and 'identity'. And researchers and processes from the past become 'beacons', I'd say, more like a false southern cross (like Elkin's prose and Winterbottom's gaze) on 'authority' and 'representation' of and for our people. The definitive IK research protocol is a way of bordering that relationship exchange to the specific time and place and space of the researched interfaces.

Ultimately, it is Indigenous communities involved and their representatives who decide what their research is 'for' or not aligned with their expectations. IKS Lab, AIME, Stronger Smarter are all examples of Indigenous education Institutes that have a high level of Indigenous senior leadership visibility. In the 'power-relating' modelling, it is important to take steps back and see how organisations are reflective or abusive/ignorant in this relationship. Is Indigenous leadership in an organisation purporting Indigenous educational equity and design an embedded safe space Indigenous leadership model, or is it a shell, based on the 'one' (not more than three) Indigenous senior management expertise?

As we are the most researched people in the world, our access and ability to say no, waga, kabi, yugam, should not be restricted to how the higher education space oversees and rules on ethics and permission experiences. The right to say 'no' proper way is in the active participation in joint research which the labs call kolab space (Davis & Coopes, 2022; Fletcher et al., 2023) or wrong way research, which is predicated on what the system or authority wants or needs. The inequitable roll-out of previous government wage-garnering schemes (QATSIF, Queensland Aboriginal and Torres Strait Islander Foundation, and SEAMs, School Engagement and Attendance Management) are good models of and on how our decision-making voice is thwarted.

The best flow and articulation of deep and regenerative IK research is to enable 'open accesses' and check-in points on multiple parts of and on a research protocol. Too often do our non-Indigenous researchers get adept at following the 'latest policy', latest steps in proceeding with research ethics. This colloquially is referred to by mobs as 'ticking a box'. What *Riteways flows* speaks to, the need to weave in and out of ways of working and relating together, is a research protocol process which weighs the ethics and balance of assumed research power to the 'researched'. So at all tracks and junctures of a particular research project or process, the Indigenous voice has right to negate and reform a process.

Currently, my home community has had great success in the social and emotional wellbeing and services space by applying these protocols as guiding principles for partnership brokerage. As an active collaborator and

Figure 11.2 Yarning circle in action (Liz Kupsch, ~Waanyi).

113

writer in this process and development of protocols, I can share our work of and on EqPs (shared earlier). Where an education group or collective in Logan like Durithunga years ago vied for 'space' or to be seen, now in the 2020s, our collective Indigenous polity has a firmer and stronger sense of space and identity and is 'asking more' from the governments and so-called change agent NGOs who come in droves to our most complex communities. I use *most complex* in reference to original PhD research which used SEIFA (Socio-Economic Indexes for Areas) (Davis, 2018).

In this space still, after leaving the field from active teaching and aiding in state-wide education program delivery, out of catchment principal roles, I returned to our 'safe space', community-controlled circles within my hometown of Logan, to a social services diaspora which had no mechanisms for recognising the community-controlled 'voice' of wanting and needing 'more equitable funding' supports.

Within a complex community like Logan City, extra funding and support dollars are given to our area with little forethought to the equity and cross-cultural power relating that exists. The protocol to balance this power differential, developed by us, has been the articulation and creation of 'Equity Partnership' (EqP) documents and contracts. Foregrounded in this approach is the common-stance and common-sense mantra of 'First Nations first' service delivery.

IK Research Multi-Staged Protocol (Davis, 2018)

Stages	Description
(i)	Proposal for study
(ii)	Permissions + reciprocation lines
(iii)	Researcher " critical circle " established for feedbacks
(iv)	Researcher presence at locale yarning (sit + listen)
(v)	" Critical circle " updates / feedback
(vi)	Researcher proposal of process + possible date claimers (share)
(vii)	Yarning circle — multiple perspectives (captured first)
(viii)	Member checking
(ix)	" Critical circle " updates / feedbacks
(x)	Us/ 3 yarns + storying — individual perspective x3
(xi)	Member checking
(xii)	" Critical circle " updates / feedbacks

Figure 11.3 IK research multi-staged protocol.

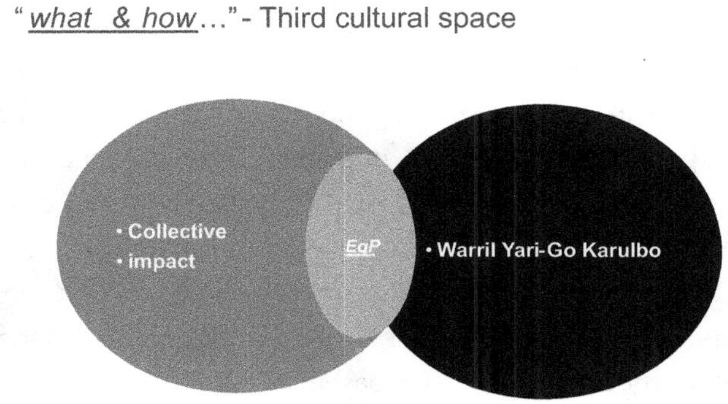

"*what & how*..."- Third cultural space

Figure 11.4 EqP: Equity Partnership and relationship designs.

Figure 11.4 has been a great process to be involved in as lead research and designers. EqP cuts at the heart of the 'Cultural Competence' type of modelling and 'othering' of us or externality of identity politicking. Up front, EqP[1] demands a recognition of and on 'First Nations First' leadership paradigm. EqP works off the premise that within our Indigenous communities, social service and not-for-profits that come to 'engage' with in Logan, apply their great 'win' in funding from a range of sources, must actively engage with 'First Nations first' and clearly articulate how the power relating will unfold and develop in time. Not lockstep community into social impact already-defined designs, the meted-out response of ongoing steering and so-called 'reference groups', but articulate up front how organisationally funding partners will engage with the strengths that exist within the local community.

When the latest 'Close the Gap', 'response to racism', or 'early years intervention' ensues or is inflicted on us as local communities, EqP has been developed and designed in the Indigenous community–controlled diaspora and will become a new language and tool for our people to use when negotiating and navigating the so-called 'collective impact' space. And its power in design is the 'contract', which firmly moves us as 'partnership' brokers and members (previously) on steering committees and asks the intervening agency to up-front the dollar value for Indigenous voice. Our community-controlled organisations are savvy enough and have worked long enough on the 'smell of oily rags' – tight and fiscally sound budgets (audit approved). What the EqPs relationally offer is a power reset or rebalance whereby the intervening agency must engage in a clear contractual agreement to renumerate the strengths our community members bring and have always brought to the social services tables. So in time with the design, we always aim back to our beginnings – relating and connecting/grounding as the key element to eventually equally land on – so EqPs in time can become models of EqP: Rs (relations).

In all the processes to share, it is essential that specific curricula and scaffolded tools exist and are developed to lay some tracks and offer ways forward through the complexities of Indigenous community collaborations and learning space developments. The *Riteways* 'lore' marker deepens when these multiple place-based responses are developed or listened to from within the country context they are based. The *Riteways* layer indicators to follow will share further articulation and refraction points on what has happened and what has sustained as good teaching and learning tools within a *Riteways* context.

Note

1 EqP language and thinking were originally directed and shared by the red dust thinking and communities of western New South Wales. Specifically, we had support and engagement of a great Aboriginal consultant, Jacky Beetson – Ngumpa. He gifted the language and 'other way' ideas at network forums; we created the Logan EqP model. And collectively, the 'we' I refer to is the Warril Yari-Go Karulbo, First Nations Logan City leadership circle.

References

Barlow, A., & Best, Y. (1997). *Koombumerri – saltwater people*. Melbourne: Heinemann Library.

Bunya Mountains Elders Council (Eds.). (2010). *Bonye Buru – Boobagun Ngumminge – Bunya Mountains Aboriginal aspirations and caring for country plan*. Bargara: Burnett Mary Regional Group.

Davis, J. (2017). *Binung Tjanga: Davis family storybook* (Limited ed., Family History Book). Bunya Mountains.

Davis, J. (2018). *Durithunga: Growing, nurturing, challenging and supporting urban Indigenous leadership in education* (Unpublished PhD thesis). Queensland University of Technology, Brisbane.

Davis, J., & Coopes, R. (2022). Our fire stories: Emergence through the circle work-process at the Indigenous knowledge systems lab. *Journal of Awareness-Based Systems Change, 2*(2), 85–108. doi:10.47061/jasc.v2i2.3892

Delpit, L., & Dowdy, J. K. (2002). *The skin that we speak: Thoughts on language and culture in the classroom*. New York: The New Press.

Fletcher, G., Waters, J., Yunkaporta, T., Marshall, C., Davis, J., & Manning Bancroft, J. (2023). Indigenous systems knowledge applied to protocols for governance and inquiry. *Systems Research and Behavioral Science*, 1–4. doi:10.1002/sres.2932

Kirwin, D. (2012). *Aboriginal dreaming paths and trading routes: The colonisation of the Australian economic landscape*. Brighton: Sussex Academic Press.

Martin, K. (2008). *Please knock before you enter – Aboriginal regulation of outsiders and the implications for researchers*. Teneriffe: Post Pressed.

Moreton-Robinson, A. (2000). *Talkin' up to the white women*. St Lucia: University of Queensland Press.

Pascoe, B. (2014). *Dark Emu: Black Seeds: Agriculture or accident?* Broome, WA: Magabala Books.

Singh, S. (Ed.). (2001). *Aboriginal Australia and Torres Strait Islands*. Footscray: Lonely Planet Publications.

Stronger Smarter Institute. (2017). *Implementing the stronger smarter approach*. Brisbane: Author.

Stronger Smarter Institute. (n.d.). *Stronger smarter leadership © training posters on 'Cultural Competency'*. Brisbane.

Ungunmerr-Baumann, M. (2002). *Dadirri inner deep listening and quiet still awareness*. Emmaus Productions. Retrieved from http://nextwave.org.au/wp-content/uploads/Dadirri-Inner-Deep-Listening-M-R-Ungunmerr-Bauman-Refl.pdf

Walter, M. (2018). The voice of indigenous data: Beyond the markers of disadvantage. *Griffith Review*, (60), 256–263. Retrieved from https://search.informit.org/doi/10.3316/ielapa.586241932732209

Walter, M., & Anderson, C. (2013). *Indigenous statistics: A quantitative research methodology*. Walnut Creek: Left Coast Press.

12 Culture and Language

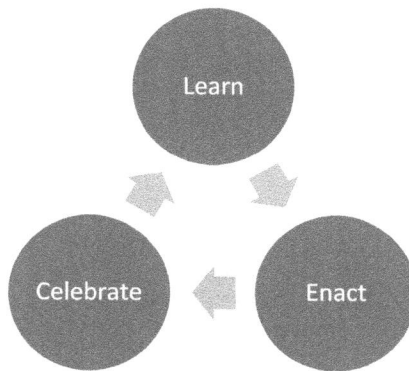

Figure 12.1 Cultural Curriculum cycle.

This is one of the strongest knowledge layers, where teachings and learnings are most palpable. Cultural practice is already grounded through the 'lore' of setting circle, and there needs to be more explicit times and tasks with focused learning on 'culture and langauge'. Why? Because the focus of the *Riteways flow* is 'ember blowing' part of *Riteways* education. In the 2020s, there is no hiding from the fact that no anthropological redefinition of 'lost tribes' or 'noble savages' can deny the impasse and impact of colonisation. There is *no part* in Australia which does not interact with Migloo culture. So how do we continue to blow the flames on IK learning? We deepen learning experiences through Indigenous culture and centre our approach and voice through Indigenous languages.

The process 'to learn', the pedagogical approach, is signpost earlier. Three parts to effective and sustaining 'cultural and language' programming –

DOI: 10.4324/9781003298717-12

'learning', 'enacting', then 'celebrating'. Language is a timely, ongoing *Riteways flow*. Sequentially, 'languages' can follow a national curriculum (ACARA) rhythm which is yearly/mapped to learning sequences related to Language Revitalisation to expert delivery. Specific Cultural Curriculum, we've found, produces and reproduces more energy if it is tailored towards a specific six- to eight-week learning/term juncture or runs into an event/celebration/showcase (a specific example in action to be shared in the last part of this section).

Language is essential to the sustenance and sustainability of pedagogy and curriculums of the land. First must be the Traditional Owner language, then growing connections and strength for own home community languages – this builds a nest or central cradle for all Cultural Curriculum work to grow and flow from. We write this perspective from a 'revival' point of view (*www.acara.edu.au* – Framework of Aboriginal and Torres Strait Islander Languages). That is, the 'language learning' framework our home country languages are 'in' and we are working with locals and school communities on. Depending on where your community is along the language's continuum, you would grow your place-based response from there. We have written, co-designed, and enacted three sustaining Indigenous Language programs. These are all based in the south-east, Yugambeh as a LOTE (2010 onwards), Yuggera as a LOTE (2012 onwards), and Barrungam as an on-country study (1997, 2010, and 2013 onwards). Specific references can be found at Yugambeh as a LOTE (Davis-Warra et al., 2011; Stronger Smarter, 2017), Yuggera (Mills et al., 2016) and Barrungam (Davis, 1997, 2017; Bunya Mountains Elders Council, 2010a, 2010b).

This work can be done, and is being done, to revitalise 'sleeping' languages for communities across Australia. If local area languages aren't sleeping, then there's massive strengths and opportunities to deepen learning further through a local community of speakers. And we have learnt from the previous footprints of bilingualism in Northern Territories and Western Australia. On the eastern sides, the language lead of Koori education, specifically Gumbaynggirr language, has been a Story of Strength we from the east coasts draw from and provide the mechanics on how to enact Language programs. Further west, the Language programs of the Barkandji specifically have provided fertile ground and modelling of taking First Nations languages through to tertiary – an ATAR pathway.

Every education iteration should include or embrace Indigenous languages. This flows from greetings to 'Acknowledgements' and 'Welcomes of Country' to 'naming' spaces. The more we hear, practice, learn, and locate our languages, the more their usage grows. Always at the centre of this approach is Traditional Owner direction, application, and ownership. It can, and in some places does, extend to teaching of and in the traditional language – a practice seen in schools with deep links to SSI (Stronger Smarter Institute, 2019). This is an important evolution in how schools position themselves in relation to the local community they serve.

Indigenous language models exist all around the country. The position a proficient educator would find themselves in is based in this important and essential element of ember blowing. The languages research and outputs we have co-designed and collaborated with in south-east are all predicated on the ways we speak, and language speakers recall our spoken voice. Again, Jutjas like Pa Noel Blair of Jinibara and Cobble Cobble nations refer to the concept of 'rolling our tongue' (Davis, 2017). This is an important linguistic and guttural definition on 'how we speak' as a people. What is key in developing any front-facing Language program is to design and redefine the languages position not from a Western linguistic and anthropological lens of learning but layer and learn from and allow the Traditional Owners to drive Language Revitalisation and bilingual programs.

The programmatic timetabling of languages is a clear signal to all community members of the importance and centrality of learning the oldest-living, surviving languages in the world. Languages, in effect, speak to power. The great work of Barkandji language holders and local lead Indigenous principals of Menindee and red sands areas shows another enactment part of *Riteways* modelling in action. The languages themselves are not separate from the next level or layer of school learning. Barkandji language as a subject can be taken from the nesting and after-school programs of the people to a nationally accredited, university-level pathway. 'Aboriginal students in the town of Menindee were creating history. At the Menindee Central School, students are taking part in a pilot program that sees Indigenous language studies as an elective subject in the HSC' (Welcome to Country, 2017). This high-order modelling and higher expectation of where we can take our Indigenous languages has to be at the forethought and directional paths of program designs and ultimate enactment.

The flow-on effects of the language design and enactments are exponential. Take the Menindee model as an example. Elders through Land Council and local AECG articulation have built, taught, and worked overtime in refining and redefining Barkandji language work and activities. So the community layers of strength, Land Councils, AECGs, Elders provide the base to launch the educational response. From here the Indigenous principalship, Indigenous teachers, and liaisons provide the structural support to see the languages seeded in current educational settings. The local Aboriginal language nests, centres, colleges attached to universities are the places where specific professional learning is and can be provided to guide the speakers in contexts of learning and embedding language praction. The gundoos – the students – respond as a way of having their language linkage their identity embraced in the curriculum for which they are assessed.

The exponential and strength-based over-performance in a space like languages is shown through the scope of people, cross sections of institutes and businesses which can enable further enactment to occur. A powerful 'Welcome to Country' process we enacted recently on country with our Western Downs was sing-song and language from the Downs. After introducing and setting the table, our mayor provided all with 'Welcome to Country' plates. This was a great way to see, smell, and taste the language of the land. We enjoyed an appetiser of local winna Murray cod to set the rest of the tone of the night/welcome to dignitaries visiting our Downs area (Governor General Visit, Western Downs Council event at Dalby, 2022).

When language and local protocol are infused in country and systems who 'care for' country, this opens safer space possibility and opportunity for our gundoos. This way, the social distancing from our gundoos is less and less of being able to see themselves be able to dream of roles within these same spaces. Indigenous languages pathway shifts our social justice mantra of 'you can't be what you can't see' to reality. Speaking, singing, dancing, painting, and referencing language in pedagogy and curricula require our people to do that circle work. Languages as a *Riteways* layer provide an extremely focused and fertile ground for further exploration and social success factors as designers and do-ers can effectively 'pick up' work or become the next-generation scholars, knowledge holders, teacher, or principals within their own native tongues.

There are key weaves of difference here in the development design and enactment of languages in programming. The successful embodiment of languages comes with whole of staff planning, training – we utilise, and I highlight, Stronger Smarter training here. Specific macro Indigenous-led professional learning is essential for the elasticity and stretch of Indigenous Knowledge thinking and applications. Coupled with this, as the Western Downs examples show, are further spaces of language enactment, whether they be through food, choral – through choirs and rendition of regular ceremony pieces like singing of national anthems or, in recent times, articulation of individuated Indigenous languages. This approach, individuating or translating into Indigenous language, has been a core research translation piece for the upcoming referendum on an Indigenous Voice to Federal Parliament. The Uluru Statement from the Heart is widely translated in traditional languages for 'sharing of meaning' and translating the wish of our people (https://ulurustatement.org/the.statement/translations/).

This piece, as my Budin Yadgie is a co/designer and writer of the Uluru Statement, has been our recent Barrungam (our country) translation of the statement.

Barrungam language translation of the Ulruru Statement from the Heart: . . .

Budin gungdu wanagi, gundir ngue maras. Tjanga djungu: Dguan djimben gung ngin budin gung dganganbarras. Gurangindau duwur. Gurangindau tjanga. Dguai djimben Gaiwar. Duwur – djah, djumnge, gunda. Djuan dgimben dghanum gambargan migloo. Waangi migloo bianga gurangdai waga. Gurangadai djah, dgumge, gunda tjanga?! Tjanga bullyman budin barras. Ngurama gundoos gunnin gunnin. Djimben garis? Gari gambas gunnin gunnins. Dangi tjanga migloo gambargan waga gamba.

Gnua budin gundju guni Australia. Mimburi gundoos tjanga. Gaung gundoo gundamena duwur ngin baulan tjanga.

Gundamena budin gundju, gawung gundamena – 'VOICE', Gundamena gambaragan 'makaratta' – 'TREATY', Gundamena gawung gambaragan gunge – 'TRUTH'.

Gung ngin budin gungs budin gundju tjanga 'makaratta commission'.

1967 gnuar barras guni Australia.

2017 bianga guni Australia.

Yanande gundju tumba dganganbarras – budin gung ngin gung gungs. Guni Australia gaung dguinga jinung du-ur gamba gamba bouls . . .

(see *Riteways* Flowbook sample, p. 177, for fuller definition/translations)

---)))--<

What the preceding design shows is an example of and on how to embed IK through the lens of language development and articulation. The opportunities in our languages are limitless and have been practioned well around the country already. By definition or articulation of deeper *Riteways* learning opportunities, 'culture and languages' provide a highly visible and recognisable layer of learning and learning potential for educators. What's essential in all learning forums is, the visceral, live energy and positive spirit language flows are not hemmed or hampered by the limitations of and on third space thinking and modelling.

Extended knowledge time on Aboriginal and Torres Strait Islander Studies and Arting and Storying – creating Cultural Artefacts is another key exemplar of deeper Riteways enactment. Learning blocks of and on significant historical moments contextualise the learning of us within the broader Australian teaching and learning space as well as deepening connections to kin and kith, learning and understanding of Stories of Strength. There is an enfoldment of learning (Martin, 2008) whereby the central topic areas are juxtaposed then rolled into the next layers of learning. This, again, is why the *Riteways flow* model is not defined through compartmentalised segmentation but is rather crafted on following the contours and patterns created through circle work. Each layer of the *Riteways flow* intersects with the other. All layers are impacted on by 'spirit'. And its movement is not linear or shaped in a box. *Riteways* model for movement is a flow.

The recording and reflection of enactment is an important interrogative and deeper analytic process to engage through the 'doing' of each layer. Specific ways to, and willingness to, do research in sustaining and regenerative ways are shown in the next marker: 'identity'. However, using the Bunya Bunya Mountains as an example, a space where we share yarns (and have so far in this book), we can extrapolate and explain further how a process like artefact making – art and story – can be practioned *Riteways*.

To finish on the sharing on 'culture and languages' practice, I wanted to (share) *gift the Arting and Storying teaching and learning cycle used across multiple macro and micro contexts*. To sustain a culture for over 60,000 years, we, as Indigenous people, didn't randomise our approach or practice adhockery (Bunya Mountains Elders Council, 2010a, 2010b; Kirwin, 2007; Pascoe, 2014). To be able to create a culture of sustainability and regeneration, we have developed over time methodologies and approaches which sustain learning and connection to place. The archetypal Dreaming or story place yarns are great exemplars of this. Song, dance, and art are other elements of Cultural Curriculum and pedagogical practices.

Despite the intense colonisation of an area like my country, south-east Queensland, we didn't 'forget' songs and dance and story: the lore of country. In areas that were so heavily colonised, especially in relation to everyday language, we refer (as earlier stated) to languages as 'asleep', needing a *Riteways flow* to blow on the embers to enact the living memory which already exists in the land. In this area of intense colonisation, gathering and trade songs/sharing songs are still heavily sung, remembered, revered, and taught. One such song, the centre of wanjau – exchange – is gari ina narmi (Davis, 2007, 2017; Bunya Mountains Elders Council, 2010a, 2010b). This is a Bunya Bunya song. And I write that in reference to a time and place where, on country and with sharing like the bunya harvest provides, calling out 'who you are' and 'where I am from' is an essential part and continues to be of reference referring and revering one's country.

As a song in language – both Kabi and Wakka Wakka languages – the song has varied meanings. In Kabi context, the song refers specifically to country, 'where I'm from', 'everyone wants to claim my country, I am not from this flat country. . . .' And the Wakka translation sings specifically about gathering the nuts, 'climbing bonye tree and handing down the cones to share' (Lydon Davis, personal communications 2022). The strength of this song and storyline lies in the 'nuance', the rhythm and motion of the dance to share and learn, together. At the height of colonisation, the 1800s in Queensland, this is a song and storyline which kinnects us all in the south-east of Queensland (Davis, 2017; Gala, 2004; Geia, 2016). A song shared along the 'great bunya Highway' which Kirwin details extensively in his historical research (2012).

The Bunya ceremony extended for over three months on country. Mobs from as far north as Rockhampton and south of the Tweed would come and gather at the special site of mimburi (Gaiarbaru in Steele, 1984). Gari ina narmi is a favourite song of our people, remembered and sung at our times of gathering now. As a result of the diversity of mobs who came for the Bunya ceremony, there are variations of Gari ina narmi which have been passed down which are in the different languages and movements of the people who came to the Bunya Bunya.

In spite of colonisation, the creation of three or four intensive prison camps and stations (close by), and the mixing of our mobs together, the reverence for Bunya Bunya and the singing of this important song remained and remains as a link in the south-east to Gaunrindgindu – dreaming time, time before Migloos. At our most recent opening of the auspicious Bunya Bush University, this song and this storyline were (and continue to be) an import-ant part of retelling and sharing the significance of the bunya nut harvest, the intermeshing of extended relationships between salt- and freshwater people since time immemorial.

These cultural practices don't just 'reappear'; they are learnt and taught through a constant loop of sitting, listening, seeing, observing, then doing. It is because of the greater Collective Knowledge System in existence before colonisation that a song like Gari ina narmi is able to sustain from a time of great impact and intensity – colonisation and now regrow well after coloni-sation. This grounding for us on country has meant the pattern to relearn or re-sing songs now – tjanga is very much a positive reaffirmation of and on culture. There is a methodology and practice in performance of culture that is essential to *Riteways* models. This model draws strength from the practices exemplified in the south-east and connected to different groups around the country.

The *Riteways* method we use in Cultural Curriculum teaching and learn-ing is shown through the following diagram.

This learning best comes through an intensive six- to eight-week teach-ing and facilitation focus. In this cycle, there are three parts. The 'learn' cycle involves knowledge deepening through listening, observing, and recording. Then there is 'enact'(ment), which is practicing culture through 'doing': applying what has been taught and observing others who are doing to sharpen my practice. Here there may be multiple lessons/practices to

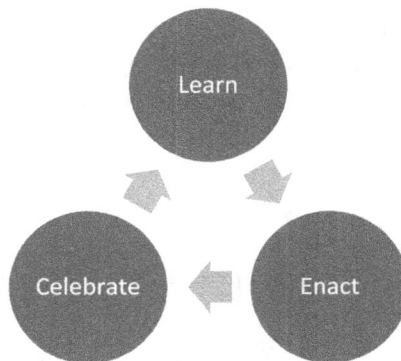

Figure 12.2 Cultural Curriculum teaching and learning cycle(s).

learn and get right the songs, story, and position of gundoos and staff – does everyone know and engage in their role in the flow?

Once the initial cycles are enacted, there is a performance or demonstration, or 'Celebration' of culture and the cultural knowledge shared. This is an important part of the cycle because the act of listening and learning must be reshown to the teachers, the Elders, in a respectful loop of 'doing'. Depending on the type of task or learning that the cycle is being applied to, this is a six- to eight-week process. *Celebration is successful application of learnings. And these learnings should be assessed.* All parts of the cycle are essential and form part of the discipline of 'circle work' which enables a knowledge thread to regrow and strengthen.

This is a tried-and-true method of IK translation and curriculum articulation. The models of place bases (shared at start of the book) provide insight into the kinds of spaces where this learning has occurred through a similar way. Areas of deeper *Riteway flows* include on country – dgangunbaras ngin Warra Warra ngin Bunyas (Bunya Mountains Elders Council, 2010a, 2010b) – as well as Logan City, Yugambeh and Yugggera country (Exley et al., 2016).

The 'Cultural Curriculum Work' referred to (earlier and in what follows) relates to the performance and dance of Barrungam song and story. What is most important in the learning cycles are the segues leading up to and a part of the overall 'Cultural Work' flows. Exley and Dooley provide a good breakdown of and on set activity and cycles of learning a part of a regular weekly learning space called the 'Dream Circle' (Logan, off country) (Exley et al., 2016). Distinct learning processes are created and shared by jarjums (young people) and Elders alike in these learning scenarios. Again, what is distinct and definitive about the praxis are the clear learning junctures – beginnings, middles, and ends to rebeginnings of the process.

Setting circle process was essential, which Exley et al. frame as *Activity 1* (Exeley et al., 2016, p. 41). So our circle setting in this context was a 'transition into' the teaching and learning space. This would be signalled by a 'didj in' or 'chant in' to circle. Local Traditional Owner language would come first. All translations begin in local language before English translation. We share, we show. You welcome, you share, we do together. 'It is expected that participants introduce themselves in the Aboriginal language taught at the school' (Exley et al., 2016, p. 42).

The next phase of activities was 'breaking bread', which Exley frames as *Activity 2*: sharing food (p. 42). A process which 'is not only integral to Indigenous cultural practices, but also an important nutritional lesson'

(Exley et al., 2016, p. 42). Followed by 'homework', 'Jarjums engaged in conventional academic work in a culturally safe extracurricular space' (Exley et al., 2016, p. 43).

To progress successfully through each learning layer led to the final 'cultural activity' (p. 43). And there is deep discipline again to this most important activity. 'All cultural activity is carefully introduced by an Indigenous elder' (Exley et al., 2016, p. 43). Establishing understanding of the importance of deep listening and observation. Just like the deadly eagle, they are about to dance, or the kangaroo, they are about to jump line, embrace your countries' senses. Look hard at what the dancers are showing you. See how they move. Can you do that move? Do you want dancers to show you how? 'Jarjums acquire rites and rituals around permission to introduce story through song and dance' (Exley et al., 2016, p. 43).

Listen to the beats. The clapsticks and boomerangs are fast and slow throughout the songs. Can you hear the different rhythms? Can you feel it?

The evidence base recorded from visiting educational scholars was prevalent in the way Indigenous students 'held themselves' and wove across the whole school community.

> The Jarjums have . . . repositioned themselves in terms of their Indigenous identity: They have taken a strong and proud role in educating the mainstream community about Indigenous Knowledges . . . including Indigenous dance, dance, song, art and languages.
>
> (Exley et al., 2016, p. 44)

Within boul, these rhythms can take an hour of 'practice'. This is the first learning and enactment cycle. Gundoos must watch and observe and earn their time into the circle. Circles are set, safe circles created because our gundoos claim and own the space. And in the richest sense, they are seeing their country, their people, their faces, 'teach' – noonthalli.

One of the greatest learnings or research translation challenges I had within an all-Indigenous school was creating assessment bridges for teachers, who, in their curricula-centric and preservice-text worlds, were 'taught' by our higher-learning institutes how to map progress along a prescribed criteria yet when asked to stretch or think on the broader application of a gundoos skill set would find the third space that creates the most challenging.

Within the Indigenous school parameters, we had a team of exceptional (travelling the world) Indigenous dancers. Rather than read report cards that didn't reflect that 'excellence' at the end of semester, I challenged the learning cohorts to capture that excellence. 'If young ones are performing and excelling in front of thousands of people at sold-out football grounds and asked to perform oversees, how are we allowing that identity to be assessed/connected within their schooling world?'

Such a provocation has recently led to a change in Australian design of Vocation education capture, which is a good thing, and again, our application of *Riteways* should not be an 'exceptional' anything but a part of the norm and regular praxis of educational flow.

References

Bunya Mountains Elders Council (Eds.). (2010a). *Bonye Buru – Boobagun Ngumminge – Bunya Mountains Aboriginal aspirations and caring for country plan.* Bargara: Burnett Mary Regional Group.

Bunya Mountains Elders Council (Eds.). (2010b). *The Bunya Mountains – multi-stakeholder project.* Bargara: Burnett Mary Regional Group.

Davis, J. (1997). *Cobble cobble: Davis family storybook* (Unpublished Family History Book). Eagleby.

Davis, J. (2017). *Binung Tjanga: Davis family storybook* (Limited ed., Family History Book). Bunya Mountains.

Davis, W. (2007). *Spear making* (Unpublished master's thesis). University of Queensland, St. Lucia.

Davis-Warra, J., Dooley, K. T., & Exley, B. E. (2011). Reflecting on the "dream circle": Urban Indigenous education processes designed for student and community empowerment. *QTU Professional Magazine, 26,* 19–21.

Exley, B., Davis, J., & Dooley, K. (2016). Empirical reference points for Bernstein's model of pedagogic rights: Recontextualizing the reconciliation agenda to Australian schooling. In P. Vale & B. Exley (Eds.), *Pedagogic rights and democratic education – Bernsteinian explorations of curriculum, pedagogy and assessment* (pp. 33–46). Oxon: Routledge.

Gala, J. (2004). *Gari Gynda Narmi.* Retrieved from Cheryl Colan: Free Download, Borrow, and Streaming: Internet Archive: https://archive.org/details/gari-gynda-narmi

Geia, J. (2016). *Gurri Ngindin Narmi.* Retrieved from Gurri Ngindin Narmi – song and lyrics by Joe Geia | Spotify: https://open.spotify.com/track/0Qwdrkd3nTTsr HtUOB5cfk

Kirwin, D. (2007). *Aboriginal heroes: Dundalli a "Turrwan" an Aboriginal leader: 1842–1854.* Nathan: Griffith Institute for Educational Research, Griffith University.

Kirwin, D. (2012). *Aboriginal dreaming paths and trading routes: The colonisation of the Australian economic landscape.* Brighton: Sussex Academic Press.

Martin, K. (2008). *Please knock before you enter – Aboriginal regulation of outsiders and the implications for researchers.* Teneriffe: Post Pressed.

Mills, K. A., Davis-Warra, J., Sewell, M., & Anderson, M. (2016). Indigenous ways with literacies: Transgenerational, multimodal, placed, and collective. *Language and Education, 30*(1), 1–21. doi:10.1080/09500782.2015.1069836

Pascoe, B. (2014). *Dark emu: Black seeds: Agriculture or accident?* Broome, WA: Magabala Books.

Steele, J. G. (1984). *South East Aboriginal pathways*. St. Lucia: UQP.

Stronger Smarter Institute. (2017). *Implementing the stronger smarter approach*. Brisbane: Author.

Stronger Smarter Institute. (2019). *Stronger smarter field notes 2014–2019*. Brisbane: Author.

Welcome to Country. (2017). *Meet the first Aboriginal students to complete an Indigenous language HSC exam*. Retrieved from https://www.welcometocountry.org/first-aboriginal-students-indigenous-language-hsc-exam/?fb_comment_id=1470 637376359772_1617480261675482

13 Identity

○ **IDENTITY:**

Figure 13.1 Identity.

Identity refers to the reflection and articulation of knowledge of self, under-standing self. *Identity* in *Riteways flow* refers to a 'Whole → Part → Whole' way of knowing. This involves knowing and understanding the whole self and knowing and connecting that identity as part of a broader collective then redefining self within this collective. For this IK our way, an individual can't be Indigenous, identify as Indigenous, without understanding Indigeneity from within. To understand or know yourself within the whole is essential in the *Riteways flow* model. IK theorists have explained this process as 'related-ness' (Moreton-Robinson, 2000; Martin, 2008). That is why in HR and for the want and desire for staff to kinnect to both their and their clients' identities, a model like the 'Mani model' formed and has been enacted. Always knowing self and articulating my role, showing your understanding of your role in flows, situating own identity is a key part of the *Riteways* pattern.

There are essential teaching methods and materials to develop and weave into this wanjau. We will list some of the main methods and materials for

DOI: 10.4324/9781003298717-13

future reference and provide an example to drill down into. Knowledge of self is an integral part of emancipatory education (Sarra, 2011; Gilbert, 1977; Fesl, 1993; Martin, 2008; Sheehan, 2012; Nakata, 2007). An integral element of *Riteways flow* is to learn from different points of Indigenous cultures and, if 'off country', always relate back and kinnect to your learning, your footprint, your country. This is another essential element differential from other ways of learning through culture, song, and dance. *Riteways* models of learning would grow from the central point of location – where is the local area knowledge, the Traditional Owner footprint and stories? How can we learn from there, the central point of *Riteways* knowledge base?

Learning Processes as a 'Whole' – Us/All

- Understanding and walking *Country*
- Local footprints
- PLPs – together
- Family story
- Researching and recording local history (Davis, 2007, 2018; Craven, 2011; Grant, in QSA, 2000)
- Macro area studies

This 'whole' knowledge of and on identity is a baseline to develop further flows. It is foundational, as the first part is connecting on country where I am. Understanding and defining local knowledge, story, and footprints. Once connected to this broader map, individual reflections flow – hand-printing to family storying. Woven into the pedagogical pattern again is the Cultural

Learning processes as a 'whole' - us/all:

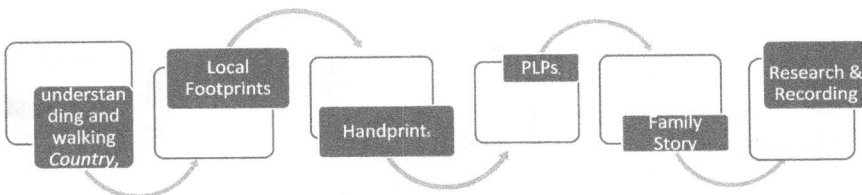

Figure 13.2 Phase 1.

131

Curriculum elements, where 'celebrating' shifts to more personal research of and recording on own knowledges of self.

Once foundational learning is mapped and patterned, gundoos and communities can move through a second phase of curriculum and pedagogical development and refinement. In the figure to flow next, the main 'foundations' remain the same, Country, hand-printing, PLPs, and there is a subtle or next phase shift in learning. After establishing the Traditional Owner baselines, roots (Davis, 2018), next phases of study can grow and flow to broader topic areas. First phases are a closer definition of country and obligation, and second phases are an expansion, and thus demonstration, of enactment, what gundoos and community have learnt and shown. So local area stories shift in next phases to macro – broader area studies. And the onus after the initial cycles of 'research' moves into demonstration, articulation, and assessment or showcase of what has been learnt. This element of movement is shown in the second phase (below) through the last cycle of 'research and sharing'.

- Understanding and walking *Country*
- Macro area stories
- Handprints as principles of and for knowledge
- PLPs – together
- Our Stories of Strength
- Researching, recording, and sharing local stories
                    (Davis, 2007, 2018; Craven, 2011; Grant, 2000)

These are integral to deepening knowledge of self. Just as in the enactments of 'culture and language' explained earlier, a discipline, a regulatory motion, is required. I just returned from Bunya Bunyas as a Traditional Owner of country working with my countrymen and countrywomen – further extended from my Cobble Cobble line (see Bunya Mountains Elders Council, 2010a, 2010b). And here I sit and set in circle not as Dr John Davis

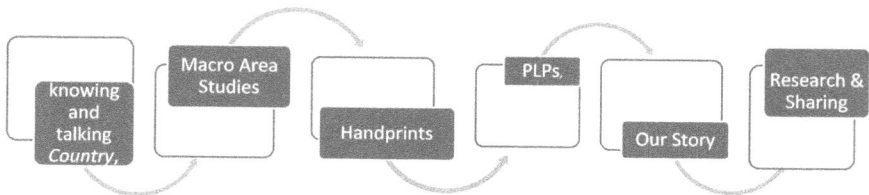

Figure 13.3 Phase 2.

but as JD, gungi Davis, the younger brother of my clans. Noonthalli, a teacher who has knowledge of song, story for country and is part of brighter and broader pattern of relationships of Bonye Buru – Boobargun Nguumonge. And in this space, I am (as I always flow and know) in awe and amazed at the rich vein of knowledge, knowledge holders that continue to spring from the deep wells of Bunya Bunya. As an 'academic' now, trialling *Riteways* in IKS Lab (based at Deakin University), I learnt from and was overwhelmed with the richness of story, culture (carvings), primary and secondary source materials shared – wanjaued on country of country. Shout-outs to Darlows, bandji Dino, local area and fellow family historian. His archives of knowledge are matched by his wisdom of and on country, now centring and basing his identity, caretaking on country at our Bunya Bush Uni site. And his brother, Shannon, now Head Ranger of our Bunya Murri Rangers team. He has texts, codified and carefully recorded, on his electronic hard drives. The meticulous note-taking and research capture the means Language Revitalisation work of our Western Downs, country we refer to as Bunya Barras, can be more easily 'blown onto' the embers of the burnt-down language fires. His access and archiving were and are the next step of our Traditional Owner knowledge to be stored and re-storied through the data or electronic footprints.

This is the power of 'relatedness': whether you are blessed in your own country or respectfully weave as a new historical Indigenous member, there is a way of relating and being which has been layered and laid by our ancestors since time immemorial. The *Riteways flow* direction point is to set your work on that continuum. This individual work builds collective knowledge strength. And when you, as individual, a responsible and responsive human being in the pattern of relationships, do it well, it opens another way of learning and exchanging.

And the lore of the learning environs, with regular check-ins and setting of Yarning circles, means the sensemaking that happens thematically and spiritually for participants is shared (allowed to be shared) in constant cycles of feedback.

The personal journey of individuals is a lifelong learning path. I guess that is the key learning I am sharing of yarns from Bunya Mountains. Blessed to write and provide insights on Indigenous education from my learning journey, and am still learning and in awe of the collective knowledges that exist in and between our Traditional Owner family groups. We are not burning the right fire, putting logs on the collective campfires if we don't go out yarn, take time to listen, and 'be' on country – bianga (Davis & Coopes, 2022).

This is an important part of this segment of *Riteways flows*. The activities listed earlier – PLPs, family stories, researching – are a part of an ongoing cycle of learning. Kabi Kabi Elders of the south-east like Garmi Jenny Thompson speak of the individual need in Kabi circles to link 'seven generations of learning' (Thompson, n.d. in Davis, 2017). This standard in family storying gives a Traditional Owner a benchmark to map family trees and kinnections. The greater the depth of learning and knowing on seven generations, the greater the depth of relatedness or being able to make and map the kinnections of others (relatives or not) around you.

In my previous experiences as an Indigenous educator and leader within independent Indigenous schools, blended learning spaces, both state and catholic education, the impact of individualised learning and focused personal goal setting and story making cannot be understated. PLPs refer to Personalised Learning Plans. In NSW, early on in my Stronger Smarter experience, I saw these being implemented and referred to the most by exceptional NSW colleagues and practitioners. An individuated learning and 'compact' between gundoos/families and the schools (Sarra, 2012; Stronger Smarter, 2017). They have, and the process of individuating learning has, grown more widely as a common practice, which is a good thing – shown through leading specialist in the Special Education space, development in social justice education of the unique 'identified' – LUI as well as the mainstream data wall (Sharrat & Fullan, 2012) models.

For ease of translation here and reference to the work I'm grounded in and *Riteways flows*, we will stick with the language of 'personalised' as it matches the pattern of self related to the hand – na.

Sample:

→ *Part – us/only*:

A powerful us/only metaphor for identity mapping is our handprints. The previous PLP design highlights the importance of the 'space' of centring any design within the individual identity. At the forefront of the sample PLP is a 'hand-printing' exercise. IKs shared along the east coasts refer to the handprints as markers of identity. The identifiable marker of self apart from all others is the individual mark of a handprint. ~Gamilaori Elder statesman Uncle Reg Knox (RIP) shared the knowledges of his people through 'handprint designs' and artistic works. While forging his work at a local Durithunga

Sample:

Personalised Learning Plan – PLP

Links to our care plan way of thinking and doing. Either place or make your hand design visible. Listen to how noonthallis explain and show the 'Hand Design'.

NOW – your turn. *Take time to think. You can start this and finish at the end (signature process) or make time now and finish your PLP design.*

The middle – the palm is your design – what image or designs represent you?

The fingers our indicators of identity represent you. Who's your mob? Where's your family from? How many in your family? What do you love to do? What are you good at? What is something unique about you?..

(see fuller PLP design in 'Flow book' samples pg171–176 onwards).

Figure 13.4 Personalised Learning Plan – PLP.

→Part – us/only:

Figure 13.5 Part – us/only.

school, Uncle would teach the observing classes that 'the handprint is your individual marker. No one would have the same handprint. This is why my people's caves are filled with handprint stencils'. He then would contextualise to contemporary Australia, 'You all watch crime shows? Who done its?? What do they use to track people in crimes, what do police use? . . . Fingerprints! My people knew this for thousands of years before Sherlock Holmes' (personal communication, 2007). As an IK tool, handprints, or hand-printing as an activity, is a way to celebrate individual identity.

Uncle Reg imported and supported IK in a way that was warm, welcoming, and soothing of the soul. When I was a young Murri teacher (now older), my weaves with him and his daughter Missy Knox and family came through the doors of the safe 'third space' created called Knowledge House at Loganlea SHS.

Uncle Reg translated and inspired IK in a way that welcomed all and maintained an integrity and point of significant difference. His layering of knowledge came from an older time and way of knowing and being. And through the mechanism of art, he transmitted (and still does) knowledges that make meaning today.

I have, over the years, led collaboratives as a teacher of HASS to embed Indigenous curriculum and identity into the scholastic programming. This, in turn, led to further mobilisation of opportunity designs shifting across the Australian and curriculum to sciences. While specific micro program developments, the individuated 'lesson' and learning times associated with subject matter, what were essential elemental pieces were the macro whole of school 'whole context' to embed and ultimately build sustainable curriculums and pedagogy. Naidoc days, art murals, an international thread, and adopting 'of learner' and 'place' within local schools were essential (Davis & Grose, 2008).

Our roles as educators were to create and provide safe space for IK to grow in and, at Loganlea, be a part of the living knowledge fabric. The simple item of learning place and story design was through the handprint design process. Here the gundoos sense of place and space was fixed and embraced by the whole school. Before creating Knowledge House, at my first stint at Loganlea is a picture of my students in front of the mural – macro, whole-school design. Painted and positioned in a central gathering location for sports, Ag students, drama, hospitality, in front of the office next to B block, HASS, and performing arts. Key part of 'display' is IK exposure – art to be seen. Create good energy.

And the gundoos excelled in looking after the art – their IK. In my years at Loganlea, my first stint (early 2000s), the artwork remained 'untouched'. Even over Xmas and Easter school breaks, where local young people would move through schools and leave their marks – graffiti over a range of buildings – the murals remained untouched. And this was a pattern reciprocated Logan City–wide: a respect to the Gamalaroi Elder and knowledges from his family group that he imparted on our young ones with vigour and richness and an integrity like no other.

Ironically, I wanted to seek an Uncle Reg art piece as it was a Logan City school's 'calling card'. I knew from growing up in the area and having my teaching pracs across Logan City that a definitive moment in teaching IK (back then) in Logan was to have an Uncle Reg masterpiece adorn your buildings. To weave in Uncle's IK was a marker of respect both on country and off country Elderships. Yugambeh, in their articulation of Yugambeh lore through YRACA, relate to us as non–Traditional Owners, living 'off country' as historical people. Through the diplomacy of their ways, they refer to this as 'autonomous regard' (personal communications, 2023).

For us as Indigenous families, it was a recognition of respect we have for our Elders and, for Gamilaroi, the strength of being able to carry such knowledges through contact time to our burgeoning diaspora of a multicultural Logan City. And in storying place, *Riteways*, Uncle painted the original school's emblem, a recognition of the mimburi of place to eagles – specifically white-bellied sea eagles – the main totemic ancestor of the local Yugambeh people. And he told this story and linked it to the 'new', now Loganlea emblem of 'the stars' – ad astra.

What Uncle could do tjanga is link IK thought worlds of and on 'place' and 'story' and your individual role in flow – the handprint. Every gundoo, every staff member, mattered and matters – an affordance and celebration of identity which should be multiplied to the maximum across all social services. His pieces done with humility and strength covered all bases of a rich and higher-order teaching and learning task and ask. And the very output – the final design – was imbued with a sense of togetherness – us all, a part of a richer mosaic that we had been connected through this deepening of IK.

And in my hometown, it is great to see a pattern of new Logan artists emerge and define education spaces across the city. Foremostly, Traditional Owners now holding regular and deeper patterns across the learning environs and off country, artists like Uncle Reg who pay tribute and link story back to country. Shout-out and recognition to hometown art of Chad Briggs, as well as massive mural art outside the school gates now of Traditional Owner artists like Casey Coolwell-Fisher. The visual, reinterpretation of space, creates a marker that provides a layer of knowledge which expands the safe spaces of and for learning.

This hits the us/all concepts signalled by Yunkaporta (2019). 'Bigger than me' for 'all of us'. A knowing and being which is more important than doing individually or for one's gain. For *Riteways flows*, deepening enactments and positive energies vibrations came through this mural process, a particular 'whole of curriculum' and pedagogical production. A celebration of Indigenous identity and assessable and accessible to all. This is an important part of IK stretch. The 'bigger than me' concept is also grounded in 'me'. So partaking in the overall art mural and storying as a collaborative art piece was and is just as important as laying handprints as part of the murals design.

Extrapolating this context and these concepts further is to define the parts or elements of the handprint as a design. Expert weavers and creators like Yunkaporta (2019), Marshall (2020), and Sheehan (2012), as well as countrymen like Djeripi Murray (in Davis, 2018), are explanatory, artistic masters of these elements. What I will share are specific insights from taking the imagery of a hand, na, and translating that to the thought and thinking process of self-reflection and definition: 'Who am I?' 'Why do I matter?' 'What is the purpose of my role?' 'What do I believe, and why is that important?' It is essential to share more in these definitions as models in a culturally competent or 'aware' phase of working myself select and 'try out' the designs without digging deeper into the interrelated meanings. Often, earlier re/interpretations of and on our ways, our words, our metaphors are reinterpreted purely in an aesthetic way – like 'that art looks nice'. *Riteways flow*, when proficiently enacted, makes us as educators and learners look at the in-between spaces – the whisps of the smoke, what is known as liminal spaces of design (Davis & Coopes, 2022). Seek meaning and create connections.

Questions evolve in the design process of hand-printing and may include, 'What are five things, people, or places that represent you the best?' A blank handprint stencil can be used to make a representative art piece/design. These designs act as great signifiers of individual identity and are for gundoos, families, teaching teams only (not for public display). As an activity (PLP shown earlier), this is a great personalisation technique and connection to successful Indigenous education models, like PLPs or Individual Education Plans.

The handprint reframes as a great 'knowledge builder' as well. In masterclass designs, I have and we, collectively, as learning Institutes, used the 'handprint' design to build focus and intent on IKs in higher-learning research focus.

The earlier process has been used *Riteways* to get adult educators to reflect on their strengths, work through more meaning of self, to ultimately build a more relationally responsive research piece. As the preceding design is focused on culturally competent practitioners in the field of Social Sciences and research, it requires a two-part, and sometimes three-part na, reflection process. Within this learning environ, it requires a staged process as researchers tend to be bound in an academic daze of so-called researcher objectivity (Western science–based), where they can disembody themselves and 'research about' others without making a connection to self (and by default recognition of deep biases).

For all Indigenous people of this country, understanding and knowing self – who I am, where I am from, who I am kinnected to – is so important to create relatedness and grow a 'seven generations' knowledge depth. This is where the method of circle as a pedagogical approach is so significant.

o **IDENTITY:**

What's my hand in research?
What strengths do I bring to the challenge??
How can I further write/design/ flow them??
Complete a further x2 parts to your design.
Is your research 'identity' clear here???

Figure 13.6 Identity: What's my hand in research?

→ *Whole – us/altogether:*

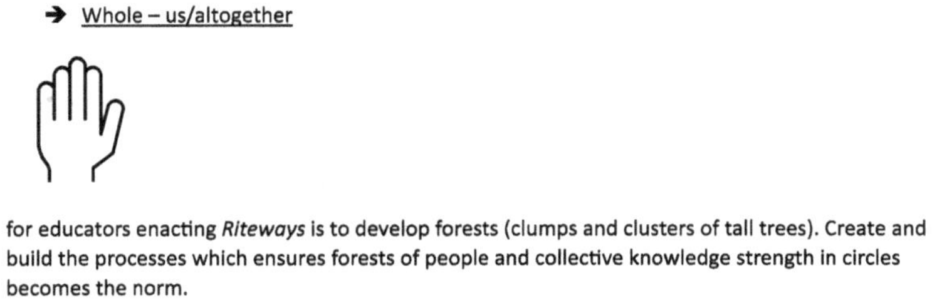

➔ Whole – us/altogether

for educators enacting *Riteways* is to develop forests (clumps and clusters of tall trees). Create and build the processes which ensures forests of people and collective knowledge strength in circles becomes the norm.

Figure 13.7 Whole – us/altogether.

Kinnected to the deeper understanding of self is knowledge that you are setting circle with like-minded individuals, creating 'Collective Knowledge Bouls'. Seeing self within circle is just as important as acknowledging oneself. This is because we are all human beings. We all connect as beings. We grow strength as individuals or in our identity when we can see within circles, ourselves as part of the whole.

Points of individual identity celebration and articulation of and on the esteem of self, positively identifying with Indigenous heritage, are essential building blocks and sustenance to the robust articulation of an Indigenous individuated political spheres. Not knowing 'who we are' or where we're from is an extreme challenge in and of itself for any of us, more so magnified in Indigenous communities and realities. As aforementioned, no one polity across the country has not been exposed to Migloo cultural lens or society. So as a modern Australian polity, we are challenged as Indigenous people with the encroachment, continuity, of Western culture and ways of being within our own lives. Providing our younger generations with more tools and directions of when and how to interest with greater or broader knowledge circles or places **provides an empowerment opportunity** and exploration point to know more of self than is afforded in current educational settings. Not knowing mobs or power and strengths of our people is a malaise we all must work hard to fight and push back because the encroachment of Western identity is as subtle as Jutja Noel says so poetically as 'rolling our tongues' (Davis, 2018). *Being hyper-cognisant of when who and how we are speaking, sounding, touching, feeling, and tasting experiences and showing/expressing our Indigeneity. This is core to articulating knowledge of self, placing self. Wanjaus then goes beyond our individuated parts of identity and seeks ourselves to be selfless.*

Symbolically and symbiotically, the learning junctures of past successful schooling community models can be remodelled and followed to enable deeper identity enactments to occur. Successful learning tools have been explicit instruction of and on individual identity, like the handprint model. Expanded, the handprint design can also be shared and shown as a Personal Cultural Portfolio, which tracks paths and activities of cultural enactments. Again, arting, weaving, and design are great examples of how this identity can be accented and celebrated further. Gundoos successfully completing program elements can auspiciously own or make their own artefacts. The productions and 'end part' of receiving show theirs and others (part and whole) contributions to significant IK layers. Examples (practioned previously) could include Didj men, collective art shirts, connective art, kangaroo and/or possum skin cloaks.

The onus is on us as proficient educators to co/design and collaborate (kolab) with communities to tap into what works locally and then ground our educational response in a more intricately woven way. This way, the power and energy produced through extremely successful individuated programming become the benchmark and opportunity wanted to be grasped by other younger generations, rather than an accepted norm of social distance and non-exceptionalism that is offered in a number of current educational spaces. This non exceptionalism is clearly shown through the gap data and, when reintegrated or overlain with latest curriculum and pedagogical foci of STEM, can be articulated as low-balling or ill-preparing our next generations for the next waves of opportunities which can develop in a field they are actually really well suited for but aren't being seen by an educational gaze which favours white Australia (Tynan & Noon, 2017).

This is the exponential potential *Riteways* offers individuals. *Riteways* forces educators to look and find Indigenous exceptionalism. Because as a teaching premise is the unassailable belief that we have the right stuff, we have the tall trees already in existence in our home communities. The onus in *Riteways* is for educators to see and then grow more learning opportunities which propagate and sustain the next generation of tall trees. Sustainability-wise, this means we move from seeing more than standout exceptional 'tall trees' in and across our Indigenous social landscape. The challenge for educators enacting *Riteways* is to develop forests (clumps and clusters of tall trees). Create and build the processes which ensure forests of people and collective knowledge strength in circles become the norm.

On a macro level, we wanted to share some models or expansion of us/all collective knowledge. Examples and exemplars of praxis have been shared in the preceding identity marker sections, like reflections on the Bunya Bunya Traditional Owner knowledges. Now, definitively, we will share good spirit indicators of and on what has worked well in 'Collective Knowledge Bouls' and responding to the right conditions and indicators, regenerated.

Firstly, the shares on processes which have grown specific Indigenous community leadership in Logan and shared around the country (through forums like Stronger Smarter and now at the IKS Lab). This again follows the pattern of 'whole' own school/context learning, followed by 'part', individuated learning experience, then 'opened up' to 'whole' again, which is an informed and should be a 'broader Indigenous identity'/collective that we, as individuals, are hyper-connected to.

When you're positioned in a society with your identity as a deficit, as a negative, it can be a draining exercise to speak lingo, to be ourselves. Everyone, every Migloo, has an opinion on Indigenous Australia and Indigenous Australians. A close friend, colleague, and fellow educationalist of mine from Germany reflected on our times at uni together. He said, '[Y]ou know John, everyone, no matter where I went and where I go now in Australia gives me an Aboriginal story. . . . They're the ones to watch out for' (personal communication, 2013).

This othering and positioning of Indigenous identity within a deficit, as a negative, is not my reality and has never been my reality in Indigenous

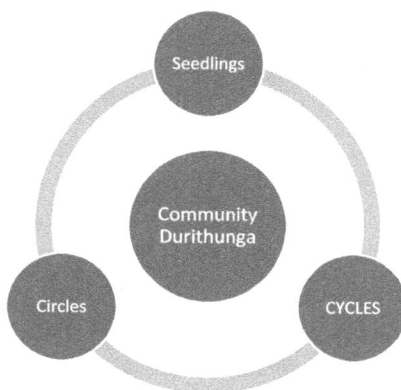

Figure 13.8 Collective Knowledge Boul (CKB), *Community Durithunga:* whole – seeds part – circle – whole – cycles.

education. In fact, growing up in, working in, and living and loving and knowing and learning in one of the most complex communities in Australia, Logan City, I had an experience that has been overwhelmingly an experience of hope, determination to succeed, high performance, and sustainability. All rich Indigenous learning practices on education sites, non-Migloo constructed realities, realities woven by Indigenous community, specifically through our methods, award-winning and high-expectations-driven, have been specifically linked to our education process known as Community Durithunga: 'Murriland, Beenleigh State High 2000', 'Bulkari Jarjums, Woodridge High 2006', 'Knowledge House, Loganlea High 2008', 'Deadly Maths, Marsden SS and Beenleigh SS 2012', 'Bariebunn Boul, Waterford West 2013' (Davis, 2018; Davis & Woods, 2019).

What is *Community Durithunga*? *Durithunga* is our processes, our way, what mob call 'proper way' (Bulman & Hayes, 2010) education. There exists between our worlds very different, very real idiosyncrasies in relation to concepts of process, 'equity', time, and feelings/spirituality. Troy Sadler, ~ Wiradjuri, reflects this in his speeches on Durithunga: '[W]e want to be sure we're for real – that it's not just a professional thing . . . as Indigenous people we're relationship based' (Sadler, in Davis et al., 2009). Community Durithunga is a weave that provides cultural integrity, ethics, and sustainability to processes of Indigenous education. Community Durithunga, in its approach, is both a leadership and community empowerment approach to education as well as a cutting-edge curriculum approach, embedding what is known locally as 'Cultural Curriculums' (Davis in Exely et al., 2016). These aren't exotic or othered; these are centred, embedded, linked to higher-order thought processes and ways of learning synonymous with any culture of learning.

Community Durithunga extrapolates and promulgates successful Cultural Curriculum approaches to embed and foster positive change in education. The research piece attempted to map Community Durithunga impacts on education to share a fuller picture of Indigenous education, not as a deficit, not as a gap to close, but as a way to develop and enshrine proper process, alter time to develop relationships to inculcate positive feelings of and towards Indigenous communities developments and success. Read in another context, another way, Community Durithunga could be perceived as a threat to current education practices, mainstream practices, not following appropriate regional educational guidelines – this is part of its reality, being 'othered' by state education systems.

This is the change we need to seek more of in Indigenous education, the embers from within. We are the leaders of change and positive directions in our collective communities. The embers burn deep within, and Community Durithunga represents one such ember which burns for positive change in education. It's not a component of the dominant Migloo hegemony; it is a grassroots approach to Indigenous education, an education footprinted in thousands of years old Indigenous method, the centre of which is the Yarning circle – the boul – the bora. From our circles are leaders, embers from within. Ironically, naturally, Murri way, our trees, like the Durithunga symbol of the great gum, needs fire to harvest and grow and create seed cycles and clear and provide healing. The embers we have are woven in a pattern of strength, bound by our circle; individually and collectively, their story, our story, is a 'Story of Strength' which is so essential to balance the stories and representation of deficits or gaps.

Community Durithunga is storied or strengthened through the leadership of Faithy Green, Enid Dirie, Bill Davis AOM, Wayne Fossey, Troy Sadler, Gary Karangari Crosby, Faith Linino, Petah-girl Hegarty, Aunt Allie Warrior, Aunty Rita Moore, Jess Holland, and Aunty B Wilson and Aunty Eileen Williams (RIP), to name some foundational members. These are parts of the whole circle; it is bound by more members, embers. The research positions itself amongst a backdrop of Eurocentric otherness where Indigenous identity and ways of being are or can be defined by Migloo interpretations and manifestations of who is and isn't achieving Migloo standards. Its focus is unashamedly on the feeling, the spirit of education that is reflected constantly by mob as 'proper way'. Community Durithunga has several successful ways and strategies to grow Indigenous sustainable success.

I am a conduit of Community Durithunga process; this research is a message back to Western education practices about 'proper way'. I am one of the Stories of Strength for and of Community Durithunga. Yet I, in my positional power of Principal and now Senior Research Fellow, am othered and filtered not through my role by Durithunga but as my spirit, as my identity, through my kinnections. In Community Durithunga, I am just as equal as, not as important as, my brothers and sisters sitting around circle.

I was blessed to base my PhD work amongst the collective knowledge circle of Community Durithunga. As a process, Durithunga operates through three distinct ways. Foremostly are the 'Seedlings' (discussed in earlier chapters). The principles, behaviours, and filters defined by Indigenous educators on how to set circle as Indigenous practitioners. Durithunga as a process is Indigenous-led only. The circle is made of Indigenous practitioners only. Through the individual work of leading Indigenous educationalists in the area came the establishment of Riteway principles and protocols to guide the expanding voice and circle work across the region. *Durithunga* itself is a regional Yugambeh translation of the word *duranga*, to grow.

The formation of Durithunga came at the behest of local Indigenous educators who had a sense that the ASSPA structures of that era were being threatened or wound up. Our Indigenous practitioners responded to the promise of having to third space and follow the direction of the state and federal systems and funders of Indigenous education to make space and demand time of these 'centres' to set Durithunga circles. That is, Durithunga, as a process, was and could be set with a rich IK focus and delivery model not at the behest of the local education nexus.

So the time to come yarn the division of leadership and leadership activity was (and has been) defined in the Durithunga Seedlings (Community Durithunga, in Davis, 2018). The Seedlings are a good organising process, as they set out and define the protocol for holding circles and expanding work and agendas. As a collective, we have as 'one of our [core] principles . . . respect. . . . That's the biggest thing . . . that we teach . . . to everyone that is there [in circle]. Be respectful of yourself and to the group' (Dirie in Davis et al., 2009). Unlike mainstream onboarding process or the feeling individual Indigenous workers had weaving within non-Indigenous or third space schooling environs, Durithungas' premise of transformative change was creating more safe spaces to 'be' and 'feel' and make sense of the local education diaspora within a burgeoning (and still growing) urban city setting. When mainstream systems pressurised our Durithunga leaders – educators in their individual spaces – to 'do consultancy work', get 'community backing', the individuals were able to speak back to power using a circle process, not bigger than me, and apply an overarching process of 'rule of three' (shared earlier).

The research itself pays homage to this process and deep IK principle of leadership by writing and capturing additionally to the 'whole group yarn', three distinct individual Durithunga leader voices, in the 'one-on-one' interviews on and about Durithunga impact. This was a powerful praction from the research, being able to embed the Durithunga protocol of 'rule of three' through all the information gathering and contextualisations of representative voices. To best reflect the activity and voice of Durithunga in research was to capture not just one individual voice for one-on-one interviews but three. Just as defined in regular Cultural Curriculum practice, the regularity and consistency of individual programming are and were a needed part for the seedings and then process of setting circle to take shape and gain momentum. A regular circle pattern of monthly meets, every Thursday, was an essential circle practice which ensured a continuous feedback loop and check-in steps in Durithunga practions and activities.

To magnify the differences and articulate a strong meshwork of relationships, Durithunga was also wedded in design on the cycle and movement of meetings and activities in and around the city. What this meant and means in design is that whenever Durithunga projects and leaders develop processes, they seek to build in a cyclical relationship between workspaces and each other. Although there were, at its height, quite significant lighthouse (and still regional best) Indigenous education spaces (Davis & Woods, 2019), the Cycle process meant no one school or learning environ dominated the meetings or were held stagnate in the one area. The movement of Yarning circles to discrete communities across Logan City meant we were called in to spaces and, although at different stages of our education journeys, allowed for or built in a practice of transdisciplinary approach to Indigenous education. And these processes, people, and transformative practions in motion have created a wave of effective and sustainable Indigenous education practice. The next model to share is an example of how community or collective sensemaking or collaborative spaces can scale up and scale out in design.

Third spaces speak on communities of practice (Lave & Wenger, 1991). What is exceptional and exponential of and on Community Durithunga experience are the ways of working and interrelating not through the education prism but through the notion of focused work, energies, and flows on leadership – durithunga to grow. Conceptually, our people came up with the design, in Logan, from country of the gathering tree, setting circles, still visible and strong across Logan, that being the gum tree. Its pattern is recorded and 'seen' across local context, yet there is a deeper, more closely country-connected story and pattern of these trees, specifically river gums, which were for the Traditional Owners to know and share on. There is open, gum tree knowledge, and closed, river gum knowledge. Our role in the pattern of leadership within and across multiple school settings was and is to create more growth amongst these mother trees. And Durithunga as an Indigenous Knowledge experience is able to tool Indigenous educators with the skills and abilities to weave ways which are Culturally Sustaining and now ultimately regenerative. And the structure itself, the regular group of Community Durithunga members weaving in regular Yarning circles, provided individual educators with a process that shielded – goomeri[1] – as well as carried, like a coolamon,[2] our Indigenous educators' collective energies and voice.

Warril Yari-Go Karulbo (now called Gnirigomindala Karulbo) in the 2020s was a live and growing example of the sustainability, and now regeneration, of collective agency. Its roots were (and are) firmly within the educational leadership and designs of Community Durithunga leadership models. When it was created form the 'interventions' of social services being accosted to the local area, the Durithunga founders and research became the way to 'speak' and be in circles of opportunity, working alongside big government and NGO services. When working on 'a new social services' model, our people looked to what we didn't have, where a range of non-Indigenous consultants and 'supports' from within big government agency are 'offered'; most importantly, our people had the inclination for self-reflection and introspection and draw on the collective knowledge strength and models which already operated successfully in the local area context.

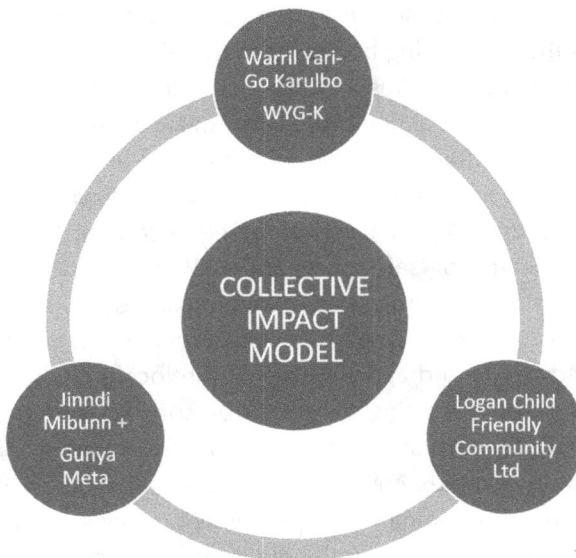

Figure 13.9 Collective Knowledge Boul (CKB), collective impact model: whole – WYG-K – part – WK hub + YG hub – whole – Logan Child Friendly Community Ltd.

The so-called social 'change agents' were being directed then to 'First Nations first' ways and the process of bouls to 'slow down' the process and institutional violence we felt and experienced as a Logan Indigenous polity. When a 'showcase' was 'put on' our community to showcase local community agency talents, our collective sat circles which would require NGOs and government agencies of the day – who supported 'showcase' processes – to look and link a proper way, a Riteway of doing, and the Warril Yari-Go collaborative was established.

This First Nations agency is essential first, as next steps flows are always directed and redirected to that root beginning. This was a way of working and weaving a Collective Knowledge Boul as a response, a shield for the fact we do not have treaty or equitable and proportional government contracts and supports to innovate and let community-controlled emergence deliver outputs. The establishment of a collaborative enables a language and agency to build collective energy to pursue broader and First Nations–developed goals.

The difference of 'collective knowledges' as compared to reference and steering committee governance structures is, the agency does not stop there. The newly forming power relations enable the collective Indigenous polities to voice 'what's next', what are further safe apace creations and activities the auspicating bodies need to deliver. In this instance, Cultural Competency training was a model purported by the collaborative for NGOs and government agencies to engage more deeply in. Organisations like Stronger Smarter, then, are able to share (and did) their effective safe space circle methodologies and pedagogies, which have been practioned to thousands around Australia and modified according to local working environs. Specifically, for 'safe space' and RAP ecology developments, the Institute has workplaces, professional learning suites, which provide tools on how systems can better create safe space realities for our First Nations people. The advocacy and agency work of the local collaborative, in this case Warril Yar-Go, was being supported by specific leadership trainings offered for NGO services and then specifically with partner organisations and leads within complex communities – Stronger Smarter. We worked, wove, and shared our community development response from 2006. Now it has regrown and spread its sustainable design or connections to broader community services sphere. The difference in design is a clear monetary articulation of what our people want and what our knowledges are valued at by us.

Individually, each organisation is important and has its own independent identity. What WYG-K did is amplify the individual difference and signify the most sustainable element, the togetherness, Karulbo. Community Durithun-gas, WYG-K circles, kinnect individuals to a broader collective strength. The principles interwoven in this process are flattening leadership hierarchies, individuated responses, and looking for more sustainable impacts. Under-standing and articulating each individual organisation's part in the collective flow means the processes can sustain in spite of shifts and change. And the previous actions and enactments can be followed, referred, and responded to.

Recent social services focus had increased significantly funding within the early years streams. Funding focus came about from the complex inter-play and mix and clash of cultures within Logan City (Birrimingham, 2013; Tapin, 2013). Government and NGO services sought to build more col-lective impact and advocacy, which was left waning when our collective peoples rioted. I remember the riots (2008 and 2012) with heavy hearts as young people we wove with, First Nations families, were openly attacked and racially vilified, leading to our most recent race riots in the area.

This is a difficult part of our joint histories that is hard to write on. We speak and advocate as educators for safe spaces institutionally within school and education, and yet outside our gates is a live and living social diaspora which brings some of the most diverse communities together in a mesh of social services and housing commission environs. When peace was made and continues to be made and brokered over the years, it is not from social service collective impact bureaucracies but from local families and tall trees our communities see.

Alongside the advocacy of a number of local family groups, in education we shout out Aunty Faith Green, who, for years, has maintained relation-ships and brokered safe space and dialogue between immigrant and our First Nations communities on the Logan Central sides of the Logan River, specifically the Pasifika. And after peace is made, rather than equity part-nering with the community-led spaces, Indigenous community–controlled social service and NGO 'leads' (largely non-Indigenous) went with 'creating a new model'. Not wanting our way and our voice listened to in the oppor-tunity of expanded and renumerating safe space targeting, which was being focussed in the early years prism, we met, as we often do, outside of the non-Indigenous brokerage circles and sought to create and make defined space of and on how we need to cross-culturally relate. Not investing in or blessing 'new models' of change and social impact but seeking guidance from country and the large First Nations advocacy nomenclature that has grown across our city for a number of years.

To articulate our way further, we, as families, connected to community-controlled and community-led organisations, sought to demand space for First Nations. And the demands led to the collective making of the impact model shown in Figure 13.9. This is essential in the building up and out of a regenerative design. Sensemaking, seeking authority, then making clear what the lines of sight and agreed actions are as Indigenous community–led praxis. The 'legacy piece' is about further along – outwards facing. The development of the Equity Partnership tool (discussed in earlier chapters) is a telling legacy of this work.

The EqP is a contract/an agreement between organising parties, purporting to weave into our complex Logan communities and 'agree' in principle, defined in dollar values, to meet our Indigenous community–controlled collaboratives as equal partners. Not come at and to our complex communities to seek change, better our lives, but seek in accordance with the lays of the lands, which we teach, preach, and each love, seek an accord which values the strengths IK collective impact experts bring to the table and potentialities that exist through fostering the strength bases of our collective communities. This recent development has meant more funding streams coming to community-controlled collectives rather than non-Indigenous NGOs.

Again, the tools themselves are not the 'end product' of and for collective impact. The processes are and have been the most important layer and liminal connective tissue. Although modelled in the x3 part circle design, at WYG-K's height (and from what I gather still remains the case) is the importance or essential component of individual community-controlled agency. Our designs aren't about bigger systems – more bureaucracy. In fact, our designs are about recognition of individual strengths, the need for collective agency, and always the thread being pulled is our own independent individual capacity. It is why our people of country have flown and grown deep time modelling on human relatedness. It is why our governance, through IKS, is based on embassy, gathering, sharing – wanjaus. And inextricably woven within the individual context are individual power and agency. Processes to flow and protocols to bind us (Fletcher et al., 2023).

Quite clearly, this process of 'Whole–Part–Whole' links to the rich depth of IK in closing and opening information. 'Learning about identity' can be a challenging space for some. Duwur ngima baulan. The 'safe space' created, the open or shared knowledge, is learning through the ways of local area stories, library, family research pieces. All these weave together to create a shared 'knowing' of self. The PLP process, together with family/kin/carers, gives another pedagogical piece to do and produce a curriculum which is shared = a part of the whole group.

Individuated or 'part' knowledges/identity work/focus like the handprint activity is a very individual/personal map of you, the individual. There are and will be, through the development of different learnings, spaces which are only shared to close ones, closed knowledges. Gundoos and we, as community of learners, can deepen this aspect by creating two hands, one of closed, individuated-only knowledge, and a design that is 'open' or can be shared. The skill and expertise of facilitators/educators are essential in determining and making these spaces as safe as possible. This kind of work has led to more recent IKS Lab activity in and around 'Digital Child' and knowing and being who I am safely within an 'IT world' (Davis & Coopes, 2022).

As I write, I am kollabbing. We're utilising past processes we've designed, like EqPs, to ensure research agency just isn't weighted to the sandstone or centralised university structures. That's what EqPs do, force relationship articulation in other ways. And in a very good fit for what has worked in the past and continues to provide great directional flow for IK works and First Nations first processes, I am wedding this new work, the Digital Child, with the Hub on the Logan central sides of the river, Gunya Meta. It is coordinated by CEO sista Faith Green, Kabi ngin Koa, a founding member of Durithunga, alongside Yadgie B Wilson, Bandjalung, a co-founder of Knowledge House at Loganlea SHS and Durithunga alumnus and lead.

Together, us/three are going to see what good practions we can develop and kollab using the Durithunga principles as a guide. We're collectively and individually moving in ways which connect projects across large areas both nationally and internationally. What we want to do or have 'agreed' in principle as Durithunga leaders is to ground what we do through the processes learnt, burnt, and etched in the Yarning circles set through Community Durithungas.

Again, the praction of evaluation, feedback, and 'check-ins' is essential for programmers to gauge the ability for gundoos and communities to work through activities or be guided another way. The regenerative element of this design is real-time practions now of this teaching and learning tool to higher-degree learning.

Notes

1 *Goomeri* means 'shield'.

2 *Coolaman* means 'carrying dish'.

References

Birrimingham, J. (2013). Boyz in the wood. *Australia, SBS*. Retrieved from Boyz n the Wood: Was there really a 'race riot' in this QLD suburb? | Programs (sbs.com.au)

Bulman, J., & Hayes, J. (2010). Yarning spaces: Dealing with depression and anxiety amongst Aboriginal and Torres Strait Islander males the "proper way". *The CAPA Quarterly (Journal of Australian Counsellors and Psychotherapists Association of New South Wales), 1*, 24–28.

Bunya Mountains Elders Council (Eds.). (2010a). *Bonye Buru – Boobagun Ngumminge – Bunya Mountains Aboriginal aspirations and caring for country plan*. Bargara: Burnett Mary Regional Group.

Bunya Mountains Elders Council (Eds.). (2010b). *The Bunya Mountains – multi-stakeholder project*. Bargara: Burnett Mary Regional Group.

Craven, R. (Ed.). (2011). *Teaching Aboriginal studies: A practical resource for primary and secondary teaching*. St. Leonards, NSW: Allen and Unwin Publishers.

Davis, J. (2017). *Binung Tjanga: Davis family storybook* (Limited ed., Family History Book). Bunya.

Davis, J. (2018). *Durithunga: Growing, nurturing, challenging and supporting urban Indigenous leadership in education* (Unpublished PhD thesis). Queensland University of Technology, Brisbane.

Davis, J., & Coopes, R. (2022). Our fire stories: Emergence through the circle work-process at the Indigenous knowledge systems lab. *Journal of Awareness-Based Systems Change, 2*(2), 85–108. doi:10.47061/jasc.v2i2.3892

Davis, J., Dirie, E., & Sadler, T. (2009). *Durithunga* [Audio podcast]. Presentation at AIATSIS National Indigenous Studies Conference – "Perspectives on Urban Life: References 203 Connections and Reconnections", Canberra. Retrieved from www.aiatsis.gov.au/research/conf2009/papers/E4.1.html

Davis, J., & Grose, S. (2008, December 7–11). *Whichway? . . . What happens when embedding Aboriginal and Torres Strait Islander perspectives in schools meets the professional standards for teachers and an accountability matrix?* Paper presented at World Indigenous Peoples' Conference on Education, Indigenous Education in the 21st Century: Respecting Tradition, Shaping the Future, Victoria Aboriginal Education Association Inc. Retrieved from www.strongersmarter.com.au

Davis, J., & Woods, A. (2019). Durithunga boul: A pattern of respectful relationships, reciprocity and socially just literacy education in one urban school. In J. Rennie & H. Harper (Eds.), *Literacy education and Indigenous Australians: Theory, research and practice* (pp. 51–69). Singapore: Springer.

Davis, W. (2007). *Spear making* (Unpublished master's thesis). University of Queensland, St. Lucia.

Exley, B., Davis, J., & Dooley, K. (2016). Empirical reference points for Bernstein's model of pedagogic rights: Recontextualizing the reconciliation agenda to Australian schooling. In P. Vale & B. Exley (Eds.), *Pedagogic rights and democratic education – Bernsteinian explorations of curriculum, pedagogy and assessment* (pp. 33–46). Oxon: Routledge.

Fesl, E. (1993). *Conned!* St Lucia: UQP.

Fletcher, G., Waters, J., Yunkaporta, T., Marshall, C., Davis, J., & Manning Bancroft, J. (2023). Indigenous systems knowledge applied to protocols for governance and inquiry. *Systems Research and Behavioral Science*, 1–4. doi:10.1002/sres.2932

Gilbert, K. (1977). *Living Black*. Melbourne: Penguin Press.

Lave, J., & Wenger, E. (1991). *Situated learning: Legitimate peripheral participation*. Cambridge: Cambridge University Press.

Marshall, C. A. (2020). The role of Indigenous paradigms and traditional knowledge systems in modern humanity's sustainability quest – future foundations from past knowledge's. In R. Roggema (Ed.), *Designing sustainable cities. Contemporary urban design thinking*. Cham: Springer. doi:10.1007/978-3-030-54686-1_2

Martin, K. (2008). *Please knock before you enter – Aboriginal regulation of outsiders and the implications for researchers*. Teneriffe: Post Pressed.

Moreton-Robinson, A. (2000). *Talkin' up to the white women*. St Lucia: University of Queensland Press.

Nakata, M. (2007). *Disciplining the savages savaging the disciplines*. Canberra: Aboriginal Studies Press.

Queensland Studies Authority – QSA. (2000). *Aboriginal and Torres Strait Islander senior studies senior syllabus*. Queensland Government: Brisbane.

Sarra, C. (2011). *Strong and smart – Towards a pedagogy for emancipation: Education for first peoples*. New York: Routledge.

Sarra, C. (2012). *"Good morning Mr. Sarra" – my life working for a stronger, smarter future for our children*. St. Lucia: University of Queensland Press.

Sharratt, L., & Fullan, M. (2012, December). Putting faces on the data. *National Association of School Principals, Principal Leadership Magazine*. Reston, VA, pp. 48–52.

Sheehan, N. (2012). *Stolen generations education: Aboriginal cultural strengths and social and emotional well-being*. Woolloongabba: Link-Up Queensland.

Stronger Smarter Institute. (2017). *Implementing the stronger smarter approach*. Brisbane: Author.

Tapin, F. (2013). Racial tension in Brisbane as Aboriginal, Pacific Islander groups clash. *ABC News*. Retrieved from https://www.abc.net.au/news/2013-01-15/an-logan-tension/4465040

Tynan, M., & Noon, K. (2017). *Indigenous STEM education project first evaluation report September 2014 – June 2016*. Canberra: CSIRO.

Yunkaporta, T. (2019). *Sand talk: How Indigenous thinking can save the world*. Melbourne: HarperOn.

14 Wanjau

Wanjau:

Figure 14.1 Wanjau.

The scale and timing of the Bunya gathering, together with the unique reciprocation rights observed as part of neighbouring relations, sets the Bunya Festival apart from other Aboriginal ceremonial gatherings.

(Bunya Mountains Elders Council, 2010, p. 14)

Wanjau is what grounds and sustains, then regenerates, the *Riteways flow*. For *Riteways* models to work and take shape, it must interrelate with and between different knowledge systems, curriculums, and activities. This grounding principle, the centre of flow, provides the conditions for the circles of knowledge to expand and contract, leaving distinct layers or markers to follow. Wanjau is our 'how'. 'Wanjau – regeneration and our "weaves" to home our inquiry in real-time research translations as a motile state of shared focal ever-becomings' (Yunkaporta in Fltecher et al., 2023, p. 3).

DOI: 10.4324/9781003298717-14

When doing individual marker activities or enactments, they are coordinated and completed with clear designs and purpose. We build the best flows of and aim towards wanjaus when we base what we give on the rhythms of what we have made and practiced and articulated and have more to share. Each marker, when the layer activities are enfolded, practioned, and completed, these aren't prescriptive end points or ends to learning junctures. That's why, again, the end in our rebeginnings is the design captured within the pattern of a boul. The learning cycle done becomes part of a new rhythm way and flow of learning.

Each layer, when designed for delivery, kollabed, and enacted through consistent activity, what has been defined earlier as the 'discipline of circle work', builds knowledge strength. The repetition of the enactments, the mastery of *Riteways* by us/all, ultimately fills the pattern toward wanjaus – over-abundance. This is the original design of our land. This is the power of dgangunbara mirrored through a place like Bunya Bunyas. When we *Riteways flow*, we build the energy to create and make more safe space learning, which, when judged to be moving toward completion, means we should get to the best space, the place to share.

Always aiming our enactments to respond positively, the spirit of our land is to share more. Wanjaus reveal themselves in each individual context. If we are giving more, looking after country more, seeing and celebrating our Elders more, being in our Elders' homes and care places, this creates positive energy flows. Sharing our knowledge of self and knowledges learnt, like

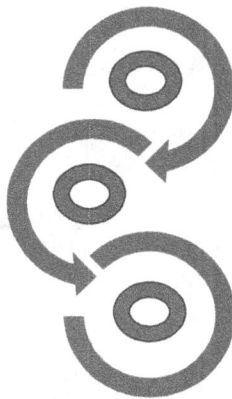

Figure 14.2 Pattern of the boul.

learning from local libraries and showcasing in art centres. We are performing on country or for country at festivals and local community events. We are researching and breathing on our fire, making good smoke for our next generations learning at local Homework Hubs or within school rooms and classes, whatever the educational form.

There are optimal times and spaces of wanjau revealed through each layer's circle work (enactments are explored in more detail from p. 123 onwards). *Riteways flow* enactment becomes highly visible through the deepening of each marker activities through the layering of curriculum and pedagogical delivery (see enactments Figures 15.1 onwards). To fully enact, love, experience, and celebrate all these markers of *Riteways* creates the conditions to deepen wanjau knowledge exchange and collectives. Enactment of *Riteways* is 'ember-blowing education', as it is not reliant on starting from a position of 'otherness' or 'meeting in a middle' or third cultural spaces (Davis, 2018; Bhabha, 2004; Chilisa, 2012). *Riteways* centres Indigenous education within curriculum and pedagogical exchanges and hyper-extends it. This is a map for Traditional Owners, Indigenous Community Organisations, Historical people, and Indigenous Education Experts to utilise in developing, growing, grounding, comparing, and contrasting further IK models that work (Davis, 2007, 2018; Denzin et al., 2008; Grant, in QSA, 2000; Steffenson, 2020).

The focus of *Riteways* is regeneration. The ACARA-type models aspire to be responsive to our Indigenous identities; however, it is not centred or aimed at sustaining IK practices. We are a circle culture and identity whose systems of thinking and understanding patterns and developing responses to our unique environs are not fully understood by Western knowledge systems (Pascoe, 2014). And with the impact of colonisation affecting all Indigenous people, re-setting our identities within our own world views, processes, and practices reinforces our resilience as a people, as a polity. Transformational, emancipatory education for us, our gundoos, can only occur by embracing *Riteways* and embracing IK to inform and frame Culturally Sustaining and regenerating flows.

Knowledge Exchange and Cross-Overs

How did and do we do business? Along the songlines – the storylines – on country to protect and nurture. This great land was created for us. The patterns of these relationships and storying remain in the land and kinnected to the people of the land. Ngai Cobble Cobble Warra: our knowledge connect and wanjau we'll do and we must get to comes from along the Bunya highway. Migloos focus on distance, GPS tracker millimetres. We focus on connections.

The Bunya Feasts are unique, as

- they were generally triennial rather than annual or seasonal – demonstrating a complex system of conservation practice;
- the supply of Bunya nuts was vastly larger than could be consumed by Aboriginal groups; and
- specific fire management regimes were employed in preparation for the feasts

(Flood, 1976 and Fensham & Fairfax, 1996 in
Bunya Mountain Elders Council, 2010, p. 14)

My country, djanganbarras, Warra Warra, is a place steeped in a long line of exchange culture and broad meshwork developments. The perspectives I share are deep, freshwater knowledge exchanges kinnected to the Bunya Bunya (Bunya Mountains Elders, 2010; Davis, 2007, 2018). I feel great love and respect for my fledgling knowledges and understandings, our deep knowledge, and for our people. So when I write to share, wanjau knowledge it is to place my learning, which is largely open (allowed to be shared), in context, give context, and seek meaning. The Bunya Bunya provided regular nourishment for our people, and then on the bumper season of bunya cone production, every three years, multiple tribes were invited to share in the overabundance in our summer – hot seasons (Bunya Mountains Elders, 2010). This triennial ceremony would go for as long as the bunyas bore fruits from December till March. And when completed, multiple tribes would reassert boundary lines, make further connections through marriages, settle disputes. Most importantly, to share, exchange, wanjaus, the bunya gatherings, provided an access point for Traditional Owners in colder months – May till July – gave permission for Bunya hosts to visit saltwater country and share in the bountiful fish runs (namely, mullet and taylor).

Of all these big affordance times, fire, cooking, burning for hunting, and clearing the earth was (and remains) an essential element to care for and look after country. When we burn our woods and place our leaves on top to create more smoke, it is to cleanse or clear, bathe or heal. Its antithesis is water. To know us is to flow like us (see Flowbook samples, p. 167).

Knowing Others' Stories and Maps

When you know your story, you have more of your map. Wanjau – kinnected to Bunya Bunya – is patterned all along the Bunya highway. Because it is the back of Budin Guju. Remembrances of that light and energy are left on country as mimburi – sites of flow. Boobargun Ngummin is a site of flow. Geriward further south in snowy mountain country is a sight of flow. Bogong, Nganawall, is a place and space of flow where our contemporary parliament, Canberra 'gathering place', is based.

OUR story is being able to see and make more connections. Let's sit, talk . . . yarn and show who you are, where you're from. That's YOUR responsibility . . . AND if you don't know, that's OK. You are Murri, Koori, Goori. You are Aboriginal or Torres Strait through whose side? YOU do know.

Maps are understandings of beliefs and boundaries of country. Sometimes our maps overlap, and sometimes in Native title maps overlap, AND that's OK. Our people are sophisticated people. Migloo politics has gotten to a height of stagnation where our parties sound very much the same – ×2 main heavyweights. Migloo law system and governance are based on adversarial parties, the Westminster system of governance. Murri politics is built upon a system of *knowledge exchange and reciprocal relationships*. My Bunya Elders describe Eldership as 'Leadership'.

> Leadership in the Aboriginal community is not a foreign concept. . . . Leadership is earned with skills and knowledge and often a fair amount of debate. . . . The term Elder in the Aboriginal community does not mean a person of age – you can be an elderly Aboriginal person without being an Elder and you can also have the term bestowed upon you when you are quite young.
>
> (Bunya Mountain Elders, 2010, p. 11)

Our Elders go further in their articulation on Aboriginal Leadership circles by explaining the differing layers of responsibility. 'Aboriginal concepts of consciousness and responsibility demand that the responsibility for managing relationships is taken by all parts of the kinship system, to differing degrees, because all of the parts regulate each other' (Bunya Mountain Elders, 2010, p. 11).

Regulation of boundaries, understanding who and who cannot 'speak for country', is part of Indigenous conceptualisation on space and time, which 'is misunderstood in some oral histories, in much anthropology and within colonial and later history' (Bunya Mountain Elders, 2010, p. 11). Wanjau wasn't and isn't a straight, given to 'share'; *we had to bama = fight too* (*Steele, 1984*; Bunya Mountain Elders, 2010; *Davis & Coopes, 2022*). And we had sophisticated and have sophisticated law exchanges, where boundaries, disputes on resources were held in our systems and ways of working. *That's what Makaratta is, an old system* of law being offered as a way forward through the latest Aboriginal and Torres Strait Islander rights agenda through a referendum vote. Makarata is more important than law as it is lore.

So at sights of great exchange and eventual ceremony were also spaces to settle law, differences of opinion. *Bunya Bunya had recognised bambes.* These were mostly held at the bottom of the mountain – settle disputes and disagreements before heading up. Heading back to Boobargun Nguumonge, you shouldn't be fighting, yeah? Watch our national political system based in Canberra, our law in action now. It is based on adversarial law. When Bunya Bunya bamas are held, it is about equal representation to 'sort out' disputes. So when bigger ceremony like heading to Boobargun Nguumonge was held, bigger dispute resolutions had to be completed. Stylised fighting equals spear attacks. *And these bambes are recorded in Settler/Invader journals everywhere* (Kirwin, 2007, 2012; Pascoe, 2014), all over our map.

The recent Australian political context of dealing with Indigenous rights is a great indicator of or for change. For years, our people, through the law systems, have advocated for more voice, treaties, and truths (Davis & Williams, 2021). What will the new system exchange bring? The current federal government is promising a referendum. The 'Opposition' is already voting 'No'. One part I know in truth, from my perspective, is that the migloo system is fucked. And now more than ever, we need systems of IK that give us more voice on systems that impact our lives, enable truths to be told unabashedly through teaching voices for reconciliation and treaties to recognise our individual First Nation rights. So much to learn from, deepen our current Australian lives of and on – deepness of IK. I wonder if Makarata is too hard for Western thinkers – migloos – to grasp? I guess our upcoming referendum will show us – provide an indication.

Bamas at bunyas were important not to show one group's strength. Bamas or Pullen Pullens provided a space of truths to be told then settled. **Why? Because that's what our systems are based on – caring and sharing.** You couldn't get to the best part – the share the equalification to be on mothers' milk – unless you had cared enough to settle and air all past grievances.

> My people believe that every living thing on this earth was linked spiritually and each and every one of us must respect the earth and each other as equal. . . . My ancestors walked through this land, the land speaking to them. . . . We belong to this land, the land is our Mother. We are part of a spiritual structure. That's Aboriginal culture. That is Boobarran Ngummin, the Bunya Mountains, our Mother.
>
> (Jerome in Bunya Mountain Elders, 2010, p. 12)

When we change mindsets and aim back to the best version of ourselves, within living memory, I have Garmis, who had Jutjas, who were honour fighters. Some of the knowledges I share with you today, not only are they living, but also still they are thriving and regrowing. You don't have to know everything. The minute details, the *wonderful wondering pattern of the oldest-living, surviving culture*, are not like it was pre-1788. *However, we are still here.* I look around every community across Australia, and although we are 3% of the total Australian population, we are here. **We are strong. The patterns are here. We are the link to the oldest-living and thriving culture. Wanjau is about taking responsibility for that pattern of relationships.** These tracks have been laid; you tune in or you tune out. We don't force you to learn *Riteways* – you are shown *Riteways,* and you make sense of it, weave back in the patterns or create new patterns. **It's here to learn from and see.**

So in the spirit of wanjaus, with our ends being 'rebeginnings', on the following final pages, kinnect to *Riteways* enactments. *Riteways flow* samples recorded to support the development of IK-centric education and community designs. When you turn the pages, it is your responsibility to refer and enact *Riteways.* And share. Come to Bunya Bunya at our Bush Uni. Set circle at your local community collectives. Jump on the Lab website if you need to track us down. The essential element for more educational regeneration is to pattern the relationships needed for regenerative IK design and delivery. And continue to yarn and share with us/all on how *Riteways* happen in your space and time.

Na gamba...

Figure 14.3 Na gamba.

Eyes like nyal

Binna like gooraman

Mouth like yuggera

Nose like barrunga

Gujumba

Dgumge yonyung

(BIUN BIUN poem extract)

Figure 14.4 Riteways Na.

Weave your way through the last parts of flow in this book and blow life on.

Draw an outline of your hand, 'Na Gamba'. Bring IK to the front and map what makes you strong.

This is the start of our *Riteways* journey together. **On the next page, draw your other hand, '*Riteways* Na'. Write the Riteway markers in your fingers: /HOLISM/LORE/CULTURE and LANGUAGE/IDENTITY/. Draw the symbols of each in the outline of your fingers.** As a Culturally Proficient educator, draw symbols that relate and tell the *Riteways* markers for you.

The deep time element is wanjau. **Wanjau makes a print pattern in design.** How do we get to Kondaii ngima Warmgas? Wanjaus are the key.

And all around and between the finger markers, make ripples, another outline, and then another.

Do this many times, till you feel you have captured a clearer symbol of and for spirit.

What are your hands in *Riteways flows*? Take time now to think and write, draw, and record what makes you strong, what you believe in, what keeps you grounded.

Eyes like nyal
Binna like gooraman
Mouth like yuggera
Nose like barrunga

Gujumba
Dgumge yonyung

References

Bhabha, H. (2004). *Bhabha: The location of culture*. London: Routledge Press.

Bunya Mountains Elders Council (Eds.). (2010). *Bonye Buru – Boobagun Ngumminge – Bunya Mountains Aboriginal aspirations and caring for country plan*. Bargara: Burnett Mary Regional Group.

Chilisa, B. (2012). *Indigenous research methodologies*. Thousand Oaks: SAGE.

Davis, J. (2018). *Durithunga: Growing, nurturing, challenging and supporting urban Indigenous leadership in education* (Unpublished PhD thesis). Queensland University of Technology, Brisbane.

Davis, J., & Coopes, R. (2022). Our fire stories: Emergence through the circle work-process at the Indigenous knowledge systems lab. *Journal of Awareness-Based Systems Change, 2*(2), 85–108. doi:10.47061/jasc.v2i2.3892

Davis, M., & Williams, G. (2021). *Everything you need to know about the Uluru Statement from the heart*. Randwick: UNSW Press.

Davis, W. (2007). *Spear making* (Unpublished master's thesis). University of Queensland, St. Lucia.

Denzin, N., Lincoln, L., & Tuhiwai Smith, L. (2008). *Handbook of critical and Indigenous methodologies*. California: SAGE.

Fletcher, G., Waters, J., Yunkaporta, T., Marshall, C., Davis, J., & Manning Bancroft, J. (2023). Indigenous systems knowledge applied to protocols for governance and inquiry. *Systems Research and Behavioral Science*, 1–4. doi:10.1002/sres.2932

Kirwin, D. (2007). *Aboriginal heroes: Dundalli a "Turrwan" an Aboriginal leader: 1842–1854*. Nathan: Griffith Institute for Educational Research, Griffith University.

Kirwin, D. (2012). *Aboriginal dreaming paths and trading routes: The colonisation of the Australian economic landscape*. Brighton: Sussex Academic Press.

Pascoe, B. (2014). *Dark emu: Black seeds: Agriculture or accident?* Broome, WA: Magabala Books.

Queensland Studies Authority – QSA. (2000). *Aboriginal and Torres Strait Islander senior studies senior syllabus*. QLD Government: Brisbane.

Steele, J. G. (1984). *South East Aboriginal pathways*. St. Lucia: UQP.

Steffenson, V. (2020). *Fire country – how Indigenous fire management could help save Australia*. Melbourne: Hardie Grant Publishing.

Riteways Flows

Figure 15.1 *Riteways* flows (a).

DOI: 10.4324/9781003298717-15

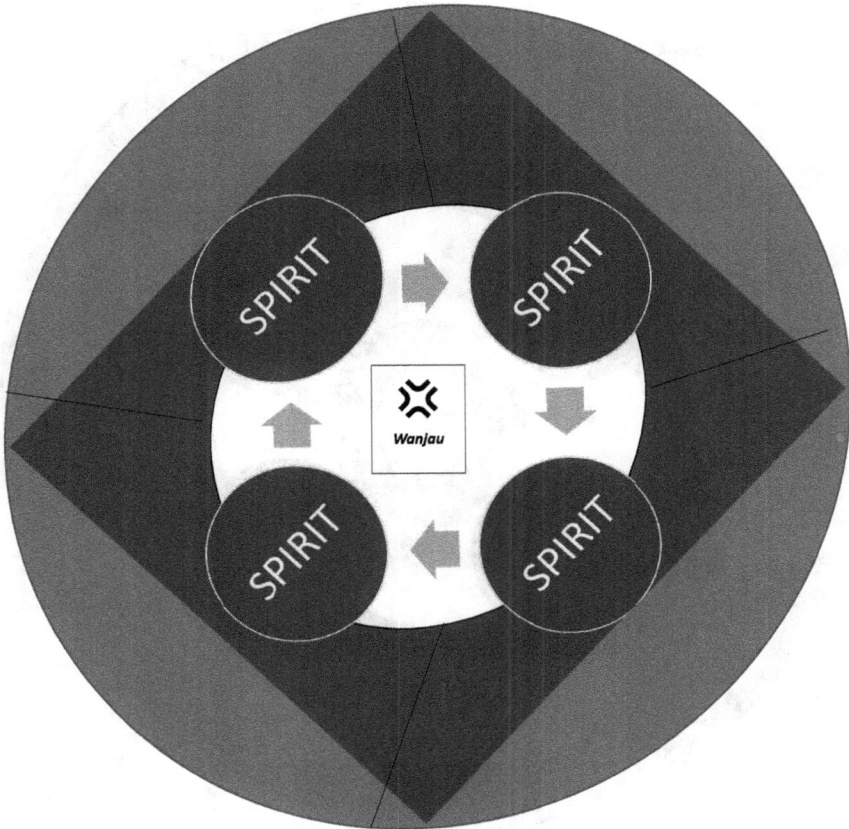

Figure 15.2 Riteways flows (b).

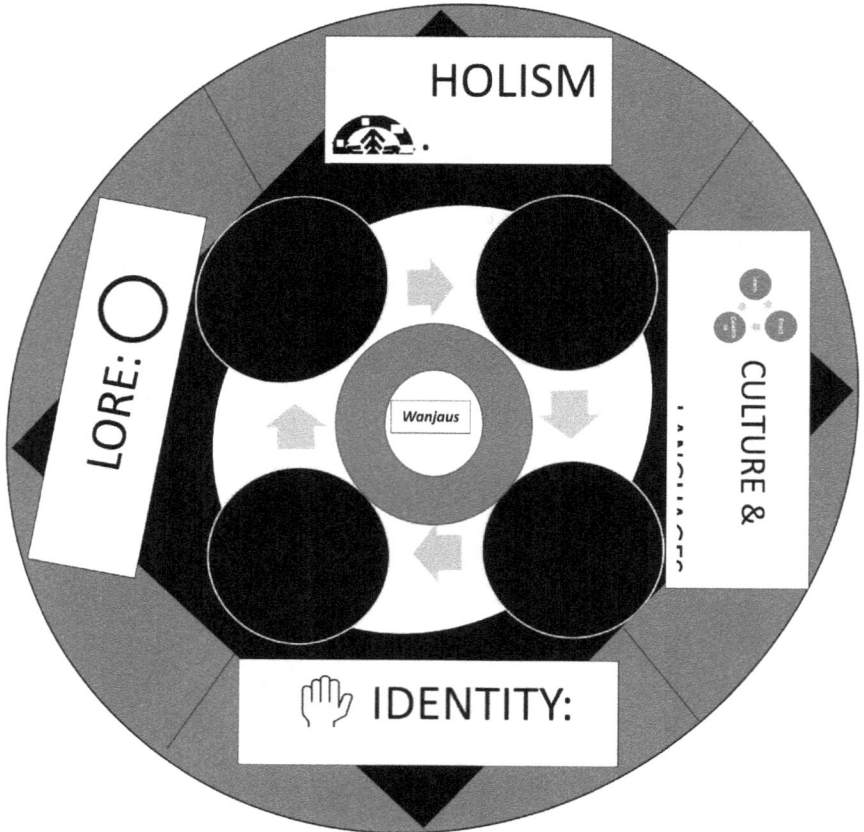

Figure 15.3 Riteway flow markings (c).

Riteways flow Model = SPIRIT -< HOLISM: CULTURE & LANGUAGE: LORE: IDENTITY = *Wanjau*

SPIRIT-<   INDICATORS   *Wanjau*

Riteways HOLISM flows:

set flows
SPIRIT

increase
HOLISM
enactments

wanjau
abundance

SPIRIT --<

- o Check in on the lay of the land. How and where is Community & Country feeling?
- o Provide safe spaces for this knowledge flow to feedback into layer activities...

HOLISM enactments:

- o Use of current Holistic Learning tools to guide programming
- o Local Area Stories on Holisim
- o Articulation of own Local Area Stories

Wanjau

- o Public display of Local Area Stories
- o Invitational forum on specific 'Stories of Strength'
- o Kap mauri yarns

Figure 15.4 Riteways indicators for enactment.

Riteways LORE flow:

set flows
SPIRIT

increase
LORE
enactments

wanjau

SPIRIT --<

- o Check in on the lay of the land. How and where is Community & Country feeling?
- o Provide safe spaces for this knowledge flow to feedback in to layer activities...

LORE enactments:

- o Na – tjina Cultural Proficiency process
- o Circles in multiple contexts
- o Circle work applying strength-based approaches like 'Stories of Strength'
- o Broader system protocols
- o Applying our methods and methodologies like EqPs

Wanjau

- o Visual representations of Lore from art – artefacts, static displays.
- o Invitational EqPs – creating 'First Nations First' agreements for partnership.

Figure 15.4 (Continued)

Riteways CULTURE & LANGUAGE Flows:

set flows
SPIRIT

increase
CULTURE & LANGUAGE enactments

wanjau
abundance

SPIRIT --<

- o Check in on the lay of the land. How and where is Community & Country feeling?
- o Provide safe spaces for this knowledge flow to feedback into layer activities...

CULTURE & LANGUAGE enactments:

- o Embedding Indigenous Languages – whole year programming
- o Translation activities
- o Use of 'Cultural Curriculum Cycle' in designs
- o Complete 6-8 week 'Cultural Curriculum Cycles'
- o Artefact & Performance pieces

Wanjau

- o Indigenous spaces renamed and reclaimed in local language.
- o Local area story capture, local language story and place
- o Own language definitions are known, articulated and shared between own circles.
- o Showcase of 'Cultural Curriculums' – art displays, dance performances.
- o Sharing artefact and performance pieces to Elders and own family groups.

Figure 15.4 (Continued)

Riteways IDENTITY Flows:

set flows
SPIRIT

increase
IDENTITY
enactments

wanjau
abundance

SPIRIT --<

- o   Check in on the lay of the land. How and where is Community & Country feeling?
- o   Provide safe spaces for this knowledge flow to feedback into layer activities...

IDENTITY enactments:

- o   Whole – us/all 'Identity Curriculum' Phase 1 & 2
- o   Part – us/only 'Hand printing'. Own story and use in research.
- o   Whole – us/together 'Collective Knowledge Bouls'. Learning about and being a part of.

Wanjau

- o   Personal Cultural Portfolio
- o   State Library research
- o   Collective Impact organisational membership

Figure 15.4 (Continued)

Flowbook samples...:

Personalised Learning Plan – PLP

Links to our care plan way of thinking and doing. Either place or make your hand design visible. Listen to how noonthallis explain and show the 'Hand Design'.

NOW – your turn. *Take time to think. You can start this and finish at the end (signature process) or make time now and finish your PLP design.*

The middle – the palm is your design – what image or designs represent you?

The fingers our indicators of identity represent you. Who's your mob? Where's your family from? How many in your family? What do you love to do? What are you good at? What is something unique about you?..

Figure 15.5 Flowbook samples – PLPs.

Student Name; _____

Age; _____ **DOB;** _____ / _____ /

Year Level; _____

Date of PLP; _____

Proposed date of review; _____

Critical Information about the student (e.g. verification, medication, family circumstances)

Additional Information available (e.g. NAPLAN results, report information, absentee information

Student Plan

How each student can participate in their own learning plan.

Figure 15.5 (Continued)

What are my goals at school? (What do I want to achieve at school?)

Think in threes = what would I like to do in the future? what are 3 examples of jobs – the kind of work I would like to do??

What are my long term goals for senior years at school and after school? (School work, TAFE, University, Sports goals?)

How can I achieve my goals?

Figure 15.5 (Continued)

Educational Information to assist specific Teaching and Learning Strategies

Contributions by Teachers, IEW, Counsellor, Assistant Principal and/or Principal

What other goals do I want my child to meet? (e.g. Sporting, Social, Behavioural)

Who is in an integral part of seeing my child succeed? (e.g. Family, Friends, School)

Figure 15.5 (Continued)

Is the student working to year level? If not, estimate at what year level (this can be different for different learning areas). Specify Literacy and Numeracy levels.	
What strategies best suit the students learning style?	
What specific goals need to be considered to bring the student upto year level standard, or to exceed it?	
What area/s does the student struggle in?	
Suggest ways to assist the student with difficult areas. What additional strategies can be implemented to maximize learning?	
What classroom strategies can assist the student?	
What support needs does the student require? What resources are needed/utilized?	
What strategies can the whole school implement that will see the student meet goals and increase their level of achievement?	

Figure 15.5 (Continued)

Parent Plan

How each parent/guardian can contribute to their child's learning.

What academic goals do I want my child to meet? (e.g. Literacy, Numeracy, ATAR)

Endorsement Plan

This is an agreement that states each party is satisfied that the students educational needs are being met, and that individual goals are being observed.

Student; _____   Date; __/_____/_____

Signature; _____

Parent/Guardian; _____   Date; __/_____/_____

Signature; _____

Parent/Guardian; _____   Date; __/_____/_____

Signature; _____

Teacher; _____   Date; __/_____/_____

Signature; _____

School Counsellor; _____   Date; __/_____/_____

Signature; _____

Assistant Principal; _____   Date; __/_____/_____

Signature; _____

Principal; _____   Date; __/_____/_____

Signature; _____

Other Stakeholder; _____   Date; __/_____/_____

Signature; _____

Other Stakeholder; _____   Date; __/_____/_____

Signature; _____

Figure 15.5 (Continued)

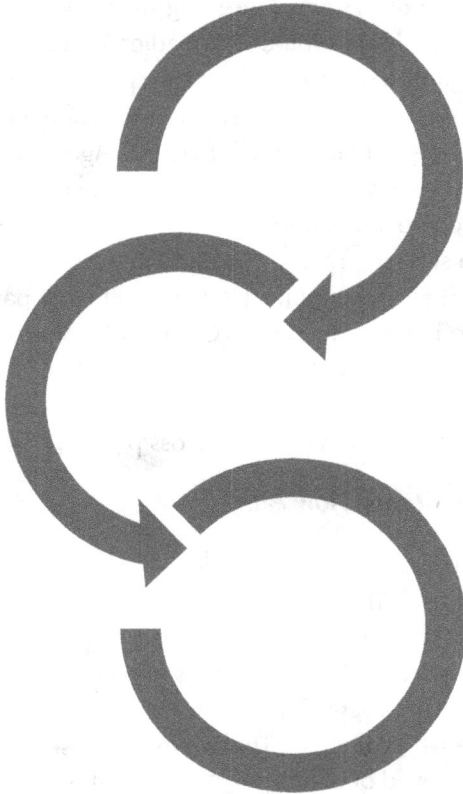

Figure 15.6 Activity: Let's make bouls.

Flowbook samples:

Circling is a pattern, an old pattern, bouls; LORE is held in circles. We need to live boul, breathe boul, act in boul.

Activity: Let's Make Bouls

Look around. Can you see? Tighten up. When I talk, can you hear?
  Now, which way? What are you doing when I talk? Speak back.
  OK, you are showing boul . . . respect in circle. You can't care and share for thousands of years unless you have a sophisticated and acknowledged system.

So in boul let's set our system. I'm going to use Wiradjuri ways here. Deadly Wiradjuri psychologist brother Troy Sadler. Whenever he works with mobs, he now, Tjanga, has our mobs claim the space.

To do this, we have to define what 'respects' mean and then 'sign up' with our mark/our handprints to make a final 'Respects Agreement'.

Share with everyone so we are all on the 'same page' and have the same reference when we come into circle.

OK! Now we can set our circles on Wanjau flows.

Group creates RESPECTs wanjau… How we will cross paths…:

Yarn on the above in separate circles. Once we've shared, bring back to bigger circle to explain what 'RESPECTs' mean to us.

As a whole circle the Group combines both yarns and insights to make a final Respects Agreement on how we will cross paths…

Activity: Explain the Riteway Flow Path

Waterflow, watermarks . . . filters of fresh flow – sands as a cleaner . . . mussels regurgitate the 'trash'. Think on the markings.

Now let's go see at the park . . . down the path . . .

Markers that exist are . . . ? What did you see? What did you observe?

Activity = Output post program… We circled:…

Use Local Knowledge as guides… This is strength-based evidence of what works and can be achieved of country, for example the Bunya Bunya – Boobargun Nguumonge story.

Provide a Case Study map on what x3 major parts of process "stood out", ring true as the closest translation on and of what worked well in recent programmatic circles.

Activity: Wanjau Djeripi…

Figure 15.7 Activity: Wanjau Djeripi.

Activity: Wanjau Djeripi

OK, let's set our circles on Wanjau flows.

~Spirit.

The tingle on skin, the hairs standing up. The light wind on the back of your neck. Storytelling is the most important part, 'the feeling'.

What can we do for you, Uncle Peter?

What can we do for you, Aunty Minda?

Instead of the 'what if' thinking/project design, look at our tall trees, who help and enable us to flow today. What good spirits do these Cultural Teachers, Elders, Advisors bring to our circles?

In meaningful ways, then, 'what can we do' to show our love and support for our people, who guide and look after us and country? Map the ways we will show wanjau through the relational weaves of exchange. And remember to ask our 'tall trees', **'What more could we do?'**

#Wanjau# . . . Knowledge exchange and cross overs . . .

How did we do business? Along the songlines – the storylines on country to protect and nurture. This great land was created for us. The patterns of these relationships and storying remain in the land and kinnected to the people of the land.

Wanjau – kinnected to Bunya Bunya is patterned all along the Bunya highway... Because it is the back of Budin Guju... Remembrances of that light and energy are left on country as mimburi – sites of flow... Boobargun Nguumonge is a site of flow... Geriward further south is a sight of flow... Bogong – Nganawall is a site of flow connected to Canberra 'the gathering place'...

To know us is to flow like us. When you know your story, you have more of your map . . . OUR ~story. Able to see and make more connections. Let's sit, talk.

Yarn and show who you are, where you're from. That's YOUR responsibility. AND if you don't know, that's OK. You are Murri, Koori. . . . You are Aboriginal or Torres Strait through whose side? YOU do know! Let's flow.

Activity: Story Back

'Speaking for' tests your knowledge strength and listening. You only get to know and develop more flow if you listen. Our old people would purposely speak soft; you got to tune your binungs in, move closer. You share your yarn with one other. They set circle to listen. Then when you have yarned your story = you now listen. After both have yarned, when we return to full circle it is the job of the "listener" to share what they've learnt & heard about each other's map…

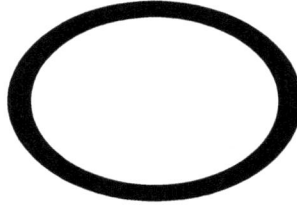

IK in research context

Honour & Healing

Reclaimation

Decolonisation

International IK Models

National IK Models

Localised Knowledge

Figure 15.8 Lore circle & IK in research context.

. . . .
. . . .))):--<

Bunya Bunya cyclic wanjaus…

• **Ngin healing** ~ dganganbarra: Tumba Tjina treks 1à 3 & beyond
  Bunya Bush Uni opening April 22! Barrungam Languages & Cultural Studies

• **Reclaimation:** IKSL

• **International IK:** WiPCE, Te Akatea, Turtle Institute, Cynefein, Catalyst of Change…

• **National IK:** Stronger Smarter Institute, NATSIPA inc, AIME, IMBIR, Warril Yari-Go Karulbo ngin Collective Impacts – Collaboration for Change

• **Localised** (place based) **IK:** Community Durithunga, Yugambeh Museum, Jinndi Mibunn, Bunya Murri Rangers, Warra Historical Society

• **Decolonisation:** Stronger Smarter Leadership Program, Spirits of Redsands,

• **Honour** ~ Barrungam lingo: story: art: song

Figure 15.9 IK in research context explained – Examples of each cyclic ripple from Healing through to Honour.

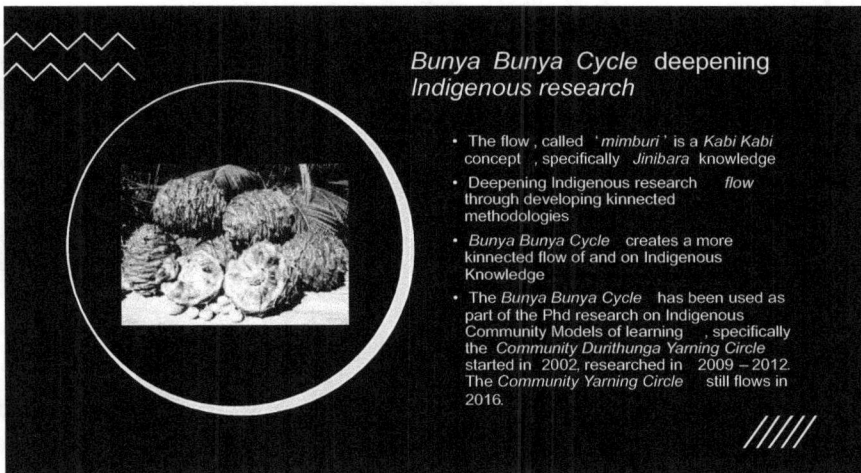

Figure 15.10 Bunya Bunya Cycle deepening Indigenous research.

For country... Bunya Bunya ngin Barrungam ✋

- "the Little Red Yellow Black Book " - AIATSIS
- "Dark Emu" - Bruce Pascoe
- "Secondary Dark Emu in the Classroom " - Simone Barlow & Ashlee Horyniak
- "Country" - Bill Gammage & Bruce Pascoe
- "Songlines" - Margo Neale & Lynne Kelly (links to web): Regenerative Songlines Australia (regenerative -songlines.net.au)
- "Dark Sparklers" - Bill Yidumduma Harney & Hugh Cairns
- "Sand Talk" - Tyson Yunkaporta (links to web...): Tyson Yunkaporta discusses Sand Talk: How Indigenous Thinking Can Save the World   - Bing video
- "Warrior" - Libby Connors
- "Bonye Buru" -
- "Everything you need to know about the Uluru Statement from the Heart   ..." - Megan Davis (Cobble Cobble) & George Williams (links to webs): Home - Uluru Statement from the Heart
- "Story About Feeling ..." - Bill Neidgie (spirituality + country)
- "Fire Country" - Vic Steffenson (links to web): Welcome to The Living Knowledge Place
- "Bussamari"..."Goodbye Bussamarai: The Mandandji Land War, Southern Queensland 1842 -1852"- Patrick Collins.

Figure 15.11 Applying the IK in research model.

Activity: Us/Together in Group Yarns

Apply the IK relational map, 'IK in research context', to the Bunya ngin Barrungam resource list earlier. What resources are closer to the local area/ Traditional Owner footprint? What is further away? Be prepared to share your reasoning.

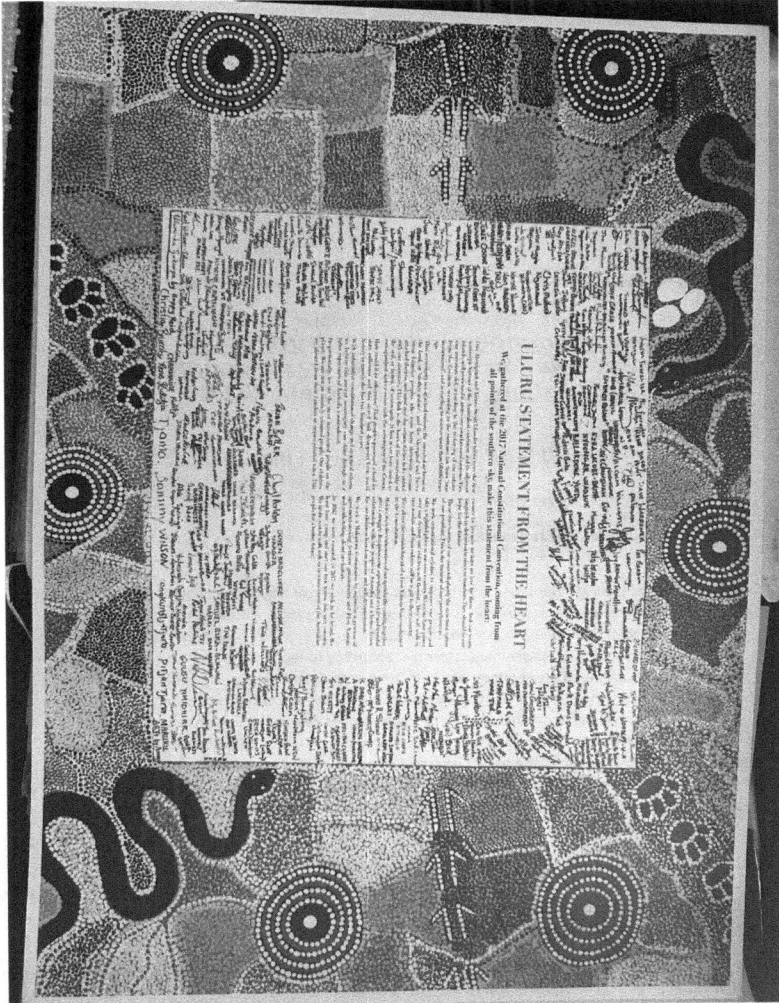

Figure 15.12 Activity: Macro area stories – enacting the Uluru Statement from the Heart.

Activity: Macro Area Stories

Reflexive praxis on the Uluru Statement from the Heart.

How are we enacting the 'statement from the heart'?

Use the 'our truth-telling' story that follows to review where your work sits now.

Our "***truth-telling***" story is made up of:

- o Australia was invaded , not settled or discovered .
- o Now is an opportunity for First Nations to tell the truth about history   in our own voices .
- o An opportunity for mainstream Australia to hear our voices   . Reconsider history & national stories told . An opportunity to listen   – Dadirri .
- o This will be challenging   & the truth about invasion needs more space to be told .
- o A recognition that truths have been told well through   : "the Bringining them Home Report ," the "Australian Law Reform Commission 's work on Customary Law ", the "Council for Aboriginal Reconciliations " Final report .
- o There's a strong belief in 'truths being done ', now need a more coordinated approach .
- o What's important is process being done at own pace and be   'bottom up'.
- o Examples 'in action ' are public art / museum displays .
- o ***"The most common method of truth telling espoused by the First Nations dialogues was through the education system ..."*** **(Davis, et al., 2021)**

Figure 15.13 How do we build more truths?

ULURU STATEMENT FROM THE HEART:

From country, translate the statement in the local context. Below is our country, Barrungam – west of the Bunyas...

We, gathered at the 2017 National Constitutional Convention, coming from all points of the southern sky, make this statement from the heart: Our Aboriginal and Torres Strait Islander tribes were the first sovereign Nations of the Australian continent and its adjacent islands, and possessed it under our own laws and customs. This our ancestors did, according to the reckoning of our culture, from the Creation, according to the common law from 'time immemorial', and according to science more than 60,000 years ago. This sovereignty is a spiritual notion: the ancestral tie between the land, or 'mother nature', and the Aboriginal and Torres Strait Islander peoples who were born therefrom, remain attached thereto, and must one day return thither to be united with our ancestors. This link is the basis of the ownership of the soil, or better, of sovereignty. It has never been ceded or extinguished, and co-exists with the sovereignty of the Crown. How could it be otherwise? That peoples possessed a land for sixty millennia and this sacred link disappears from world history in merely the last two hundred years?

Budin gungdu wanagi, gundir ngue maras. Tjanga djungu:Dguan djimben gung ngin budin gung dganganbarras. Gurangindau duwur. Gurangindau tjanga. Dguai djimben Gaiwar. Duwur – djah, djumnge, gunda. Djuan dgimben dghanum gambargan migloo. Waangi migloo bianga gurangdai waga. Gurangadai djah, dgumge, gunda tjanga?!

With substantive constitutional change and structural reform, we believe this ancient sovereignty can shine through as a fuller expression of Australia's nationhood.

Tjanga budin gundju, budin gundju bianga djuan djumge yverringi guni Australia gungu.

Proportionally, we are the most incarcerated people on the planet. We are not an innately criminal people. Our children are aliened from their families at unprecedented rates. This cannot be because we have no love for them. And our youth languish in detention in obscene numbers. They should be our hope for the future. These dimensions of our crisis tell plainly the structural nature of our problem. This is the torment of our powerlessness.

Tjanga bullyman budin barras. Ngurama gundoos gunnin gunnin. Djimben garis? Gari gambas gunnin gunnins. Dangi tjanga migloo gambargan waga gamba.

Figure 15.14 Uluru Statement from the Heart – from country, translate the statement in the local context.

We seek constitutional reforms to empower our people and take a rightful place in our own country. When we have power over our destiny our children will flourish. They will walk in two worlds and their culture will be a gift to their country.

Gnua budin gundju guni Australia. Mimburi gundoos tjanga. Gaung gundoo gundamena duwur ngin baulan tjanga.

We call for the establishment of a First Nations Voice enshrined in the Constitution. Makarrata is the culmination of our agenda: the coming together after a struggle. It captures our aspirations for a fair and truthful relationship with the people of Australia and a better future for our children based on justice and self-determination. We seek a Makarrata Commission to supervise a process of agreement-making between governments and First Nations and truth-telling about our history. In 1967 we were counted, in 2017 we seek to be heard. We leave base camp and start our trek across this vast country. We invite you to walk with us in a movement of the Australian people for a better future...

Gundamena budin gundju, gawung gundamena – "VOICE",

Gundamena gambaragan 'makaratta' – "TREATY",

Gundamena gawung gambaragan gunge – "TRUTH".

Gung ngin budin gungs budin gundju tjanga 'makaratta commission'.

1967 gnuar barras guni Australia.

2017 bianga guni Australia.

Yanande gundju tumba dganganbarras – budin gung ngin gung gungs.

Guni Australia gaung dguinga jinung du-ur gamba gamba bouls ...

ACTIVITY: Language works

Visit the Uluru website. Log on to 'translation'. Search and see if your country is represented. If not seek permission for what could be an on-country translation of the Ulutru statement. Celebrate the process by marking in local curricula or adding to the resources of the Uluru Statement: www. Translations - Uluru Statement from the Heart

----

Figure 15.14 (Continued)

ULURU STATEMENT FROM THE HEART:

From country, translate the statement in the local context. Figure 15.14 includes the statement for our country, Barrungam, west of the Bunyas.

Activity: Language Works

Visit the Uluru website. Log on to 'translation'. Search and see if your country is represented. If not, seek permission for what could be an on-country translation of the Uluru Statement. Celebrate the process by marking in local curricula or adding to the resources of the Uluru Statement: https://ulurustatement.org/the-statement/translations/

> **Dgumge yonung, dgumge yonyung,**
>
> **Bianga bianga...**

(BIUN BIUN poem excert).

Dgumge yonung, dgumge yonyung,
Bianga bianga . . .

--00))—<

References

Davis, M., & Williams, G. (2021). *Everything you need to know about the Uluru Statement from the heart*. Randwick: UNSW Press.

16 | Dgagunbara Bianga

○ *BIUN BIUN . . .*

Dgumge yonyung, dgumge yonyung,
Bianga bianga

Mi waga
Binung waga
Keeam waga
Muru waga
Warra bianga
Na marrang
Dgumge

Nyal ngima mi
Gooraman ngima binna
Yuggera ngin murun ngima keeam
Barrunga ngima muru

Gujumba
Dgumge yonyung
Bianga biun biun . . .

DOI: 10.4324/9781003298717-16

Figure 16.1 Dgagunbara bianga.

References

Dolzan, T. (2022). Dgagunbaras – research fellas IK translation as art/mapping country.
Yunkaporta, T., & Davis, J. (Hosts). (2021, June 21). Research fellas. In *The Other Others* [Audio podcast]. Anchor. Retrieved from https://anchor.fm/tyson-yunkaporta

Index

Note: Page locators in *italics* indicate a figure. Numbers followed by "n" indicate a note on the corresponding page.

practions (practicing/mastering skills)
7, 16, 27, 60–61, 64, 82, 111,
146, 151
praxis: circle sharing 20, 58; in
education knowledge 63, 68, 78,
81, 84, 126, 128; identity 103,
142; reflection 45, 49, 59, 182, 183;
sustainability 98
process: circle 31, 73, 95, 126,
145–147; closure 36, 96; rule of
three 71, 145; sharing 3, 42, 56, 73,
108; *see also Riteways*
professional: development 22, 71, 74,
100; learning *21*, 22, 33, 81, 121, 148
programs: educational 94, 96–97;
federal 51; innovative 75, 82;
language 97, 104, 119–120;
leadership 21, 88
protocols 6, 22, 87, 99, 104, 111, 113,
114, 145, 150
Purcell, Michal 12, 47

Quampie (saltwater mussel) 7, 20
Quandamoopah (saltwater country) 7,
20, 92
QUT (Queensland University of
Technology) 20

racism 27, 36, 75, 115
RAP *see* Reconciliation Action Plan
reciprocity 73, 100, 112
recognition 6, 8, 25, 30, 49, 69, 85, 88,
115, 137–139, 150, *184*
Reconciliation Action Plan (RAP) 37,
41, 148
Reconciliation Australia 66, 92, 106
regenerate 21, 32, 34, 38, 59, 81–82,
95, 98, 142, 154
regeneration 13, 16, 31, 47, 71, 104,
123, 147, 154, 156, 160
relatedness (IK reference) 7, 20, 130,
133–134, 139, 150
relationship: high-expectation 34, 45,
82–83; with land 60, 101; pattern/

design 2, 28, 38, 59, 75, 103,
133, 157, 160, 179; reciprocal 32,
34–35, 46, 110, 112, *115*, 143, 158
(*see also* connection); Equity Partnership;
with spirit 68, 74, 79, 109
research: Indigenous 26, 78, 112;
methodologies 16, 31, 41–42, 49,
50, 71, 123; relational 6; theory-
of-change 79, 83
researchers 84–85, 104, 108, 111–113,
139
respects agreement 178; *see also*
handprint
Reynolds, Henry 50
Rigney, Irabinna 19
Riteways: circle/cycle 60, 72;
ember-blowing 69, 71, 80, 118, 120,
156; enactments 61, 66, 71, 88, 93
(*see also* Stories of Strength); focus of
25, 27, 67–68; journey 162; modelling 51, 61, 63, 79, 100, 120
Riteways flows: deeper learning 30, 56,
68–69, 100; development 7, 10, 12;
education 19, 27, 37, 45; enactment 71–72, 156, *167–170*; focus
68–69; identity 134, 138, 162, *164*;
markings 53–54, *166*; mastery 155;
opportunity 66, 87; spirit 79, 87–88,
165–166; third cultural space 63
rivers 2, 5, 55, 79, 100, 146, 151
Ryan, Cass 12

Sadler, Troy 143–144, 178
safe space: community 13, 47–48, 97,
114; creation 10, 137–138, 145,
148–150; work 78, 95
saltwater 2–7, 58, 157
Sambono, Joe 20, 64
Sand Talk (Yankaporta) 25, 66
Sarra, Chris 12, 41, 49, 82–83
Schein, Edgar 50
scholar 16, 36, 75–76, 85, 121, 127
Science, Technology, Engineering, and
Math (STEM) 26–27, 141

For Product Safety Concerns and Information please contact our EU
representative GPSR@taylorandfrancis.com
Taylor & Francis Verlag GmbH, Kaufingerstraße 24, 80331 München, Germany

www.ingramcontent.com/pod-product-compliance
Lightning Source LLC
Chambersburg PA
CBHW052005270326
41929CB00015B/2792

9 781032 288369